The Downsized Warrior

Advance Praise for the Book

"How do we move from a Cold War army to a smaller force while retaining the best officers, keeping morale high, and maintaining an effective military force? A decorated veteran of Desert Storm, with unrivalled access to internal Army documents and to the commanders who did the planning, David McCormick has given us a model study to answer this question. He lucidly narrates the story of the Army's efforts, analyzes the results, and offers convincing recommendations for change." —Richard H. Ullman,
author of *Securing Europe*

"Managing growth, relatively speaking, is a snap, but the acid test of an institution's resilience is how well it copes with decline, which lays the foundation, for better or worse, of the next exigent expansion. This is analogous to Napoleon's oft-quoted maxim that there is no operation more hazardous than withdrawal. David McCormick's superb—no, that's too mild an adjective—brilliant study of the U.S. Army's 1990's drawdown will someday be regarded as prophetic."   —William L. Hauser, Chief, Military Manpower Team,
Department of the Army Task Force,
Presidential Commission on
Governmental Efficiency, 1982–83

The Downsized Warrior

America's Army in Transition

David McCormick

NEW YORK UNIVERSITY PRESS
New York and London

NEW YORK UNIVERSITY PRESS
New York and London

Copyright © 1998 by New York University

All rights reserved

Library of Congress Cataloging-in-Publication Data
McCormick, David, 1965–
The downsized warrior : America's army in transition / David McCormick.
p. cm.
Includes bibliographical references (p.   ) and index.
ISBN 0-8147-5584-4 (acid-free paper)
1. United States. Army—Organization. 2. United States. Army—
Operational readiness. 3. United States—Armed Forces—Officials
and employees—Dismissal of.   I. Title.
UA25.M18   1998
355.3'0973—dc21   97-21219
                           CIP

New York University Press books are printed on acid-free paper,
and their binding materials are chosen for strength and durability.

10 9 8 7 6 5 4 3 2 1

Contents

	List of Tables	vi
	List of Diagrams	vii
	Acknowledgments	ix
1	Introduction: A Legacy of Downsizing	1
2	The Politics of Downsizing: The Dark Side of Defense Policymaking	25
3	Reducing the Ranks: Anatomy of a Decision-making Process	63
4	Lean and Mean: Changing Attitudes and Behaviors in the Muddy Boots Army	117
5	An Agenda for Reform: An Officer Corps for the Twenty-First Century	157
	Epilogue: The Army's Future Course	195
	Notes	203
	Acronyms	231
	Bibliography	235
	List of Interviews	253
	Index	259
	About the Author	267

List of Tables

Table 2.1. Base Force Endstrengths	29
Table 2.2. From the Base Force to the Bottom-Up Review	40
Table 3.1. Summary of Officer Downsizing Programs	71
Table 3.2. Officer "Quality" and the VSI/SSB (1994–1995)	79
Table 3.3. Changes in the Distribution of Officer Authorizations (1987–1997)	81
Table 3.4. Downsizing's Effects on Diversity (1990–1994)	85
Table 3.5. The Thurman Legacy	108
Table 5.1. Battalion Commander "Seasoning": Past, Present, and Future	164

List of Diagrams

Diagram 1.1. Active Army Endstrength, 1940–1995 — 8

Diagram 1.2. Army Officer Corps Endstrength, 1940–1995 — 8

Diagram 2.1. Service Budget Authorizations, 1989–1997 — 27

Diagram 2.2. Military Endstrengths, 1989–1996 — 27

Diagram 3.1. Organization of the Army Personnel Community — 66

Diagram 3.2. The Downsizing of the Army Officer Corps, 1990–1995 — 69

Diagram 3.3. Percentage of Line Officer Positions Filled, 1989–1995 — 83

Diagram 3.4. Impact of the Gulf War on Downsizing — 93

Diagram 3.5. Enlisted to Officer (E/O) and Company to Field Grade (CG/FG) Ratios during Downsizing — 115

Diagram 3.6. Promotion Opportunity during Downsizing, 1985–1995 — 115

Diagram 3.7. Changes in Promotion Timing during Downsizing, 1985–1995 — 116

Diagram 3.8. Battalion Command Opportunity during Downsizing, 1991–1996 — 116

Diagram 4.1. Sources of Uncertainty and Anxiety in a Downsizing Army — 122

Diagram 4.2. Changing Attitudes in a Downsizing Army — 124

Diagram 4.3. Confidence in Army Leadership
during Downsizing   128

Diagram 4.4. Changes in Career Intent Because
of Downsizing   134

Diagram 4.5. Willingness of Officers to Recommend
a Military Career   136

Diagram 4.6. Changing Behavior in a
Downsizing Army   137

Diagram 4.7. Changing Career Choices in a
Downsizing Army   147

Acknowledgments

In writing this book, I have incurred many debts, which I can acknowledge though never fully repay. My principal debt is to the men and women of the army officer corps, without whose cooperation and assistance this book would not have been possible. From my own service as well as my interaction with this institution since departing the army, I know it to be one of the most talented, patriotic, and devoted groups in America. This book is in no way meant to suggest otherwise.

In particular, I would like to thank Lieutenant General (ret.) Theodore Stroup, former Deputy Chief of Staff for Personnel, who served as the primary sponsor for this project and who urged me to tell the army's story as honestly and comprehensively as possible. Also among those who have served or remain in the army, I owe special thanks to Lieutenant Colonel Leonard Wong, Lieutenant Colonel (ret.) Thomas Wilson, Colonel (ret.) Raoul Alcalá, Colonel Barbara Lee, Colonel Charles Henning, Lieutenant Colonel Neil Fulcher, Dr. Morris Peterson of the Army Research Institute, Dr. James Yarrison of the Army Center for Military History, and Dr. Donald Snider, Lieutenant Colonel Michael Meese, Lieutenant Colonel Robert Gordon, and Major Richard Lacquement of the Social Sciences Department at West Point. My thanks also to Dr. Thomas Hickok, a fellow student of downsizing, to Jayne Bialkowski who gave me superb administrative support for my research, and to my colleagues at the Woodrow Wilson School at Princeton where I wrote an earlier version of this book as a doctoral student. Finally, I owe a special debt of gratitude to Colonel (ret.) William Hauser, Colonel (ret.) Paul Miles, and Lieutenant Colonel Mike Colpo who have been good friends and sources of wisdom over the past several years. All of these individuals contributed to this study in important ways.

Also from my time at Princeton, I would like to thank John DiIulio who served as a dissertation advisor and carved time out of his extraordinarily busy schedule whenever I needed it most. Special thanks also to Richard Ullman who, in addition to being an official advisor for this project, has for the last five years been a teacher, mentor, and friend. My greatest debt is to Aaron Friedberg who guided this effort from the very beginning, supported me in obtaining generous grants from the Smith Richardson Foundation administered through the Princeton Research Program in International Security, and enabled me to study and teach with him during my years as a graduate student. My gratitude is extended also to Niko Pfund, Director of New York University Press, who showed genuine enthusiasm for this project from the very beginning and helped clarify my thinking and improved the prose on many of these pages. Each of these men has my sincere appreciation and my deep professional respect and personal affection.

I am particularly thankful for the universal support given me by my family and by friends too numerous to mention over these past several years. My mother, who finished a similar project a few short years ago, was a source of constant inspiration as well as a meticulous editor. Likewise, Amy Richardson has been a constructive critic, conscientious editor, and constant supporter during the research for and the writing and revision of this manuscript. Because of her, this book is much better than it would have been otherwise. I am forever indebted to her for her support and companionship.

1

Introduction
A Legacy of Downsizing

> When a nation loses its military spirit, the career of arms immediately ceases to be respected and military men drop down to the lowest rank among public officers. They are neither greatly esteemed nor greatly understood.... The army is always inferior to the country itself. In this state it is called into active service, and until war has altered it, there is danger for the country as well as for the army.
> —Alexis de Tocqueville, *Democracy in America*

Alexis de Tocqueville made this observation in 1840, but it reflects an enduring truth in American history: following every war, the United States has dramatically reduced the size of its army and with it the regard it shows for its professional soldiers. This apathy has bred unpreparedness, and when war has inevitably returned, the country has paid a price for its indifference in blood and national treasure. More often than not, America's army has prevailed in the long run, only to see the cycle repeat itself. Such was the case in 1919, in 1945 particularly, and to a lesser degree in 1953.

In November 1989, the United States again emerged victorious from forty years of war. It was a cold war, however, fought not on the plains of western Europe, but by professional soldiers in classrooms, training areas, and simulation centers across the United States. If the situation today in some ways compares to those that have preceded it—and if Tocqueville's admonition is accurate—several obvious questions arise. In this period of transition, what steps should military leaders take to secure the resources necessary to maintain an army robust enough to avoid such misfortune? How can the army reduce its ranks in a way that maintains a vital and capable corps of professional soldiers? And how are "military men" likely to be affected by the accompanying uncertainty and change? In short, how is a democratic army to remain viable when the nation it serves loses its "military spirit"?

Between 1989 and 1996 the active-duty army was cut from roughly 770,000 to 495,000 personnel. The officer corps shrunk from 91,000 to 69,000, with more cuts to come. This book evaluates the manner in which the army has adapted to and been affected by this externally mandated organizational change. It considers how effectively the army has managed downsizing and how its effectiveness has been influenced by it. "Downsizing" has a variety of meanings, but it simply refers here to purposeful actions taken on the part of institutional leaders to reduce the number of people in the organization.

The term "military effectiveness" is equally ambiguous. Ultimately, a military organization gauges its effectiveness by its ability to fight and win wars. But this capacity depends upon a multitude of overlapping and interdependent activities, many of which take place in the months and years that precede a war. Existing measures of military effectiveness generally fail to capture fully the complexities of military organizations and the range of heterogeneous activities that contribute to effective fighting power. These activities take place across several dimensions. Military effectiveness is dependent on adequate preparation for and conduct of war at the political, strategic, operational, and tactical levels. But it is also dependent on numerous simultaneous and interdependent military and nonmilitary tasks that successful armies must execute proficiently. An adequate evaluation of overall military effectiveness requires assessments across this range of activities (Millett et al. 1988, 2).

In examining the downsizing of the army, therefore, I consider the army's political effectiveness—the ability of its leadership to articulate the army's role and garner needed resources in an increasingly treacherous political and budgetary environment.[1] I also evaluate the army's organizational effectiveness by examining its objectives in downsizing, the appropriateness of these objectives, and its success in achieving them. Finally, I examine how downsizing has affected military professionalism—the morale, commitment, attitudes, and behavior of the army officer corps—an intangible yet crucial aspect of overall fighting power that is too often overlooked.

It is the goal of any writer to have a single, transparent message that runs through his or her work from beginning to end. If I were forced to compress the main arguments of this book into one pithy statement it would be that dramatic downsizing has compromised the army's institutional health in ways not fully acknowledged or completely understood and that qualitative reform measures are needed to restore the army's vitality. This statement, however, is a poor substitute for the much more complex story that these pages tell and the far more complicated arguments they make.

The downsizing of the army is a story of both failure and success. The army's leadership failed to make a persuasive case to civilian leaders against dramatic cuts in the army's personnel strength and budget; consequently, other aspects of military effectiveness have been jeopardized. Conversely, the army's leaders successfully planned and implemented dramatic personnel reductions, particularly within the officer corps. The army achieved its downsizing objectives, and these objectives were for the most part appropriate. Despite the army's best efforts, however, prolonged and incremental downsizing has taken its toll on the officer corps, undermining morale, commitment, and professionalism. The army's outdated officer management system and the legislation that governs it have exacerbated these undesirable effects. The army's leadership has been painfully slow to recognize this fact and to reform its officer management system to meet the unprecedented challenges emerging in the post–Cold War era.

Why This Book Matters and to Whom It Matters Most

The downsizing of the army is relevant to present and future national defense policy. The versatile, high-tech army that helped win the Cold War, was successful in Panama in 1989, and more successful still in the Gulf War in 1991, will serve as a benchmark against which future professional armies will be measured. Since 1989, however, this army has incrementally reduced its endstrength by more than a third.[2] In April 1995, Secretary of Defense William Perry directed the army to cut its endstrength by another 20,000, to 475,000. Predictably, army leaders resisted this cut, and it was delayed until the release of the Quadrennial Defense Review (QDR), a comprehensive review of U.S. military forces, in May 1997. While the magnitude of the cuts resulting from the QDR remains unclear, it is evident that the size of the army will be cut well below the current force levels in the coming years to satisfy budget constraints and to support floundering defense modernization programs.

Policymakers should enter this next phase of downsizing with open eyes and clear heads. Even accounting for all the usual skepticism about arguments that downsizing poses a threat to national security—e.g., the armed forces are simply trying to perpetuate themselves and Republicans are simply looking for an opportunity to criticize the Democratic administration—surely the impact of downsizing on the ability of the armed forces to defend national interests, no matter how those interests are defined, is of critical importance. This book contributes to this end by illustrating some of the effects that prolonged and incremental reductions have had on America's army. Moreover, it details for military and civilian leaders those aspects of the army's planning and implementation that were most and least effective between 1989 and 1996, which should prove a particularly valuable service when additional cuts are made in the future. In addition, it proposes a much-needed officer management reform agenda to be considered by military and civilian policymakers.

The army's story also contributes to our understanding of organizational downsizing in a broad sense. Since the 1980s, thousands of American corporations have downsized their workforces; yet, as the effects of this process have become more apparent over time, a consensus has emerged that downsizing may be creating more problems than it solves, with many companies failing to achieve desired gains in productivity or profitability. More recently, downsizing has become prevalent in the public sector as well. The Clinton administration took office in 1992 promising to cut the federal workforce by 100,000 employees, but following the National Performance Review boosted the number to 252,000, a number subsequently raised by Congress to 272,900 in 1994 (GAO 1995c).[3]

Moreover, this study documents a significant and unprecedented period in army history that might otherwise be overlooked: unlike past reductions of conscript armies, the most recent downsizing required dramatic cuts in an all-volunteer force. This book is also important in light of the fact that the army has done a relatively poor job of recording the planning, implementation, and effects of previous downsizing efforts (Kozlowski et al. 1991, 125). It is likely that this most recent experience might also have been overlooked. There are several plausible explanations for this paucity of analysis. First, the unpleasant nature of downsizing may have led the army inadvertently to devote little attention to studying it. Additionally, studies of personnel issues—even of those related to something as important as downsizing—are not perceived in the army to have the same value as studies of tactics, doctrine, and military strategy. And military organizations are known for their resistance to introspection and self-criticism. Simply put, it is unlikely that an ambitious young officer is going to advance his or her career by scrutinizing how effectively (or ineffectively) army leaders managed personnel reductions after the last war; the priority, quite rightly, is on preparing for the next. This point notwithstanding, it is important from a practical standpoint—in order to avoid repeating past mistakes—as well as from a historical perspective, not to neglect this important period.

Finally, this book makes a significant contribution to the relatively scant body of work on military organizations. Civilian scholars traditionally have been reluctant, perhaps increasingly so since the end of the Cold War, to devote themselves to the study of military organizations. Certainly part of the explanation lies with academic vagaries, particularly the notion that the study of the military organizations or issues divorces one from mainstream scholarship in the fields of sociology, history, or political science. There are also very real constraints imposed on civilian researchers by the military's disinclination to make information available. Conversely, the analysis done by military professionals often yields critical insights but is more likely to be biased during data collection or analysis due to organizational pressures, institutional myopia, or legitimate concerns over the career implications of certain findings. Moreover, the large majority of internal studies, particularly those most critical of the army, are unlikely to be made public.

The downsizing of the army affects enlisted soldiers as well as officers, civilians as well as service members, and reserve and national guard as well as active forces. This book focuses primarily on the downsizing of the active army officer corps for several reasons. Past downsizing efforts have been especially devastating (often due to mismanagement) with respect to the army officer corps. This was particularly true of the cuts following the Vietnam War. Additionally, reducing the officer corps is much more complex than cutting the enlisted force because legislative restrictions imposed by the 1981 Defense Officer Personnel Management Act (DOPMA) constrain the army's managerial flexibility. The army's relatively rigid officer management system further hampers personnel planners, who must take into account a wide range of variables, including promotion opportunity, officer professional development, and tenure requirements. This makes the downsizing of the officer corps a more difficult management challenge and a richer, more interesting case study.

Further, personnel decisions affecting the officer corps generate substantially more interest from Congress, Defense Department policymakers, the general public, and the army's senior leaders than those involving the enlisted force.[4] The stakes are simply higher in the area of officer management. The professional officer corps is the heart and soul of the army. Its competence and professionalism have been essential to America's past military successes, and the lack thereof instrumental in its failures:

> The officer corps is critical to combat operations. It is the institutional memory of the Army, the living repository of its history, its experiences, and, above all, its lessons. It is the officer corps that reflects the values and characteristics of the Army. If the corps is corrupt or incompetent, the whole Army will be also. If the corps is of high quality, then it is possible to forge a good army.
> (Gabriel 1985, 7)

Well-trained soldiers and competent noncommissioned officers are obviously also extremely important. However, a robust, highly professional officer corps is essential to the long-term health and effectiveness of the army.

Unpreparedness: The First American Tradition

Throughout most of its history the United States has found itself unprepared for the wars that it ultimately fought (Betts 1995, 5). As a consequence, the outbreak of war has required frantic improvisation in raising, arming, training, and deploying ground forces, and America has lost many of its first battles, most notably at the Kasserine Pass in 1943 and the battle of Task Force Smith in 1950 (Dunnigan and Macedonia 1993, 42–45). These failures may be attributed largely to military establishments too small and understaffed for the tasks at hand, late starts in mobilization, deficient peacetime plans for economic conversion, outdated equipment, and inadequate training. America's unpreparedness can also be linked, however, to the precipitous and sometimes indiscriminate manner in which the armed services have reduced their forces following World War I and World War II, and the wars in Korea and Vietnam. And of all the services, the army in particular has an undistinguished record with respect to the transition from a wartime to a peacetime footing.

While these experiences inform the army's most recent downsizing, the utility of a comparison of present and past demobilizations is limited by the profound differences between the situations then and now. Because America has fought the majority of its conflicts overseas, the end of war has generally required a massive transfer of men and material back to the United

States. Previously, personnel reductions were a subset of the myriad demobilization activities that this process entailed. Many of these same activities are taking place today, but on a much smaller scale. The current situation is also distinctly different, however, because unlike the conscript forces demobilized in 1945, 1953, and 1970, today's army is an all-volunteer force. The all-volunteer army, established in 1973, is by most accounts a remarkable success story (Halloran 1984). However, the presence of top-quality volunteers—many of whom wish to stay—makes downsizing more complicated.

Past personnel cuts were not only carried out in the wake of "hot" wars rather than a cold one, they were also significantly larger in order of magnitude. Indeed, the current downsizing appears insubstantial in comparison to the massive personnel cuts following World War II, though it is comparable in relative size to the reductions following Korea and Vietnam (diagrams 1.1 and 1.2). In addition, the soldiers of past armies were less specialized. Thus, current military leaders must place added emphasis on retaining individuals with the critical technical skills needed to operate the modern, high-tech military organizations of today. The aforementioned officer management legislation also imposes different constraints on present-day policymakers.

These differences aside, however, the similarities between past and present downsizing efforts suggest the need for a brief investigation of previous experiences. In each case, the size of the officer corps was cut dramatically; in each case, there was substantial controversy between the army and Congress; and in each case, personnel cuts had devastating consequences for the army.

World War II

Military leaders fastidiously planned the personnel reductions in anticipation of the end of World War II. Unfortunately, political pressures for more rapid demobilization following victory first in Europe and then Japan were so great that the army lost control of the process and the detailed plan initially in place was thrown out the window (Dunnigan and Macedonia 1993, 51).[5] In June 1945, the army had a total strength of roughly 8.2 million men (including the Army Air Force); by the end of 1948 it had been pruned to 554,000, roughly one-sixteenth of its earlier size. The army officer corps went from 890,000 in October 1945 to about 70,000 by the end of 1948, where it stayed until the beginning of the Korean War in 1950. The pace of demobilization was determined largely by the availability of transportation

8 | *Introduction*

Diagram 1.1. Active Army Endstrength, 1940–1995

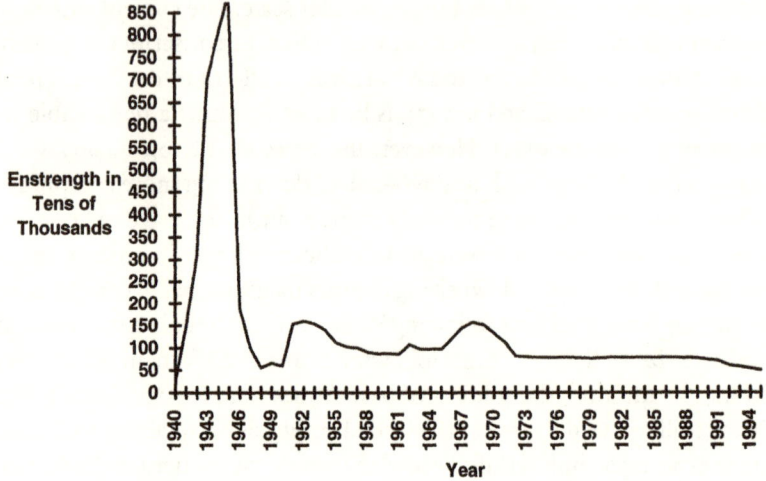

SOURCE: *Historical Statistics of the United States, Colonial Times to 1970*, U.S. Department of Commerce, 1141; *Statistical Abstract of the United States, 1995*, U.S. Department of Commerce, 364.

Diagram 1.2. Army Officer Corps Endstrength, 1940–1995

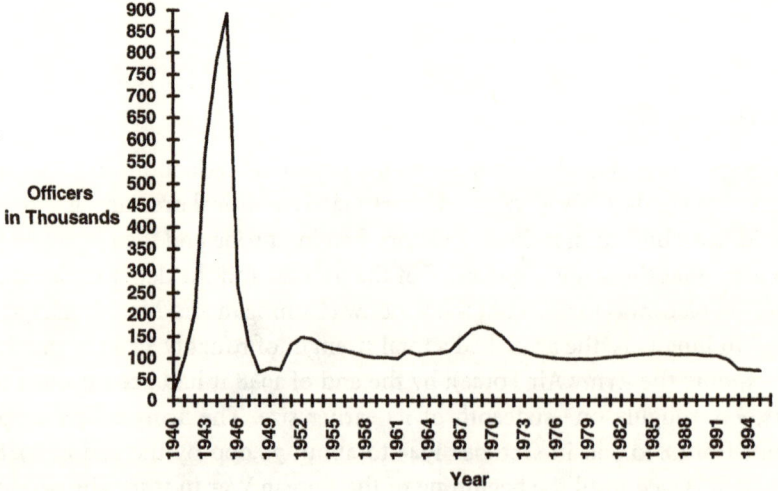

SOURCE: *Historical Statistics of the United States, Colonial Times to 1970*, U.S. Department of Commerce, 1141; *Statistical Abstract of the United States, 1995*, U.S. Department of Commerce, 364.

and administrative personnel to "bring the boys home" rather than by a decision about the size or shape of the future army.[6] Additionally, the failure of civilian leaders to give firm guidance concerning the army's occupation duties and other postwar requirements made it impossible for the army to control or efficiently manage the reductions of officers and enlisted soldiers (Coakley et al. 1968a, 133).

Certainly military and civilian policymakers managed some aspects of the demobilization process well. As the large majority of soldiers were conscripts, the army designed its program around individual rather than unit separations and relied on a point system to determine eligibility.[7] The required number of points for separation was lowered more slowly for officers than for the enlisted; thus it was possible to keep the needed number of officers during the final stages of the war and in the years immediately after (Coakley et al. 1968a, 26).[8] As the war ended, the majority of reserve officers were released from active duty, though an effort was made to integrate the strongest performers into the regular officer corps *(Demobilization Series Study No. 9*, 8–10). Additionally, beginning in 1944, the Roosevelt administration provided extensive aid—separation pay, education benefits, and unemployment insurance—to assist the large majority who left the army to make the transition back to civilian life (Steward 1993, 7).

But significant problems arose. Although military leaders were initially conscientious about informing the rank and file about demobilization plans, they did not sustain this as the war progressed and the plan continually changed (Sparrow 1952, 191).[9] The majority of the force remained uninformed, and this contributed to declining morale and a deterioration in discipline that plagued that army during and after the war (Collins 1971, 11). The discharge of millions of men, almost overnight, left the army with a skyrocketing ratio of officers to enlisted men—an issue to which Congress devoted substantial attention after the war (Peppers 1988, 151). Finally, public pressures for more rapid reductions led military leaders to downsize with a haste and imprecision that resulted in dramatic reductions in personnel readiness.[10] As Major General Clair Street wrote to General Hap Arnold, the commanding general of the Army Air Force in 1945:

> We have gone overboard to demobilize the Army under a system which to me is not only unsound but positively dangerous, we are not coppering our bets. It is perfectly apparent that when the present point system ... [has] taken its toll, the Army Air Force will be left with ... nothing but a potpourri of warm bodies inadequately seasoned by too few regular army officers and enlisted men. The basic structure of what has been our Air Force will have been dissipated.[11]

Street's predictions proved chillingly accurate in the opening days of the Korean War, when the army and the newly created air force suffered for their unpreparedness.

Korea

Unfortunately, we know little about the army's post-Korea downsizing experience; the little that has been written about this period is piecemeal and scattered across a variety of sources (Kozlowski et al. 1991, 124). Personnel cuts took place primarily between 1953 and 1957 in the midst of a major shift in strategic policy away from the mobilization strategy of the Truman administration to an increased reliance on nuclear deterrence under President Dwight D. Eisenhower's New Look (Huntington 1961, 82).[12] Inherent in the New Look, which translated to a 33 percent reduction of the army, a 16 percent cut in the navy and marines, and a small increase in the size of the air force, was a much smaller role for the army.

To army Chief of Staff Matthew Ridgway, these cuts represented an attempt "to reduce [the army] to a subordinate place among the three great services that make up the country's shield," and he fought vigorously against the New Look throughout his short tenure (as cited in Collins 1971, 19). Ridgway's impassioned but unsuccessful dissent put him at odds with the President and the Secretary of Defense, and he resigned in 1955 after serving less than two years as Chief of Staff (Geelhoed 1979, 118).[13] The army's fortunes did not improve substantially until after the 1960 presidential election and John F. Kennedy's subsequent embrace of General Maxwell Taylor's Flexible Response.

There are numerous reports of substantial problems within the army after the war. To meet mandated officer reductions, the army instituted early release programs between 1953 and 1955 but restricted the eligibility of officers in branches with shortages (Coakley et al. 1968b, 143). But as with the post–World War II experience, reserve officers, rather than regulars, suffered the brunt of the cuts, and the officer-to-enlisted ratio grew noticeably as a consequence of personnel reductions (Luttwak 1985, 292–95). Although performance was the criterion used for separating officers, the army purportedly lost many of its most capable "warriors" because a college degree was seen as being more important for retention than performance in combat (Dunnigan and Macedonia 1993, 56).[14]

Morale during this period was reportedly low due to the unpopularity of the Korean War at home, and poor recruitment and low retention after the war were indications that a military career was quickly losing its luster. The army sought to address these problems by raising pay, introducing new uniforms, increasing educational opportunities, instituting a reenlistment bonus, and ensuring that officer promotion opportunity remained at or close to wartime rates (Collins 1971, 17). These efforts, however, produced only limited success (Coakley et al. 1968b, 116).

Vietnam

Richard Nixon won the 1968 presidential election on the promise of a secret plan to extricate the United States from Vietnam. Soon after taking office, his administration called for a shift from a national military strategy founded on having the ability to fight two and a half wars simultaneously to a one and a half war strategy. These two changes set the stage for dramatic personnel cuts in the army between 1969 and 1975 (Kaufmann and Steinbruner 1991, 12). During this period, the army's endstrength was reduced from roughly 1.5 million to 780,000 men and the officer corps was cut from 173,000 to 103,000. The army's planning was complicated by Nixon's commitment during the 1968 campaign to move toward an all-volunteer force. This decision required military and civilian policymakers to take actions to make military service more "attractive," a particularly difficult proposition in the final stages and immediate aftermath of the Vietnam War.[15]

Army leaders were unsuccessful in adapting to an increasingly hostile political environment and in 1971 they made a miscalculation that threw existing downsizing plans into disarray. Dissatisfied with the pace of army cutbacks, the Senate Armed Services Committee recommended in May 1971 that the army reduce its ranks by an additional 50,000. The army resisted this proposal and a game of political "chicken" ensued. To the army's surprise, the Senate stood fast on its request, mandating the reduction in the 1972 National Defense Authorization Act. In a mad rush to meet this requirement, the army lost control of the downsizing process and readiness declined precipitously (McNeill et al. 1974).[16] The army's endstrength did not stabilize until March 1974, when Chief of Staff Creighton Abrams gained the approval of Congress and the administration to expand the army from thirteen and a half to sixteen divisions, but within the existing endstrength of 785,000 (Sorley 1992b, 360–65).[17]

The Reduction in Force (RIF) procedures used by the army to downsize its officer corps after Vietnam were brutal, unfair, and incoherent. Until 1975, RIFs were directed solely at reserve officers, many of whom were seasoned combat veterans, who were given little warning of the impending separation and minimal separation pay and transition assistance.[18] This resulted in tremendous turbulence and diminished morale throughout the army. Some of the best officers left, either as victims of RIF or out of disgust with the army (Dunnigan and Macedonia 1993, 102–3). Junior officers suffered the brunt of the cuts, and the officer corps became increasingly "top-heavy" and relatively larger as a whole in comparison to the enlisted force.[19] Within the officer corps, a breach developed between "regulars" who had tenure and reserve officers who were the most likely candidates for RIF (Gabriel and Savage 1978, 160). It took the better part of a decade before the army overcame the severe effects of this experience (Kitfield 1995a).

Common Threads

Several common threads run through these experiences. In all three cases the army was unsuccessful in articulating the need for less rapid cutbacks and more robust budgets in the years following war.[20] It is, of course, the responsibility of military leaders to present their best assessment of military requirements and the prerogative of civilian leaders to decide the extent to which this advice is followed. It is noteworthy, however, that among the armed services, the army stands out as being particularly ineffective in contesting cutbacks. The navy, for example, suffered far fewer reductions in size and budget during these same periods.[21] The army's ineffectiveness may be attributed to greater ambiguity about its future role and missions during these periods than existed with respect to the other services as well as its relatively larger wartime forces. Moreover, the army has historically enjoyed significantly less congressional support than the other services, perhaps partly due to its own inability to articulate clearly its role in ambiguous postwar environments. Regardless of the reasons, "the Army has most reflected the consequences of changing external requirements in terms of its posture, personnel levels, etc. over time" (Lewis 1989, 25).

In each case the army's leadership did a relatively poor job of managing the downsizing process, particularly with regard to officers.[22] The army failed to develop a systematic and equitable process for determining who should be released and who should be retained. As a result, when subjected

to political pressures, it repeatedly lost control of the downsizing process. Moreover, the quality of the officer corps in each case suffered as the army lost some of its brightest young officers. Reserve officers in particular, many of whom had performed admirably in war, were haphazardly separated in the reckless transitions to peace. Communication about personnel reduction plans was consistently inadequate, and as a consequence morale fell sharply. Finally, particularly after the Korean and Vietnam wars, soldiers who left the army received scant transition assistance and separation pay. This made the passage to civilian life for them more difficult and generated low morale and disillusionment among those who stayed.

Each series of cutbacks also had alarming consequences. With the exception of the period following the Korean War, a substantial decline in promotion opportunity contributed to malaise within the officer corps. In each instance, the officer-to-enlisted ratio increased substantially (the significance of this trend has been vigorously debated throughout the post–World War II period and is discussed in detail in chapter 3). In each case, personnel readiness at the unit level and army-wide declined markedly, and the army had a difficult time recruiting and retaining a qualified core of competent military professionals. Thus, following each war, the army has had to take steps to improve its image and the quality of army life.

While these observations help place the army's most recent downsizing experience into perspective, the distinctive characteristics of today's army also set it apart. Indeed, in some ways, personnel cuts of an all-volunteer military organization are more comparable to downsizing in other public or private institutions—whose members are employed by choice and presumably wish to remain—than to the demobilization of conscript armies after World War II, Korea, and Vietnam.

Downsizing America

Management trends are like academic ones: today's fads are tomorrow's fall guys. Such is the case with organizational downsizing, an enormously popular practice in America's private sector over the past decade. By the mid-1990s, however, many had begun to argue that the faith corporate America had placed in downsizing was misguided. In a January 1996 editorial, Secretary of Labor Robert Reich publicly questioned the wisdom and morality of the layoff of forty thousand workers by the American Telephone and Telegraph Company (1996, 11). In March 1996, the *New York Times* featured seven consecutive front-page articles focusing on the negative effects of downsizing on individuals, organizations, and society. Three months later, a Harvard professor and a former student published a book arguing that it was the frayed trust between IBM and its workforce resulting from downsizing—and not IBM's reliance on outdated technology, as conventional wisdom had it—that accounted for the company's disastrous performance in the 1990s (Mills and Friesen 1996). By summer 1996, as public criticism grew, companies were no longer trumpeting workforce layoffs as a means for bolstering shareholder profits. Downsizing also became the subject of meaty presidential campaign rhetoric, inspired initially by the populist campaign of Patrick Buchanan. While it is difficult to determine where rhetoric ends and reality begins, the emphasis within corporate America appears to be shifting from workforce cutbacks to growth and improved efficiency (Uchitelle 1996, D1). Downsizing, it seems, is in disrepute.

It is surprising that this shift occurred so recently because the downsizing trend has been underway for years. Moreover, criticism of downsizing does not appear to extend to the public sector where President Clinton and others have enjoyed praise for making substantial cuts in the size of the federal government (Barnes 1996, 12; Kamensky 1996, 247–50). At the same time, a decade of downsizing has undoubtedly taken its toll on the American public. Data from the Bureau of Labor Statistics suggest that between 1979 and 1996, 43 million Americans lost their jobs, directly affecting one-third of all households. For one in ten adults the loss of a job precipitated a major crisis in their lives (Uchitelle and Kleinfield 1996, 1). In the last five years, job loss has been most pervasive among white-collar workers, with 1.4 million "executives, managers, and administrative professionals" losing their jobs (Hickok 1995, 3). The downsizing phenomenon has fundamentally transformed the way Americans think about present and future employment (Bennett 1990a).

The Downsides of Downsizing

For some managers, downsizing has not been the panacea they hoped it would be. Most companies downsize to reduce costs and increase profitability and productivity.[23] Yet, many downsizing efforts fail to achieve these objectives. A 1993 Wyatt Company survey of over five hundred companies found that only 43 percent of the companies saw improvements in productivity and 46 percent increased profitability. Sixty-one percent of those that desired reduced costs achieved them (Koretz 1997, 30; *Best Practices in Corporate Restructuring* 1993, 34). Similarly, a 1994 American Management Survey of companies that have downsized since 1989 found that 30 percent actually reported declines in productivity (Hickok 1995, 5). Even more startling, two-thirds of the companies that downsized ended up doing so again a year later (Cameron 1994a, 183). As William Bridges concludes: "Trimming an organization's workforce, which is being touted as the answer to America's corporate ills, is a cure that can be as bad as the disease" (1987, 2).

Certainly this failure may be attributed at least in part to ineffective management. Most companies acknowledge that their downsizing efforts are guided more by anecdotal evidence, personal experiences, and intuition than by validated principles or rigorous analysis (Cameron 1994a, 183). Moreover, numerous organizations have steadfastly relied on a cleaver rather than a scalpel when cuts were deemed necessary. By either implementing voluntary separation programs without carefully identifying the worker populations to which they should be made available or by simply relying on mass layoffs, managers have consistently lost the workers they needed most for successful downsized organizations. Consequently, they have often been forced to hire these workers back, sometimes as highly paid consultants or temporary employees, at significantly higher expense.

The disastrous experience of the U.S. Postal Service, one of the few documented cases of public-sector downsizing, is a telling example of the consequences that can result from a seat-of-the-pants approach. Marvin Runyon took the reins as Postmaster General of the United States in 1992 and immediately mandated a 40 percent reduction in all management positions within ninety days. Toward this end, the postal service rapidly created a buyout program to reduce its workforce through voluntary separations. The program was poorly conceived, however, and only one-third of the roughly forty-seven thousand workers who accepted the offer were managers—the designated target—while the remainder were clerks or mail carriers. Moreover, morale and productivity within the postal service declined dramatically. As the outcome of this inadequate planning, the postal service was forced to pay exorbitant overtime costs and hire new mail clerks and carriers to meet the 1992 Christmas postal rush. Consequently, the number of postal employees in 1994 was higher than it had been in 1992 (McAllister 1994, 28–30).

Other downsizing experiences suggest that organizational leaders often have had a difficult time retaining their best, most productive employees during and after downsizing. For example, a Wyatt Survey found that 31 percent of 531 companies surveyed had failed to retain their highest performers during downsizing (*Best Practices in Corporate Restructuring* 1993, 37). Logically, those who contribute most to an organization are prone to leave voluntarily because they have the capabilities and the confidence to succeed elsewhere (Mone 1994, 283). Downsizing also may affect an organization's capacity to attract new talent. The Wyatt study also found that 22 percent of the companies surveyed had a more difficult time attracting quality employees during and after downsizing (*Best Practices in Corporate Restructuring* 1993, 37). While the effects of these phenomena on short-term costs and productivity are not always apparent, they obviously play a prominent role in long-term organizational effectiveness and, ultimately, in profitability.

The inability of companies to achieve their downsizing objectives also stems from the devastating effects of the process on its survivors. Over the years, researchers have documented a long list of undesirable attitudinal changes in workers at all levels of an organization as a consequence of downsizing. Although vaguely defined, these effects are commonly referred to as "survivor illness" or "survivor syndrome" and consist of at least four clusters of feelings: (1) fear, insecurity, and uncertainty; (2) frustration, resentment, and anger; (3) sadness, depression, and guilt; and (4) betrayal (Noer 1993, 89).[24] These conditions are often exacerbated by the fact that work processes, intentionally or unintentionally, change as a consequence of downsizing, and survivors are often asked to do more work, different work, or less fulfilling work as a result.

Most survivors, particularly those who can identify with the departing individuals, also appear to suffer a loss of commitment to the organization (Kozlowski et al. 1991, 70). Downsizing is viewed as a breach of the psychological contract—an implicit agreement between employer and employee in which the latter has traditionally been afforded a modicum of job security in return for adequate performance and some exhibition of loyalty (De Meuse and Tornow 1993, 3). The Wyatt study found that over half of the companies it surveyed had suffered a decline in worker commitment from downsizing. Likewise, leaders appear to be more likely to lose the confidence of their subordinates; this too undermines commitment (Cameron 1994b, 195). For those who doubt the correlation between commitment and organizational effectiveness, research also shows that individual commitment is closely correlated with absenteeism, retention, innovation, and performance (Hunt and Morgan 1994).

The effects of downsizing on the behavior of survivors is equally detrimental to organizational effectiveness. The most in-depth study of downsizing to date, for example, concluded that personnel reductions led to centralized decisionmaking, increased politicization and conflict as individuals and special-interest groups fought over shrinking resources, and diminished cooperation among organizational members.[25] Moreover, the author of the report, though favorably disposed to downsizing, discovered a diminishing tolerance for risk among managers and a decreasing propensity for creative activity throughout downsized organizations (Cameron 1994b, 195).[26] In short, the predicted benefits from downsizing, namely reduced costs and increased profitability, remain elusive while the potential costs in quality, commitment, and dysfunctional survivor attitudes and behavior are extraordinary.

Best Practices in Downsizing

Experience shows that it is much easier to articulate the most effective approaches to downsizing than to implement them. Even when an organization's senior managers plan and implement downsizing "correctly," there is no guarantee that the desired objectives will be achieved. An organization's particular situation, its culture, and its leadership all significantly influence the extent to which it will be successful in achieving and affected by dramatic cuts in personnel. However, there do appear to be some common approaches, some "best practices," initiated before, during, and after downsizing that are shared by those organizations that downsize successfully.

Downsizing is not something that should happen to an organization but rather an action that it should undertake purposefully. Personnel cuts should be part of a larger effort to redesign or reshape an organization. In other words, managers should rethink their organization's goals and strategies before downsizing, and the content and magnitude of the downsizing plan should follow from this assessment (Cameron 1994b, 193).[27] Experience also shows that it is important for managers to develop clear, consistent policies on separation criteria and on how separation decisions and notifications are to be made. The appropriateness of involuntary separations versus voluntary separations is likely to vary significantly across organizations. Voluntary separation programs alleviate the need for massive involuntary layoffs, maintain the commitment of the workforce, and are less disruptive to employee morale. However, they generally require costly incentive programs, sometimes interfere with normal attrition, and risk encouraging the departure of the most valuable employees, particularly if poorly conceived. There is also some question over how rapidly managers should implement personnel cuts. Some maintain that gradual downsizing permits an organization to adjust to the inevitable turmoil and is positively correlated with successful organizational renewal and performance (Cameron 1994b, 201). Conversely, others argue that it is best to cut fast and deep, thereby avoiding "the Chinese water torture method" that exacerbates the survivor syndrome (Harback 1993, 30). The army's experience offers insight into these unresolved questions.

It is as important for practical reasons for an organization, while showing compassion for those who are departing, to maintain constant communication with those who remain: "Survivors question the procedural and distributive justice of layoffs in many ways; the more unfair they perceive them to be, the more likely they are to respond in ways that the organization would define as unfavorable (e.g., reduced commitment to the organization, lowered work performance)" (Brockner 1990, 96). It is therefore important that survivors believe that appropriate care has been shown for those departing the organization (Wong and McNally 1994). For these reasons, downsizing organizations are placing increasing emphasis on transition assistance—separation pay, education, career counseling, and training—to aid the passage of those leaving the organization (Kozlowski et al. 1991, 91). In addition, organizations have attempted to minimize uncertainty among survivors by installing "hot lines" and creating transition monitoring teams (Bridges 1987, 4–7).

In the wake of downsizing, managers should take steps to mitigate its negative effects and restore a healthy climate within the organization. Most organizations fail in this area. Among other things, leaders should alter as necessary their appraisal, reward, promotion, and development processes to reflect the goals and values of the downsized organization (Cameron 1994b, 210). Managers should also make an effort to clarify and communicate new career paths and opportunities open to workers (Brockner 1992, 26). Finally, given the turmoil and uncertainty produced by more than a decade of downsizing, organizations should make explicit a new covenant, redefining the relationship between employer and employee: in return for strong performance and a commitment to institutional purpose from employees, employers would be responsible for enhancing an individual's employability inside or outside the organization through training, education, and development experiences (Waterman and Waterman 1994, 88).

Unresolved Questions

Despite all that has been written about downsizing, the literature has surprisingly little practical value to managers faced with the prospect of dramatic personnel cutbacks. Most of the research focusing on downsizing at the organizational level is based on a small number of interviews with senior managers across a number of organizations. As a consequence, the conclusions drawn from this work are too general and the recommendations too generic to be of much use to managers struggling with the complexities of impending personnel cuts. In addition, the existing work on this subject fails to question why some organizations effectively manage downsizing while others do not. Organizations that deviate from the best practices are likely to do so not because they do not know any better or do not care but for more complex reasons that remain unexplored. For example, organizational culture and bureaucratic politics are both likely to influence the decisionmaking process, yet they receive little mention. Downsizing is among the more painful forms of organizational change, with clear-cut winners and losers. Knowing who these winners and losers are, and where they come from within an organization, might shed light on the content and implementation of downsizing plans.

Additionally, despite the fact that public-sector downsizing has accelerated in the past several years, there has been surprisingly little written about this process. In the absence of such research, there is a disturbing tendency among academics and public managers to suggest that the findings from research in the private sector may be applied across the board to public institutions (Hardy 1990). There is ample reason to believe, however, that the implementation and effects of public-sector downsizing will be dramatically different. To a much larger degree, the decisions of public managers are governed by the constraints imposed on the organization rather than the tasks assigned to it. Public managers cannot allocate the factors of production—labor and capital—as they deem necessary or choose the organization's goals or objectives.[28] Moreover, they are constrained by legislation that not only regulates the hiring, but also the firing, of personnel.

In addition, the ability to gauge the effectiveness of downsizing in the two sectors differs greatly. In the private sector reduced costs, increased productivity, profitability, and shareholder value generally drive downsizing.[29] But in the public sector there is no bottom line, and absolute levels of public productivity cannot be estimated (Downs and Larkey 1986, 31). Public-sector downsizing is generally undertaken to cut costs, though sometimes the contraction or elimination of a public agency is an end in and of itself. Sometimes, reducing or eliminating a public bureaucracy may be more costly than leaving it untouched. The differences between public and private organizations are particularly apparent for the military services. Unlike General Motors or Chrysler, army leaders do not set their own force levels or have the option of lateral transfer or hire. And they are hostage to a retirement system in which individuals are not vested until after twenty years of service and to very strict legislative constraints that stipulate not only when and how "career" soldiers may be separated but also the rate at which they may be promoted.[30]

While private-sector downsizing may be planned in secret, public-sector personnel cuts, particularly those involving military forces, must be considered publicly in congressional hearings; this, too, greatly influences the dynamics of decisionmaking. For these and a host of other reasons a simple list of "best practices" in downsizing has only limited applicability for public managers, particularly military leaders. The military is unique in that the "expertise" of the professional soldier has only limited applicability outside the military. Moreover, professional soldiers are exposed to dangers surpassing those of most other professions. Thus, the relationships among professional soldiers, and between them and the institution, are different than those that exist in other private or public organizations.

Finally, though the short-term effects of downsizing on survivors is well documented, there is little understanding of the potential long-term effects of this process on organizational effectiveness. For example, we know little about how downsizing affects the willingness of employees to pursue traditional or nontraditional career paths or an organization's propensity for sustained creativity or innovation. Similarly, while some suggest the need for "revamping" personnel practices in the aftermath of downsizing, there is relatively little work on how evaluation, reward, development, and selection processes should be adjusted to counter "survivor syndrome" and to meet the needs of a newly downsized organization. These are issues with which private and public managers will surely struggle in the coming years.

The wisdom gained from a decade of experience in the private sector is a useful starting point for considering the range of issues involved in downsizing, though for the reasons already stated it has only limited applicability to the army's experience. The reverse is also true with regard to the findings of this book. Some of the lessons and observations from the army's post–Cold War downsizing will surely apply to other organizations; many will not. Nonetheless, it was my intention in writing this book to provide insights into aspects of organizational downsizing about which we know relatively little.

How This Book Is Organized

In 1945, John Steinbeck likened his approach to writing about life on Cannery Row to the collection of certain marine invertebrates "so delicate that they are almost impossible to capture whole, for they break and tatter under the touch." Instead, one had to permit them to crawl of their own will onto the knife blade and slip them gently into a bottle of seawater before lifting them up to the light and examining them whole (1945, 3). The same approach might be recommended for digesting this book.

It is a study of two very different armies. On one hand, it is an examination of how the leadership of one of the largest bureaucracies in the world, the "corporate army," resisted, planned, and finally implemented dramatic personnel reductions. But it is also a study of the "muddy boots army"—the lieutenants, captains, majors, and colonels in today's field army who are the survivors of this process. Downsizing required myriad complex and overlapping activities at various levels of the army and has produced equally varied effects. Thus, to understand fully the complexities of this process, it is best to permit the entire story to unfold chapter by chapter before lifting it up to the light and viewing it whole.

While the distinction between the corporate army and the muddy boots army is in some ways misleading, it is nonetheless important to capture the differences between these two aspects of the military institution.[31] In one army, scrupulously groomed generals in pressed uniforms and spit-shined shoes ready themselves for battles over budgets and endstrength on Capitol Hill. In the other, captains in wrinkled fatigues and dusty combat boots prepare their overworked units for uncertain missions in unknown places. In order to understand fully the downsizing of America's army, one must examine both.

The army's downsizing story begins with the political decisions that precipitated the personnel reductions in the first place and then traces how the army adapted to and was affected by these decisions as they filtered through the organization. Chapters 2 and 3 focus on the corporate army—how it resisted, planned, and eventually implemented personnel cuts. Chapter 4 provides a snapshot of the effects of downsizing on the muddy boots army on those who remain. Chapter 5 proposes an agenda for the army's leadership as it addresses the problems caused by downsizing, many of which bode ill for the army's long-term health and effectiveness. The epilogue makes some predictions about what could and some suggestions about what should happen in the future.

More specifically, chapter 2 considers the politics of downsizing—the political, budgetary, and strategic forces behind reductions in the army's size and budget. It tracks the evolution of army force posture from the development and implementation of the Base Force under the Bush administration in November 1989 to the creation and implementation of the Bottom-Up Review under the Clinton administration through fall 1995. Although primarily descriptive, the chapter makes two important arguments. First, budgetary and political considerations, not strategic ones, drove decisions about army personnel reductions. Second, the military services, and the army in particular, exerted minimal influence over the pace of downsizing and little, if any, control over the size of the reductions themselves. The chapter also seeks to explain the political ineffectiveness of military leaders, particularly army leaders, during this period.

Chapter 3 scrutinizes the army's leadership—the corporate army—and its management of downsizing, particularly of the officer corps. The chapter concludes that the army's aims in downsizing were appropriate and that it has been largely successful in achieving them. Moreover, it attempts to explain the factors that contributed to this success by chronicling the planning and implementation of personnel cuts through four successive generations of army leadership in the Office of the Deputy Chief of Staff for Personnel. The chapter argues that the army downsized with unprecedented precision, compassion, and success as a result of its post–Vietnam experience, a robust analytic capacity developed in the army personnel community over the last two decades, and generous assistance from Congress.

Chapter 4 considers how downsizing has affected the morale, attitudes, and behavior of the officers who remain in the muddy boots army, far removed from the intricacies of the downsizing decisionmaking process. It argues that the magnitude and prolonged uncertainty of downsizing has compromised the institutional health of the officer corps in ways that are neither desirable nor fully understood. Morale, career expectations, and organizational commitment have dramatically declined in the post–Cold War army. Competition and careerism have risen and initiative and cooperation have decreased. And there is evidence to suggest that perceptions may be affecting the career patterns and choices of junior officers in particular, in unrecognized and undesired ways. These attitudes and behavior are neither wholly recent developments nor exclusively the consequence of downsizing; but these pathologies have become more pronounced, and dangerously so, because of it.

Chapter 5 considers the effects of downsizing and what should be done about them. It argues that the changes in attitudes and behavior signal a notable decline in the professionalism of the officer corps, which has important implications for overall military effectiveness. The army's leadership has been slow to recognize the deleterious effects of downsizing and slower still to make the changes in its grossly outmoded officer management system needed to meet the unprecedented challenges of the post–Cold War era. Army leaders must take steps to reform current officer management practices, and civilian leaders in Congress and the administration should make much-needed changes in officer management legislation. This chapter proposes an agenda for reform.

The epilogue highlights some of the more important lessons from the army's downsizing experience that may be useful to public and private managers alike and predicts what is likely to happen if the alarming trends identified here are left unchecked and the army resists dramatic and immediate reform of its officer management system. Unhappily, as this book goes to press, this urgently needed reform appears increasingly unlikely to occur.

The most interesting books often have obvious villains or culprits—ideas, theories, people, or organizations—that may be tried, convicted, and sentenced all in the course of three hundred pages. Indeed, this binary, prosecutorial approach to research and to the presentation of that research is a salient characteristic of contemporary American discourse. Books of that sort are easiest to follow because, while the reader may become temporarily perplexed by various elements of the evidence, the identities of the prosecutor and the villain are usually evident from the very beginning, as is the fact that the overall purpose of the effort is conviction.

The downsizing of the army does not fit so neat a pattern. There are no obvious villains. Civilian leaders required the army to downsize, but few knowledgeable observers would quarrel with the need for dramatic downsizing at the end of the Cold War. Policymakers should have been and need to be more sensitive to the effects of downsizing on the attitudes and behavior of military professionals—particularly the impact of incrementally cutting the army's endstrength rather than agreeing on a credible downsizing target and sticking to it. Likewise, though its leadership ineffectively articulated the army's role and needs in the post–Cold War era, it is unlikely that a more persuasive case would have changed the outcome: the army had relatively little leverage against the overwhelming political momentum for substantial cutbacks. Its leadership should be criticized for its dilatory approach to officer management reform. The overly conservative steps the army has taken thus far are completely inadequate given the unprecedented challenges it will face in the twenty-first century. However, these criticisms are more of an indictment of method than of purpose, more misdemeanors than felonies. In short, the arguments made in the pages that follow are for the most part more nuanced and complex than a simple verdict of guilty or not guilty. Yet, while there are no obvious villains in this story, there is one obvious victim: a healthy and vital American army.

2

The Politics of Downsizing
The Dark Side of Defense Policymaking

> The military ... has characteristics normally attributed to other political institutions. But politics here ... means the exercise of power and pressures ... associated with policy-making, budgets, manpower levels, and strategy.
> —Sam Sarkesian, *The Professional Army Officer in a Changing Society*

Defense policymaking has been described as a moon with a "light side intensely explored and a dark side largely unknown to those not living on the planet" (Danzig 1989, 72). On the light side fall issues like proliferation, intervention, and peacekeeping—topics of general interest to policymakers and the public On the dark side are more arcane subjects, such as logistics, procurement, manpower policy, officer management policy, and so forth, which are seldom considered by those outside the defense establishment. This chapter is about the dark side.

Between 1990 and 1996, the active duty army was downsized by more than a third. In this context, downsizing means reducing the endstrength, or the number of soldiers, in the active army. This chapter is not about reductions in the army's infrastructure or budget (though decisions in these areas are closely related to those concerning endstrength), nor about base closures or cutbacks in the Army Reserve or National Guard (though significant downsizing is underway in these areas as well). Nor is this chapter about what the size, budget, organization, or strategic role of the army should have been during this time period, or presently ought to be. This chapter is about how and why the size of the active army was dramatically downsized from 1990 to 1996, a process that continues today.

Downsizing is in reality the by-product of two interrelated policymaking processes. Decisions about how much to reduce the size of the army are the obverse of decisions about what the appropriate size of the future army should be. To understand what happened to the army and why it happened, it is necessary to evaluate both. In examining the downsizing process, military policy may be divided into the generic categories of strategy and structure. Samuel Huntington's description of the two is gratifyingly precise:

> Strategy concerns the units and uses of force.... A strategic concept identifies a particular need and implicitly or explicitly prescribes decisions on the uses, strengths, and weapons of the armed services. Structural decisions, on the other hand, are made in the currency of domestic politics. They deal with the procurement, allocation, and organization of the men, money, and material which go into the strategic units and uses of force. (1961, 4–5)

In practice, of course, the policymaking process is highly interactive and dynamic. No sharp line exists between these two elements of military policy decisions. Moreover, they often work at cross-purposes, as decisionmakers must make explicit or tacit trade-offs between the desired ends of national security policy and inevitably scarce resources.

The United States cut the overall size of its armed forces by roughly 30 percent between 1990 and 1996. Total real defense spending was reduced by over 40 percent during this same period. Concurrently, the army shrank by more than a third, with more cuts on the way, and the army's budget authority decreased from roughly $100 billion in 1990 to $60 billion in 1997 (in constant 1997 dollars). The reduction in the army's budget was substantially larger in relative terms than those endured by the air force and the navy (see diagram 2.1). Between 1991 and 1996, the army's percentage of the Defense Department's Total Obligational Budget Authority (its piece of the annual defense budget pie) declined from 30 percent to 23 percent, where it is projected to remain until 2001.[1] Similarly, the army experienced significantly larger reductions in its endstrength than the other services (see diagram 2.2). The army's targeted endstrength has been controversial throughout this period as it has been incrementally reduced from 770,000 to 535,000 to 520,000 to 495,000 to 475,000—much like a bouncing ball, descending down a stairway.[2] As of this writing, it is not yet clear when or where the ball will stop bouncing, restoring stability to army manpower policy.

This chapter focuses on the politics of downsizing decisionmaking. It ex-

Diagram 2.1. Service Budget Authorizations, 1989–1997

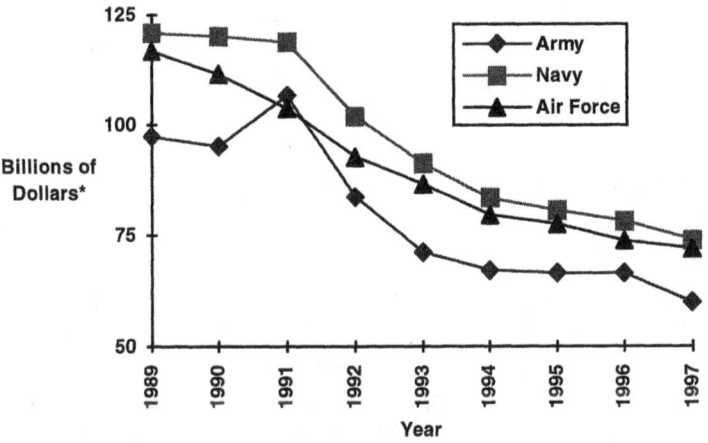

*In 1997 dollars.

SOURCE: National Defense Budget Estimates for Fiscal Year 1997, Office of the Under Secretary of Defense

Diagram 2.2. Military Endstrengths, 1989–1996

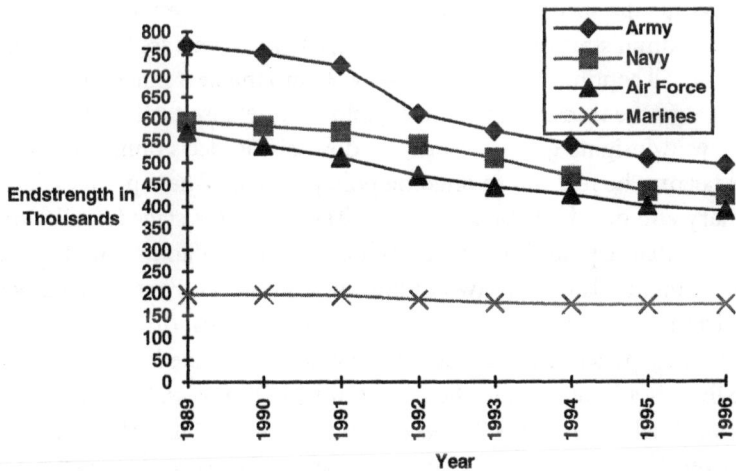

SOURCE: National Defense Budget Estimates for Fiscal Year 1997, Office of the Under Secretary of Defense (Comptroller), April 1996.

amines how the Department of Defense's downsizing proposals were received by policymakers in Congress, and how political forces outside the Pentagon ultimately determined the endstrengths of the military services. It also looks at how leaders within the Office of the Secretary of Defense (OSD), the Joint Staff, and the military services argued among themselves and eventually reconciled the trade-offs between strategic and budgetary considerations. Lastly, it evaluates how army leaders determined the endstrength they advocated in these negotiations and how effective they were in articulating the army's role and resource requirements in an increasingly treacherous political and budgetary environment.

The debate over post–Cold War defense cutbacks has proceeded in three waves. The first wave took place between 1989 and 1993. During this period the Bush administration proposed and instituted its Base Force plan—which spelled out the minimum force America needed to meet the uncertain demands of the post–Cold War era. The second wave took place between 1993 and 1995, during President Bill Clinton's first term in office. The Clinton administration's Bottom-Up Review was the second post-Cold War road map for manpower and budgetary cutbacks. The third wave is still very much under way. As this book goes to press, the Quadrennial Defense Review—a top-to-bottom scrub of U.S. defense strategy and forces—has just been released, and as a result additional army manpower reductions appear imminent. While the specifics of defense planning and budgeting for the second Clinton administration remain to be seen, all indications are that the military services will continue to be downsized well into the next millennium.

Because the transition to a post–Cold War defense establishment is still underway, insights gleaned from the downsizing decisionmaking process thus far may be relevant to ongoing policy debates. These points aside, the primary aim of this chapter is descriptive—to set the stage for subsequent chapters that explore how the army has adapted to and been affected by downsizing. It also makes two important arguments: First, budgetary and political considerations, not strategic considerations, drove the decisions about army personnel cuts between 1989 and 1996; the latter played a decidedly subordinate role in the decisionmaking process. Second, the army had minimal control over the pace of personnel cuts, and little, if any, control over the size of the reductions themselves. The special character of the army and its uniquely vulnerable political position, the common political, organizational, and constitutional constraints imposed on the military leaders of all the services, and the extraordinary influence of Chairman of the Joint Chiefs, Colin Powell, all lessened the army's influence.

Building the Base Force (1989–1993)

The period from 1989 to 1993 was one of remarkable and unprecedented change in world affairs. The reverberations of this change were felt domestically and dramatically affected the content of U.S. military policy. Civilian and military policymakers faced the dual challenges of defining the scope of a widely anticipated "peace dividend" while at the same time making sense of and planning for future national security requirements in a rapidly changing world. The Bush administration's response to this challenge was the Base Force (table 2.1).

For the army the Base Force was a bitter pill indeed. It required a more than 30 percent reduction in endstrength and contraction from an eighteen division to a twelve division active duty force, a larger cut than that mandated for the other services. Moreover, the new defense plan required the withdrawal of more than half the army forces stationed in Europe, the defense of which had been the army's raison d'être for more than forty years. Many senior army leaders opposed the Base Force cuts because they believed they were only the first round in what would prove to be a very painful and prolonged transition to "peace." For these reasons, they unsuccessfully resisted the Base Force plan in the spring and summer of 1990. Even in the most stable of times, the scope of organizational change required by Base Force personnel cuts was daunting. The army's downsizing efforts, and those of the other services, were complicated further by the Gulf War in 1990 and 1991.

TABLE 2.1
Base Force Endstrengths

Active Duty Endstrength	Fiscal Year 1987	Fiscal Year 1990	Base Force (by 1997)	Reduction 1987 Base Force
Army				
divisions	18	18	12	31.5%
endstrength	781,000	750,600	535,000	
Navy				
carriers	16	16	13	13.3%
endstrength	587,000	582,900	509,000	
Air Force				
fighter wings	24	24	15.75	29.3%
endstrength	607,000	539,300	429,000	
Marine Corps				
divisions	3	3	2 1/3	20.5%
endstrength	200,000	196,700	159,000*	

SOURCES: Reports of the Secretary of Defense to the President and Congress, January 1991, 1993; Mark Eitelberg, "Military Manpower and the Future Force," in *American Defense Annual, 1993*, ed. Joseph Kruzel (New York: Lexington Books, 1993), 135–54.

The Bush Administration

The downsizing of the U.S. armed forces is generally assumed to be the logical response to a "decline in demand" for military capabilities as signaled by the end of the Cold War. In reality, however, downsizing began in the mid-1980s, more as a consequence of budgetary pressures than the thawing of superpower tensions. Alarmed by the burgeoning deficit fueled largely by sharp increases in defense spending under President Ronald Reagan, Congress leveled the Pentagon's budget in 1985 and reversed the trend altogether a year later. By the time the Democrats gained control of the Senate in 1986, a consensus had emerged that larger cuts in future defense budgets were inevitable.[3] However, the Reagan administration largely ignored the intent of these cuts—reduced defense spending across the board—by leaving long-range procurement plans unchanged and simply adding the shortfall to future budget requests. This placed added pressure on service budgets, and by December 1987 the Department of Defense (DOD) was recommending, among other things, a ten thousand person reduction in the army to reduce its 1989 budget request. By November 1989, the army had downsized from 781,000, where it had stabilized during the late 1970s, to 770,000.

Until 1989, however, these slight alterations in the size of the army were inconsequential compared to the dramatic changes underway in the Soviet Union. In May 1989, General Colin Powell was one of the first senior military officers to suggest (at least publicly) that a dramatic reduction and restructuring of the army was inevitable.[4] Six months later, after being appointed Chairman of the Joint Chiefs of Staff, Powell became the catalyst for many of the decisions affecting the army's transition to the post–Cold War era. Powell alone, however, was not responsible for the shift in thinking that took place within the Department of Defense during his tenure as chairman. Indeed, important changes in strategic thinking were underway on the Joint Staff and the Army Staff before Powell's arrival (Lewis et al. 1992). The Joint Staff analysis, merged with Powell's own thinking, served in the ensuing months as the foundation for what he labeled the Base Force.[5] In November 1989—days after the fall of the Berlin Wall—Powell presented his Base Force concept to Secretary of Defense Richard Cheney and President George Bush. Both reserved judgment on the proposal, but encouraged Powell to continue to refine his thinking (Powell 1995, 437–39).[6]

In some ways it is surprising that a career military officer would have initiated the debate that led to dramatic reductions in the size of the armed forces. Powell appears to have done so for several reasons. First, he wanted

to ensure that the nation's military leaders played an instrumental role in developing military strategy. Second, as President Reagan's National Security Advisor, Powell had personally witnessed the changes under way in the Soviet Union and was therefore convinced earlier than most of the need for a fundamental rethinking of U.S. defense policy (Powell 1995). Third, Powell's unorthodox approach was indicative of his belief that the traditional Planning, Programming, and Budgeting System (PPBS) budget cycle was too slow and cumbersome to generate the kinds of dramatic changes that he had in mind. Finally, Powell—the consummate politician—believed that if DOD did not propose substantial force reductions expediently, it would fall prey to relentless and uncontrollable pressures from Congress and the public (Jaffe 1994, 42). The world had changed but so too had the domestic political and budgetary climates. A "preemptive strike" was necessary, or cuts would be even more severe.

Despite the growing recognition both inside and outside the Pentagon that significant force cuts were inevitable, the size and pace of these reductions were widely contested:

> Two questions had everything to do with two unstated issues of large political import outside of DOD: Who decides? Who gets the credit? Within DOD, and extending into the armed services... another set of questions was more relevant: How far would the announced reductions actually go? Whose interests would be damaged by them? Would the pain be distributed to achieve some general good, or like pork, on the basis of which particular interest squealed the loudest? How much are the announced reductions a political game to demonstrate concern about spending, after which the DOD would be forced to give in and settle for lesser cutbacks? (Hammond 1994, 164)

Because of these unresolved questions, the Base Force was a tough sell within the Pentagon to Cheney and the Joint Chiefs and on Capitol Hill, where liberal lawmakers sharpened their budget knives in anticipation of a peace dividend.

Secretary of Defense Cheney, a well-known hawk, and Under Secretary of Defense for Policy Paul Wolfowitz, were predictably slow to warm to the idea of significant force reductions. Cheney tasked Wolfowitz to conduct an OSD study to confirm or challenge the Joint Staff's analysis (Jaffe 1994, 24). By May 1990, in an unprecedented expression of cooperation between OSD and the Joint Staff, Powell and Wolfowitz jointly recommended a 25 percent reduction in forces by 1996 (Snider 1993b, 111). Disagreement remained, however, over how much the budget should be reduced to coincide with cuts in force structure. With Powell's guidance, the Joint Staff planned for a 25 percent real decline in defense spending between FY 1992 and FY 1997, but OSD projected a 10 percent decline over the same period (Jaffe 1994, 9).[7] Not surprisingly, Cheney endorsed the less dramatic cut, and in June he revealed tentative plans for a 25 percent reduction in the size of the armed forces and a 10 percent cut in the Pentagon budget in testimony before Congress (Lewis et al. 1992, 27). President Bush outlined this plan further at the Aspen Institute on August 2, only hours after Iraq's invasion of Kuwait (Hammond 1994, 163).

As Powell and Wolfowitz were fleshing out the Base Force concept, the administration submitted its 1991 defense budget, which requested "slight nominal increases [in defense spending] less than would be required to offset inflation" (Ippolito 1994, 44). The budget request, however, ran head-on into a wall of congressional opposition, ending in budgetary gridlock, negotiations, and a budget summit. Congress resisted this proposal for several reasons. First, critics contended that the FY 1991 submission was based on Cold War planning assumptions and fell far short of congressional expectations for the post–Cold War peace dividend. In addition, the annual spending reductions were to be achieved by terminating twenty weapons programs and closing sixty-seven bases, while maintaining high levels of spending for programs such as the "Star Wars" Strategic Defense Initiative (SDI) and the B-2 bomber (Snider 1993a, 24). Not surprisingly, these spending priorities were unacceptable to most members of Congress, particularly those who felt the sting of these decisions in their home districts. During spring and summer 1990, the debate over future defense budgets and force structure intensified.

While the Joint Staff and OSD studies stiffened Cheney's confidence that Base Force levels were justifiable in strategic terms, growing criticism from Capitol Hill finally made significant cutbacks a political necessity. On February 1, 1990, Powell and Cheney had each staunchly defended the administration's "no-growth" defense budget, but were met with blistering questions from members of both the House and Senate Armed Services Committees (Powell 1995, 451). Later that month, Robert Reischauer, Director of the Congressional Budget Office (CBO), gave analytic punch to the burgeoning support for more substantial defense cuts. He proposed five alternative force structures for the post–Cold War era, three of which called for much more dramatic cuts than those being considered publicly by the administration.[8] In March and April, Senate Armed Services Committee Chairman Sam Nunn expressed concerns over "blanks" in the administration's 1991 budget request and the absence of an overarching strategic vision consistent with the changing international environment. In July 1990, the Defense Policy Panel of the

House Armed Services Committee concluded that the administration has been "overly cautious, even grudging, in [its] appreciation of how the Soviet threat is changing" (Ippolito 1994, 46). The administration was under fire.

Cheney's admission in June 1990 that a 25 percent reduction in force structure was conceivable marked a dramatic shift in policy and temporarily blunted accusations that the administration was not serious about cuts in defense (Towell 1990, 974).[9] After months of negotiations, a final defense budget, only marginally less than that proposed by the Bush administration, was agreed upon in October 1990 as part of a larger deal aimed at deficit reduction.[10] The Omnibus Budget Reconciliation Act and the Budget Enforcement Act of 1990—the outcome of this agreement—were, according to President Bush, "the centerpiece of the largest deficit reduction package in history" (Ippolito 1994, 50). These were historic agreements, establishing "nonnegotiable" defense appropriations for fiscal years 1991–93 and a moratorium on defense to domestic transfers during this period (Snider 1993a, 31). The administration's scaled-down defense plan, however, came mostly from the hide of the military personnel budget.

On the basis of the Base Force structure and the spending limits imposed by the 1990 budget agreement, the Bush administration developed and submitted to Congress the Future Years Defense Plan (FYPD) for fiscal years 1992–97 in early 1991. Unlike past plans, which requested unrealistic appropriations, the administration's FYPD was deliberately within the agreed-upon budget limits.[11] This approach, along with several other factors, tempered congressional criticism for the remainder of 1991 and much of 1992. Despite disagreements over projected savings, the Base Force demonstrated that the Bush administration was serious about downsizing defense. Additionally, the preparation for and the conduct of the Gulf War shifted congressional focus away from future defense planning, and Bush's enormous popularity immediately following the war stifled public criticism of the administration. Moreover, Congress was hesitant to risk aggravating the deepening economic recession during 1991 through accelerated defense cutbacks (Ippolito 1994, 65).

The Army and the Base Force

Throughout 1990, the service chiefs voiced strong reservations about the magnitude and pace of the proposed force reductions. As Colin Powell recalls:

They were bright, sophisticated men who could see what was happening in the Soviet Union. But each of them, as the head of a service, ran a huge bureaucratic institution with a massive investment in the past. And each chief naturally preferred to have force reductions fall more heavily on the other guy.... I knew they would not willingly contribute more than loose change as the collection plate was passed. They would practically have to be mugged, and preferred to be mugged to prove to their institutions that they had fought the good fight before the budget ax fell. (1995, 438)

And fight they did. Although Powell clearly regarded civilian leaders as his principal audience, he also took steps to convince the chiefs of the strategic and political logic behind the Base Force. In February 1990, Powell outlined the Base Force to the service chiefs and regional commanders in chief (CINCs) but found little support. Arguing that a threat-based approach was no longer appropriate, Powell posited that the focus of planning should be on the minimal forces, the Base Force, necessary to carry out superpower responsibilities. By dealing in such abstractions, Powell argued, it might be possible to avoid the precipitous cuts and the shift toward isolationism that historically plagued the military in peacetime. But while consensus behind the Base Force slowly gelled within the administration, the service chiefs remained unified in their opposition (Jaffe 1994).

Well before 1990, the army had already taken the initiative with regard to force reductions. Chief of Staff of the Army Carl Vuono decided in fall 1987 to review the army's force structure, particularly in Europe, in light of the declining Soviet threat and the increasing likelihood of a conventional arms control treaty.[12] The resulting Anteus Study, completed in October 1989, recommended a smaller, more flexible force structure, assuming a reduction over the next decade from eighteen divisions of 771,000 soldiers to fifteen divisions of 640,000 soldiers (Lewis et al. 1992, 37). Through Anteus, the army momentarily gained the initiative, but in response to pressure from OSD it undertook two additional studies, Quicksilver I and II, in 1989 and 1990. These studies recommended the elimination of another division, bringing the army to fourteen divisions and an endstrength of 580,000 by the end of 1996, a number subsequently lowered to 560,000.[13] Despite these downward adjustments, however, the army continued to be at odds with the Joint Staff and OSD over its final downsizing target and the pace at which it was to be achieved (Alcalá 1994, 6–7).[14]

Perhaps because of the army's own internal review process and the fact that it was being hit the hardest of all the services, Vuono was—along with General Al Gray of the Marine Corps—the least amenable of the chiefs to the precipitous cuts proposed by Powell (Powell 1995; Jaffe 1994).[15] Vuono argued that these cuts stemmed not from a revised national strategy but were resource-driven. The result, he predicted, would be an army force structure incapable of supporting a force-projection strategy. He also argued against the cuts by maintaining that the army, to a greater extent than the other services, had the diverse capabilities needed for the types of nontraditional operations emerging in the post–Cold War era. Finally, from a political standpoint, army leaders believed that a strategy based on the notion of "base force" floors was naive and feared that these "minimal" force levels would soon become ceilings—a prediction that proved accurate (Alcalá 1994, 10).

Vuono also asserted adamantly that the army could not be downsized annually by more than thirty-five thousand without significantly damaging readiness.[16] A steeper ramp, he maintained, threatened to return the army force to the "hollow force" of the 1970s.[17] This ceiling, however, was as much a political calculation as a military one; there is little evidence that the number was derived by anything other than subjective analysis. As former Deputy Chief of Staff for Personnel Lieutenant General (ret.) William Reno recalls: "There simply was not a good analytical basis for 35,000."[18] By arguing that the rate of downsizing would dramatically affect readiness, however, Vuono was indirectly able to lobby for a higher endstrength at the end of the five-year budget period.[19]

Key members of Congress were skeptical. In numerous appearances before Congress in 1990 and 1991, Vuono emphasized the fragility of the all-volunteer force, the continued uncertainties in the world, and the devastating impact of dramatic personnel cuts on army capabilities in the past.[20] These arguments, however, engendered mixed reactions on Capitol Hill. While the army had a solid core of supporters on the House Armed Services Committee, the chairman, Congressman Les Aspin, was critical of the army proposals for a gradual rate of reduction. A contentious exchange between Aspin and Vuono on March 5, 1990, following Aspin's suggestion that deeper, faster personnel cuts were a necessity illustrates well the emotion surrounding this issue:

> *Vuono:* I am talking about a devastating act on the army if we were forced to [downsize as much and as quickly as you suggest], and I am using pretty strong terms ... because of the significance of what we are talking about.
> *Aspin:* You ought to look at this in terms of minimizing the damage, [rather] than by asking yourselves how we can bring this force down

with the "least" amount of damage. I take it that is the way you came up with your 35,000 number.... That number is not going to make it here. At the end of the next five years ... the Army is going be smaller. ... You are not going to just take 145,000 off the 760,000.... It will be smaller than just 35,000 a year for five years.

Vuono: I hope we are prepared for the consequences.[21]

In retrospect, there is little doubt that it was possible to downsize more quickly than thirty-five thousand a year without "fracturing" the force; indeed, in 1992 alone the army cut its ranks by one hundred thousand without the predicted consequences.[22] At the same time, Vuono and others appeared sincere in their belief that more rapid cuts would have a negative impact on the readiness and morale of the army. As one senior officer recalls: "None of us thought that things would happen as quickly as they did ... and [Vuono] and the people close to him genuinely believed that somewhere above fifty thousand, we would be unable to cope. The army was stronger than we thought it was. Those of us who survived the 1970s are perhaps to be forgiven for that underestimation."[23] Additionally, army leaders were skeptical that the savings achieved through rapid personnel cuts would be dedicated to army modernization or readiness, instead believing simply that they would be rolled into DOD cost-cutting efforts. As one of Vuono's closest advisors recalls:

> This is like the old insurance thing. Insurance salesmen say buy whole life. An investment counselor will say buy term insurance and invest the difference. The problem that we saw was that if we bought term, the difference would be taken away from us and we wouldn't be able to invest it. So we went with whole life.[24]

By autumn 1990, however, as it became increasingly clear that the escalating crisis in the Middle East would at best only delay defense cuts, the chiefs became more receptive to the Base Force.[25] With the exception of Gray, they were unsuccessful in resisting Powell's proposed cutbacks.[26] Vuono reluctantly accepted a twelve-division, 535,000 man army, bowing to concerns that if he failed to cooperate he would be viewed as obstructionist, perhaps precipitating even larger reductions.[27] In November, Cheney directed each of the military departments to adjust its programs to satisfy his new fiscal guidance, and DOD projected an active duty endstrength of 509,700 for the navy, 437,200 for the air force, and 159,000 for the Marine Corps by the end of FY 1995.[28] The army, which had started FY 1990 with authorization for 770,000 soldiers, ended it by agreeing to downsize by more than 30 percent, to 535,000—the smallest the army has been since 1939.

The Gulf War

The debate over defense cutbacks temporarily abated during the Gulf War, and in the aftermath of Operation Desert Storm its tone and content changed notably.[29] Many viewed the Gulf War as validation of the conceptual underpinnings of the high-tech, force projection strategy that lay behind the Base Force (Snider 1993b, 127). Policymakers began to focus not only on how much and at what rate to downsize but also on the mechanics of the process.[30] They grew concerned over the demographics of downsizing, in particular over which groups within the armed forces might be unfavorably affected by large personnel reductions.[31] Anxiety rose over the human costs of downsizing and the possible involuntary separation of hundreds of thousands of service members, many of whom were Gulf War veterans. Senator Daniel K. Inouye, Chairman of the Subcommittee for Military Appropriations, remarked in March 1991:

> It is somehow both ironic and disturbing that as soldiers, sailors, airmen, and marines return from their trial by ordeal in the desert, we have already embarked on a venture to drastically reduce the size of our armed services.... I feel it would be disgraceful to welcome these members of an all volunteer force home and then hand them a pink slip—well done, welcome home, and good-bye.[32]

These concerns provoked a flurry of activity within the Department of Defense and Congress. The DOD proposed and Congress authorized an unprecedented set of programs and benefits to minimize the burden of downsizing and took steps to ease the constraints imposed upon personnel planners by existing officer management legislation.[33] The FY 1991 National Defense Authorization Act (NDAA) expanded the authority of the services to separate personnel, increased transition benefits and separation pay, gave specific guidance on how force levels were to be achieved, and required DOD to develop relocation assistance programs. The NDAA for fiscal years 1992 and 1993 was even more crucial as it gave the services temporary permission to offer monetary incentives—the voluntary separation incentive (VSI) and special separation benefit (SSB)—to encourage voluntary separation of uniformed personnel (Eitelberg 1993).

The DOD was also deeply involved in overseeing and assisting the services in downsizing. As early as January 1990, the Secretary of Defense emphasized that priority should be placed on quality, grade mix, and sustained training during force reductions, and the Deputy Secretary of Defense gave specific directives about the design of service personnel reduction plans.[34] In addition, the Office of the Assistant Secretary of Defense for Force Management and Personnel regularly critiqued the services' downsizing plans, and service secretaries briefed the Secretary of Defense on their respective plans.[35]

Despite this renewed focus on the details of downsizing, the parades celebrating victory in the Gulf had barely subsided when Base Force plans were again under fire.[36] The downsizing debate was transformed by several events: the failure of the coup attempt against Soviet president Mikhail Gorbachev in August 1991, the breakup of the Soviet Union four months later, and the election of Bill Clinton to the presidency in November 1992 all strengthened support for deeper reductions.[37] Representative Aspin led the attack on the Base Force from his position as Chairman of the House Armed Services Committee.[38] In a speech on September 1, 1991, Aspin argued that the Bush administration should revisit the 1990 budget agreement, increase the rate of downsizing, and rethink the magnitude of Base Force cuts in light of dramatic changes in the international environment.[39] So began a debate over future force reductions that would last through the Presidential elections.[40] The Bush administration, which had achieved the initiative with the Base Force in 1990 and 1991, was on the defensive throughout most of 1992.

Critics of the Base Force rejected the administration's claim that it had planned for the continued erosion of the Soviet threat, insisting that the breakup of the Soviet Union had further altered not only the strategic environment, but also the politics of the defense budgeting process (Asmus 1993, 67). Aspin argued that the Base Force resulted from a "top-down" approach to force planning, the outcome of which would simply be a smaller version of the Cold War force structure with no clear relationship between ends and means (Correl 1992). Moreover, the Base Force was capabilities-based, as opposed to threat-based, a luxury that Aspin argued was inappropriate, unaffordable, and politically unsalable in the wake of the Cold War (CBO 1991, 5).

As alternatives to the Base Force, Aspin, in a February 1992 White Paper proposed four significantly smaller force structures, advocating "Option C," a force capable of conducting two simultaneous "Desert Storm-equivalents."[41] Option C linked specific threats to "building blocks" of force structure needed to overcome those threats, an approach Aspin argued was necessary to gauge the proper size for the armed forces and to sell these force levels to Congress (Towell 1992a, 479). On top of Base Force reductions, Option C proposed a cut from twelve to nine active army divisions and the elimination of an additional 217,000 active duty military personnel. From these reductions, Aspin projected savings of $60 billion over Bush's 1993 budget request (Correl 1992, 15).

Cheney and Powell tenaciously defended the force levels prescribed by the Base Force.[42] Both argued before Congress that the Base Force was designed on the assumption that the Soviet threat would continue to diminish throughout the 1990s (Lancaster 1992, A4). Powell offered to show congressmen two-year old charts that anticipated a 50 percent reduction in Soviet armed forces and a 40 percent drop in the size of the Soviet military-industrial complex (Correl 1992). Additionally, both Cheney and Powell criticized Congress for its unwillingness to sanction needed cuts in weapons programs because of the resulting job losses in their districts and emphasized the necessity of maintaining force levels capable of overcoming threats not yet known. Powell asserted, "In a very real sense, the primary threat to our security is . . . being unprepared to handle a crisis or war that no one expected or predicted" (Asmus 1993, 64). Moreover, with uncharacteristic harshness, he derided Aspin's Option C as "fundamentally flawed . . . Its methodology is unsound, its strategy unwise, and the forces and capabilities it proposes unbalanced" (Eitelberg 1993, 140).[43]

Although defense policy was not a major campaign issue, by autumn 1992 it was clear that the armed forces were going to shrink below Base Force levels regardless of who won the presidency. Following Bush's loss, his administration put on hold the plans developed to reduce the defense budget and the force structure below Base Force levels. In January 1993, President Clinton, who as a candidate had promised $60 billion in defense savings, assumed responsibility for a bloated six-year defense budget based on overly optimistic assumptions about inflation and future weapons costs, growing demands for cuts in defense spending, and an enduring controversy over the future direction and size of U.S. conventional forces.[44] The possibility of larger cuts in the army's budget and endstrength loomed ever larger.

The Bottom-Up Review (1993–1995)

Between spring 1993 and fall 1995 many of the key players changed, but the game—the debate over post–Cold War cutbacks—remained much the same. With Clinton's appointment of Les Aspin as Secretary of Defense, the political dynamics shifted: the most powerful proponent of additional force reductions moved to the Pentagon, while conservatives in Congress opposed to further cuts became more vocal and influential in their resistance. Within the Pentagon, influence over military policy shifted subtly from the Joint Staff to OSD, and force planning became explicitly threat-based, as Aspin had advocated in Option C. Following this approach, the Clinton administration's defense plan—the Bottom-Up Review—called for larger cuts in service budgets and endstrengths. Finally, due at least partly to the cuts promised by Clinton during the presidential campaign, force reductions were driven to an even greater extent than before by budgetary and political considerations.[45]

For the army, the election of Bill Clinton made a bad situation worse. The army's relationship with Aspin had never been particularly amicable, and his new role as Defense Secretary promised to strain it further. While the Base Force cutbacks had been painful, the Bush team was far more palatable to the military than the assortment of Hill staffers and second-generation Whiz Kids who accompanied Aspin to the Pentagon. Aspin proposed a "bottom-up" review of defense forces, a process designed to match potential national security threats with the defense capabilities needed to overcome them. This approach placed added emphasis on air power at the expense of the army and the navy, and required the army to reduce its endstrength to 495,000.

TABLE 2.2
From the Base Force to the Bottom-Up Review

Active Duty Endstrength	Base Force (BF)	Option C[a]	Bottom-Up Review (BUR)	Reduction BF to BUR
Army				
divisions	12	9	10	7.5%
endstrength	535,000	495,000		
Navy				
carriers	13	12	11 + 1 training carrier	23%
endstrength	509,000	394,000		
Air Force				
wings	15 3/4	10	13	9.1%
endstrength	429,000	390,000		
Marine Corps				
divisions	2 1/3	2	2	-9.4%
endstrength	159,000	174,000		

SOURCES: *An Approach to Sizing Conventional Forces for the Post-Soviet Era: Four Illustrative Options* (1992); Owens (1995).

NOTE: These numbers were subsequently adjusted, with the army's endstrength target tentatively reduced to 475,000 and the navy's projected endstrength cut to roughly 387,500 by 1999.

[a] Aspin's Option C did not include projected endstrengths. BUR endstrengths are to be achieved by 1999.

The Clinton Administration

Although conservatives feared President Clinton would cut too deeply into defense, the new administration came into office less committed than might have been expected to dramatic changes in military policy. Clinton was politically constrained in this area because of his widely publicized avoidance of military service in Vietnam and his lack of foreign policy experience. Moreover, as the first Democrat to occupy the White House in twelve years, it was politically prudent of him to appear moderate on military policy. The early controversy over the inclusion of homosexuals in the military and Clinton's reluctance to send military forces to Bosnia also prompted the president to seek a low profile on defense during his first year in office.

Because the debate over additional cuts in force structure had to some extent been decided at the ballot box, the discussions between civilian and military policymakers no longer focused on whether to cut, but rather on where to cut to generate the savings needed to satisfy Clinton's campaign pledges. In addition, DOD civilians became more assertive. To a greater extent than Cheney, Aspin appears to have viewed it as the responsibility of civilian policymakers to counterbalance the positions of senior military officers. In a manner not unlike that of a former boss, Secretary of Defense Robert McNamara, Aspin modified the traditional "rules" delineating the respective areas of civilian and military judgment. To his credit, Aspin recognized that a new strategic framework would be necessary to justify the Clinton administration's defense budgets. For this reason, he initiated a reassessment of the nation's defense strategy, force structure, modernization, and infrastructure soon after taking office, the so-called Bottom-Up Review (BUR). Aspin's whiz kids became the predominant players in the Bottom-Up Review, supplanting the military services and the Joint Staff.

In February 1993, Clinton announced that he would cut at least $88 billion from Bush's projected defense budgets for fiscal 1994–97 ($18 billion more than he pledged during his campaign), but he made only modest changes in Bush's 1994 budget proposals. Congress for the most part accepted Aspin's contention that the administration was "treading water," waiting to initiate dramatic changes until after the release of the Bottom-Up Review, though conservatives in Congress began voicing concern long before the study was complete (Ippolito 1994, 99).[46] The battle lines had been drawn, but the opening salvo was temporarily delayed pending the release of the Bottom-Up Review.

Despite their contentious exchanges during the Bush years, Aspin and

Powell were surprisingly obliging toward one another. Aspin—who earlier had argued for a "win-hold-win" strategy using air power to hold one aggressor at bay while defeating another—now advocated a "win-win" strategy, a position more palatable to Powell (Callahan 1994). Likewise, though Powell stood firm against the inclusion of homosexuals in the military, he was surprisingly pliant on the issue of force reductions (Hammond 1994, 175). As he explained to the Senate Armed Services Committee in April 1993, the BUR was part of "a necessary process of continual reassessment and realignment mandated by the constantly changing circumstances and events of our time." In comparing the Base Force with the Bottom-Up Review, Powell went on to remark:

> My dear friend Secretary Aspin and I had great fun last year arguing over who was the top-down guy and who was the bottom-up guy. But the fact is both of us have worked in a bottom up way.... The reconciliation of the two views is that we have to look at threats, but we also have to have broad capabilities.... I am comfortable with the process ... laid out by Secretary Aspin. A lot has changed since I was pitching the base force last year.[47]

What had changed, other than the occupants of 1600 Pennsylvania Avenue? Before Clinton's electoral victory, Powell argued that to go further or faster with force reductions would "break" the armed forces and that Aspin's approach was "fundamentally flawed." A few short months after the election, Powell publicly accepted the need for lower force levels and directed the Joint Staff to participate fully with the OSD in the Bottom-Up Review (Hammond 1994, 178). The "breaking point" to which Powell referred was apparently more a matter of political posturing than military requirements.

The Bottom-Up Review process included a number of working groups with participants from the Office of the Secretary of Defense, the Joint Staff, and the services under the direction of a steering committee chaired by the Under Secretary of Defense for Acquisition. Among civilian policymakers, the Assistant Secretary for Strategy, Requirements, and Resources, Aspin appointee Edward Warner, played a leading role in this effort (Hammond 1994, 170). Although the input of the working groups was considered, substantive deliberations were restricted to the highest levels, and it was largely the political appointees who controlled the process.[48] The services showed varying degrees of resistance to the force levels considered by OSD and the Joint Staff during the Bottom-Up Review analysis. While the air force benefited from Aspin's generous assumptions concerning the use of airpower, the navy was distraught over the reduction in aircraft carriers proposed by Clinton during the campaign. Following Clinton's inauguration, it launched a campaign of its own, in Congress and the Pentagon, to reverse the carrier decision (Morrison 1993). The marine corps also actively campaigned to reverse the force cuts imposed under the Base Force plan and subsequently by the BUR (Alcalá 1993, 12).

The "top-down" nature of the Bottom-Up Review is perhaps best illustrated by the fact that an initial set of force structure recommendations completed in May were sent back to the working groups to find further cuts to satisfy available funding. When the BUR was finally released on September 1, 1993, it was received with varying degrees of enthusiasm by Congress and the military services. The proposed force structure cuts were generally thought to be less dramatic than expected and were in fact less severe than Aspin's Option C. The navy effectively lobbied to maintain eleven of its twelve active duty aircraft carriers, transferring only one to the Navy Reserves; the air force maintained thirteen of its fifteen active duty fighter wings, and the Marine Corps retained all three of its active duty divisions. The army was reduced from twelve to ten active duty divisions (Owens 1995, 158). The Marine Corps emerged as the clear victor, having avoided force reductions altogether, while the army suffered slightly higher cuts in force structure than the other services.[49] In general, however, each service maintained its pre–Bottom-Up Review share of a steadily shrinking budgetary and force structure pie.

Regardless of whether or not one agrees with its approach or recommendations, the Bottom-Up Review undeniably shaped the debate over the size and content of America's armed forces from fall 1993 to fall 1995 (though the administration steadily distanced itself from the BUR during this period). In this regard, at least, it achieved Aspin's objective. Controversy over the BUR centered on two interrelated questions: (1) was the objective of being able to fight simultaneously two major regional contingencies (MRCs) appropriate and (2) were the resources budgeted by the administration adequate to support BUR force levels?[50] While the answers to these questions lie outside the scope of this chapter, a brief review of the debate surrounding them will help put subsequent decisions regarding the downsizing of the army into perspective.

Defense experts with both conservative and liberal leanings questioned the logic behind the BUR. Critics labeled the requirement that the U.S. military be prepared to fight two MRCs—almost simultaneously and on opposite ends of the earth—a "war planner's fantasy" (Borosage 1994). In particular, the assumptions that inadequate forces might tempt aggressors in one area while U.S. forces were engaged in another, and that the U.S. could or would engage in such contingencies without allied support, were viewed as extraordinarily unlikely. Some also contended that the BUR, rather than recasting the Cold War military merely shrank it. The Pentagon simply did what bureaucracies do in unpredictable environments—fit the uncertain demands of the future into existing paradigms (Snider 1996b). Finally, even if one accepted the two-MRC scenario as appropriate, there was contention over whether it was achievable with the forces prescribed by the BUR.

It is clear that the Clinton administration has proposed inadequate defense budgets to support the BUR force structure, though there is disagreement over the magnitude of this shortfall.[51] The General Accounting Office (GAO) reported in July 1994 that the 1995–99 Clinton defense plan might be underfunded by more than $150 billion.[52] In January 1995, the Congressional Budget Office estimated that the BUR force structure, along with the operations level and modernization programs proposed, were likely to cost $65 billion more than proposed by Clinton (CBO 1994a, 4). To what degree the Clinton administration was aware of this shortfall is uncertain. It is evident that the proposed force structure and budget cuts struck a middle ground: they were small enough to generate the skeptical support of many defense moderates and large enough to appease some of the more vociferous lower defense spending liberals. And, indeed, this appears to have been the BUR's intent from the very beginning.

By fall 1994, however, this mismatch between plans and resources presented decisionmakers in Congress, the administration, and the armed services with an undesirable set of choices. One option was to allocate additional funding to defense, but this possibility seemed increasingly unlikely as the fiscal climate worsened. Alternatively, additional cuts in the defense budget were possible in one of three areas: force structure, modernization, or readiness. Predictably, the armed services and conservatives in Congress resisted budgetary cuts in each. One defense analyst summarized the administration's plight in August 1994: "The administration is torn over the Bottom-Up Review. They recognize that they don't have the resources to support it, but they have no alternative. They're caught between a strategic rock and a fiscal hard place" (Dov Zakheim as quoted in Pine 1994, 5). This dilemma was felt most acutely by the army.

The Army and the Bottom-Up Review

On April 17, 1991, General Gordon Sullivan became the thirty-second Army Chief of Staff, and he led the army through the transition from the Base Force to the Bottom-Up Review. As army leaders had predicted, the Base

Force had become the ceiling, rather than the floor, and defense policymakers were immersed in negotiations over additional defense cutbacks. Sullivan, a one-time opponent of the Base Force, became one of its staunchest advocates.⁵³ In testimony before the Senate Armed Services Committee in February 1992, for example, he generously described the army's role in determining the Base Force:

> *Senator Exon* (D-NE): How did your services arrive at the numbers you did? ... Did you have input into what the numbers would be? Or were you ... suddenly presented with a number from the Secretary of Defense?
>
> *General Sullivan:* We took a look at the world in which we are living. We looked at threats. We bumped them up against the National Military Strategy and ... came up with a Base Force after looking at all that. ... We were not given a number.⁵⁴

In testimony the same day before the House Armed Services Committee, Sullivan again defended the Base Force, arguing that if the army were cut below twelve divisions, it would be incapable of achieving decisive victory.

> *General Sullivan:* Our analysis is that below 12 divisions we run the risk of not being able to achieve decisive victory. Once you start going below 12 divisions, then you start having serious problems in terms of being able to overcome the enemy.
>
> *Representative Skelton* (D-MO): There has been much discussion about a 10-division active duty Army.... If that were the case, assuming everything was equal—doctrine, morale, training, equipment and all that goes with it—could you carry on a successful Desert Storm campaign ... and concurrently a successful defense of South Korea?
>
> *General Sullivan:* No Sir, I couldn't.⁵⁵

Less than a year after Sullivan made these comments, the Bottom-Up Review—which would take the army well below twelve divisions—was well under way. However, the army played an even more marginal role in the development of the BUR than in the creation of the Base Force. Key civilian policymakers obtained analytical results from Joint Staff models and simulations. Based on this input, they developed a force structure bolstered by optimistic assumptions about the increased capabilities derived from what Aspin called "force enhancers," such as prepositioned equipment and additional sealift.⁵⁶ The BUR also made far rosier assumptions than Army Staff or Joint Staff planners about how rapidly Army Reserve units could be alerted and deployed and how quickly active duty units could be reconstituted. OSD officials argued that "force enhancers" ensured that four to five army divisions would be sufficient for each of the two major regional contingencies on which the BUR was based (Alcalá 1993, 6–8).

The details of the army's involvement in the BUR planning are sketchy, with accounts varying greatly, even among those who participated in this process. Some maintain, for example, that army leaders had minimal involvement in the final BUR decisions, did not engage in an external campaign or share alternative assessments with key supporters on Capitol Hill, and, up until the day the results were announced, were confident that the army would not suffer as deep cuts as it did from the BUR (Alcalá 1993). Conversely, others argue that the army never for an instant believed it would be able to hold the Base Force, and that it was deeply involved in the BUR decisionmaking process, and that, in the end, it was successful in arguing for a ten-division force and an endstrength of 495,000 when the OSD was lobbying for much deeper cuts.[57] These differences aside, what is clear is that the army lost two of twelve divisions and established a precarious new downsizing target of 495,000. Within eighteen months, the army's new "bottom line" was again under siege.

Critics of the BUR recommendations for the army disputed the optimistic reliance on "force enhancers or enablers" to justify a ten-division force, which, they argued, would be incapable of carrying out two MRCs. Congressman Ike Skelton (D-MO), an influential member of the House Armed Services Committee, held a hearing on army manpower levels on October 27, 1993, which was attended by senior members of the House Appropriations and Armed Services Committees, to inveigh against Aspin's proposed cuts in the army.[58] However, these arguments, were somewhat overstated. After all, the Bottom-Up Review cuts were insubstantial in comparison to those required by the Base Force. Although the elimination of two additional division headquarters did attenuate the army's flexibility and overall command and control capability, it was not the reduction in "combat power" that some critics suggested. Under the Base Force plan, the army had thirty-three combat brigades organized into twelve active divisions; thus, three divisions had only two of their three allotted combat brigades. During negotiations over the BUR, however, the army wisely spoke only in terms of full divisions. Thus, the shift from a twelve- to a ten-division force required the elimination of only three active combat brigades (CBO 1994c, 3).

The constant criticism directed at the BUR since its release suggests that its critics believe that it, like the Base Force, might be a transitional point en route to additional force reductions. As with the Base Force, army leaders became passionate supporters of force levels that they had only months before derided. In March 1994, for example, in response to questions submitted by Senator Strom Thurmond, General Sullivan underwent a second transformation:

> During ... the development of the BUR ... I initially recommended consideration of higher Army force levels to the Chairman of the Joint Chiefs of Staff and later to the Assistant Secretary of Defense for Strategy, Requirements, and Assessments. However, during the course of our deliberations, I came to the position that the Army could execute the two near-simultaneous MRC strategy with a moderate degree of risk [with ten active divisions] provided that they are fully resourced, that all force enhancements and enablers are fully executed in accordance with the BUR.[59]

The planning and implementation of downsizing has been made more difficult by the absence of a predictable "top line" (total) for army budget authorizations. The resulting plans/resources mismatch has affected the army to perhaps an even greater extent than it has affected the other services (Finnegan and Glashow 1995, 1). In November 1994, the CBO found that even at BUR force levels, the army was significantly underfunded under the Clinton administration's plan for the period from 1995 to 2010 (CBO 1994b).[60]

The army budget is essentially dedicated to three "pillars" of military capability: force structure (the number and size of army units), modernization (the technical sophistication of the forces, weapon systems, and equipment), and readiness (the capacity to deploy quickly and perform in wartime as planned). In a period of declining resources, the distribution of funds across these three areas is a zero-sum game, as dollars spent in one area require cuts in the others. Thus, army leaders have, at least in their own minds, faced an unacceptable set of choices: either cut force structure and become too small to perform effectively the missions outlined by the BUR or forgo the modern weapons and the level of readiness necessary to execute these missions successfully and expeditiously.[61]

To the limited extent that the army controlled its destiny, its leaders chose to maintain force structure and readiness at the expense of modernization (Kitfield 1993c). The army has consistently (and unsuccessfully) argued against additional force reductions during both the Bush and Clinton administrations. And, in an effort to minimize turbulence, its leaders decided on the more costly option of reducing endstrength more gradually than did the other services. It is important at this point to distinguish between reductions in force structure—divisions, wings, aircraft carriers—and personnel. The air force and navy have been extraordinarily reluctant to cut force structure but have been less concerned with the magnitude of cuts in personnel. With the exception of the Marine Corps, no service has been more resistant to endstrength reductions than the army. Because the army's personnel account comprises almost half of its budget, decisions to maintain force structure have significantly affected the availability of resources for modernization and, to a lesser degree, readiness (West 1994; Finnegan and Glashow 1995, 1).[62] Key programs, such as the development of the RAH-66 Comanche helicopter, have been cut or eliminated to generate additional funds for readiness and structure.[63]

The effects of budget cuts on readiness, however, have received the most attention. Since Chief of Staff Edward C. Meyer made the "hollow army" a source of national concern and meaty campaign rhetoric in 1980, readiness has been a priority for successive administrations, Congress, and the armed services—but particularly for the army, which suffered the most in this area during the post–Vietnam period (Owens 1995). Despite the emphasis that both civilian and military officials had apparently placed on preparedness over the years, by summer 1994 the army's readiness was being questioned. This controversy coincided with the November 1994 congressional elections and the arrival soon after of a new Republican majority in both the House and Senate. For more than a year, critics had questioned the longevity of the Bottom-Up Review. The combination of these two events led many commentators to surmise that the BUR was dead.

The Death of the Bottom-Up Review?

Between fall 1994 and the beginning of 1995, political support for the BUR eroded dramatically. In July 1994, a special task force appointed by Aspin to evaluate military preparedness had reported "pockets of unreadiness" in the armed forces, though it had found the general readiness posture of U.S. military forces to be acceptable (Morrison 1994). On November 15, 1994, the Pentagon disclosed that three of the twelve active army divisions had suffered a significant decline in military readiness due to funding shortfalls stemming from deployments to Rwanda, Haiti, and Kuwait.[64] This disclosure benefited Aspin's successor as Secretary of Defense, William Perry, when he requested $2.6 billion in supplemental funding from Congress for FY 1995 to offset the costs of these operations. On December 1, President

Clinton announced that an additional $25 billion would be devoted to the existing defense budget over the next six years.[65]

Cynics viewed the readiness flap as predictable Pentagon grandstanding. As Congressman Barney Frank (D-MA) sarcastically remarked: "If you are going to invade America, do it in November just before the budget. This is our weakest moment every year" (Black 1994, 2). To what extent the crisis in readiness was fabricated or legitimate is difficult to gauge; readiness is inherently subjective, and the judgment of it rests ultimately with senior military officers. In retrospect, it appears that the November readiness crisis was not as dire as it first appeared. On December 27, 1994, the *New York Times* suggested that the commanders of the three divisions in question had painted an overly pessimistic picture of readiness to help the army claim a larger share of the defense budget ("Are US Forces Ready to Fight?"). However, the attention focused on readiness had the desired effect. Clinton devoted additional funds to the Pentagon, and the debate over the army's size and budget gained political prominence.

The mid-term congressional elections in November 1994 marked a sea change in American politics. After forty years in the minority, the Republican Party achieved a majority in both the House and the Senate. High on the Republican agenda—the sixth point on the ten-point *Contract with America*—was resurrecting national defense. Republicans charged that the Clinton administration was spending too little on defense and that the armed forces were doing too much. The result, Floyd Spence (R-SC), the new House Armed Services Committee Chairman, concluded, was "a systemic degrading of the military's readiness" (*Gannett News Service*, November 18, 1994). Despite these calls for dramatic changes in national defense policy, 1995 was most notable for the fact that surprisingly little changed. As the consequence of a split between deficit hawks and defense conservatives within the Republican Party, the defense budget resolution for fiscal years 1996–2002 passed by Congress in June 1995 was similar in content and scope to Clinton's own budget proposal (Spring 1995). Moreover, though Republicans proposed marginal increases in defense spending, they also supported increased spending across a wider range of programs, including on SDI, which threatened to worsen the plans/resource mismatch.[66]

The first tangible crack in BUR force levels appeared in May 1995. Defense Secretary Perry directed the army to reduce its endstrength by an additional 20,000 troops, to 475,000, by 1999, a cut predicted to free roughly $1 billion annually for modernization (Stavem 1995). Although Perry's mandate was part of a comprehensive effort to raise additional funding for the army's modernization programs, it had symbolic significance as well. Throughout spring 1995, General Sullivan vigorously resisted additional force structure cuts while actively lobbying for added funding for modernization. Perry eventually allocated more money for this purpose, but it came at a price: in April 1995, Sullivan finally agreed to support a cut to 475,000, provided that additional funding for army modernization be siphoned from the other services.[67] The Army's bottom line once again proved to be negotiable.

The cycle described several times previously repeated itself. Critics of the agreement were afraid that this cut would require the army to go below ten divisions, further eroding its capacity to prevail in dual major regional contingencies; advocates applauded the decision as a necessary step toward achieving the much lower force levels required in the post–Cold War era. As of this writing, in spring 1997, the debate over funding for readiness, modernization, and force structure continues and the plans/resources mismatch remains. Barring significant increases in defense spending, it will be necessary for the army to make "painful" trade-offs between force structure, readiness, and modernization in the years ahead. There is also the very real possibility that this situation will force the present or future administrations to abandon the two-MRC scenario altogether (CBO 1995, 55–57).

In June 1995, General Dennis Reimer became the thirty-third Chief of Staff of the Army. In 1990 and 1991, as Major General Reimer oversaw one of the first downsizing efforts at Fort Carson, Colorado, the army's most senior leaders speculated that by the end of 1995 downsizing would be complete and that the role of their protégés would be to establish stability, reconstitute the force, and set a steady course for the twenty-first century.[68] The army, however, remains in transition. Although the size of the reductions that will result from the Quadrennial Defense Review is uncertain, there is much evidence that the army's endstrength will be cut further, perhaps substantially further, in the years ahead. The third wave of post–Cold War strategic thinking calls for a "portfolio management approach" to defense planning, with emphasis on the multiple goals of "contingency capability, environment shaping, and strategic adaptiveness" (Davis et al. 1996, 2). Under the more dramatic proposals being considered using this approach, the army's combat forces could conceivably be cut by another third (Davis et al. 1997, 34). Thus, while the army's final resting place remains unclear, it seems increasingly likely that cuts will continue in the years ahead.[69] In any case, by the end of 1999—when the currently projected reductions are complete—the army will have been downsizing for more than a decade. The effects of this prolonged uncertainty on the health and vitality of the army are discussed in later chapters.

The Politics of Downsizing

The military services had minimal control over the pace and the magnitude of downsizing. Budgets and politics, not strategy, drove the process. The army, in particular, had limited influence over the downsizing decisionmaking process. Why? Aaron Wildavsky writes, "Whether one listens to advocates of higher or lower spending, they all agree that the defense effort should be apportioned to estimates for the perceived threat from abroad" (1988, 379). In other words, strategic considerations should be the primary impetus behind force structure decisions. But what should be and what is are often at odds. Despite the axiom that strategy should shape budgets, defense planners have always coped with political and budgetary constraints when attempting to balance threats against capabilities (Ippolitio 1994, 149). As former Defense Secretary Dick Cheney succinctly observes: "In the real world, budgets drive strategy, strategy does not drive budgets" (Toffler and Toffler 1993, 215). This principle has clearly been manifest in the downsizing of the army, and in this regard the decisionmaking process was not unique.

In the decisions leading up to the first two waves of post–Cold War downsizing—the Base Force and the Bottom-Up Review—budgetary and political considerations were the predominant determinants of military policy. This assertion is supported by the historical record. First, since 1991, changes in the strategic environment have been minimal, yet there have been numerous decisions to make additional cuts in the size of the military services without accompanying shifts in strategic thinking. Second, between 1990 and 1995, individual policymakers altered their positions concerning the appropriate magnitude and pace of downsizing in conjunction with changes in the political environment. Third, there was significant congressional pressure on the Bush and Clinton administrations to expedite force structure cuts.

The warming of U.S.-Soviet relations and the eventual breakup of the USSR made downsizing a strategic and political possibility. These changes provided the context within which all downsizing decisions took place. By 1990, however, most of the changes in the international environment that served as a catalyst for the downsizing debate had already occurred. The August 1991 coup attempt against President Gorbachev and subsequent dissolution of the USSR reaffirmed the notion that the superpower rivalry was finally dead and made a threat to western Europe that much more remote. But Colin Powell had been preaching that "the bear is benign" since May 1989, and the Base Force was developed based on that assumption. Between 1990 and 1995, U.S. interests and the possible "threats" to those interests remained essentially unchanged. Yet policymakers continued to downsize the U.S. military forces incrementally during this period.

One possible explanation for this phenomenon is the normal lag between changes in the world and the adjustments to these changes in the force planning process. This may partially explain why many of the downsizing decisions justified as a necessary response to the end of the Cold War took place years after the Cold War was universally regarded as over. Downsizing decisions might also be explained as the consequence of shifts in strategic thinking. In other words, different strategic objectives or conflicting approaches to force planning, as were said to have existed between the Base Force and the Bottom-Up Review, might also have accounted for the incremental force reductions. In reality, however, the strategic visions and methodologies behind the two were remarkably similar.

Obviously, the international environment had to have been seen as relatively benign for large-scale reductions to have been undertaken. The Base Force and the Bottom-Up Review were based on matching assessments of the international environment and designed with the intent that U.S. forces should be capable of simultaneously fighting and winning multiple regional scenarios (Morrison 1994, 2126; Garrity and Weiner 1992, 57). One can argue over whether the Base Force or the Bottom-Up Review were in fact capabilities-based or threat-based. Powell said the Base Force was capabilities-based—that it represented the minimum forces necessary for a superpower—while the BUR planning process was openly threat-based, in the sense that Aspin directed his staff to build a force structure from the ground up capable of defeating "illustrative aggressors" on the Korean and Arabian peninsulas. The Base Force, however, was also based on an assessment of regional threats and the military capacity to confront more than one of these threats concurrently, while having the military capability needed to overcome two mid-size regional threats underlay the BUR planning process.[70] In short, the international environment, the strategic vision, and the methodologies employed in developing the Base Force and Bottom-Up Review varied only marginally. Political and budgetary pressures were the primary motivation for continued force reductions.

Second, on numerous occasions key policymakers modified their positions concerning the minimal force levels necessary in the post–Cold War era as political and budgetary pressures heightened. Both General Sullivan and General Vuono, for example, testified before Congress that the reductions under consideration would "fracture" the army and posed unacceptable levels of risk. Within a year, however, each voiced his support for the force levels he had previously opposed. General Colin Powell also came to support the lower force levels recommended by the BUR after having argued so vehemently against cuts below the Base Force. Political and budgetary pressures made hypocrites of these military policymakers, who first reluctantly supported cuts to force levels they had once opposed and then later supported these force levels in an effort to avoid additional reductions.

Third, both the Bush and Clinton administrations were influenced by the fear that if they did not take the initiative, Congress, rather than DOD, would set the parameters of the downsizing debate. In this way Congress affected the decisionmaking process, and this testifies to its increasing prominence in the management of defense policy and oversight of the defense budget (Ippolito 1994, 24).[71] Prominent members of the House and Senate Armed Services and Appropriations Committees devoted significant attention to the downsizing and restructuring of America's defense establishment. Senator Sam Nunn's speeches about the restructuring of the armed forces in March and April 1990, Congressman Les Aspin's report on sizing conventional forces published in February 1992, and Congressman Ike Skelton's hearings on the appropriate size of the army in October 1993 are but three of many compelling examples. Many of their statements were not-so-subtle threats that if the administration did not find expedient, politically acceptable compromises on force reductions, Congress would act. Undoubtedly, "administration decisionmakers were keenly aware of, and influenced by, [this] potential for independent, and undesirable congressional action" (Snider 1993a, 39).

Powell's recollection of the testimony that Cheney and he gave before Congress in February 1990 is even more compelling: "As we left Capitol Hill we knew that unless we came up with an overarching strategy to guide reductions, the Pentagon's political enemies were likely to come after us with a chain saw" (1995, 451). It was primarily as a consequence of this political pressure that Cheney proposed a 25 percent reduction in forces in June 1990. As one senior army officer concludes: "By the time Congress voted on the 1991 defense budget . . . the intellectual connection between US national security objectives and the "Base Force" had largely been discarded by proponents and critics alike (Alcalá 1994, 15). In contrast, the outcome of the Bottom-Up Review was in some ways predetermined by the fact that candidate Clinton had promised significant cuts in defense spending during his first term in office. As a long-term Senate staffer concludes: "The real world thrust of the Bottom-Up Review was ... how to downsize the Base Force to fit a lower budget ceiling. Strategic rhetoric had to be superimposed on a budget driven exercise" (Cordesman 1994, 23).

That budgetary and political considerations played such a prominent role in post–Cold War decisionmaking should not be surprising. In periods of international or domestic instability, military policy is at the center of public discussion and partisan debate. The political stakes are higher, strategic considerations take precedence, and decisionmakers devote more energy to the policy process. Structural or budgetary considerations are more salient during periods of international stability, particularly when concern over domestic ills is elevated. With the exception of the periods immediately before or during America's wars, the second set of circumstances has prevailed (Huntington 1961).

The Base Force and the Bottom-Up Review were developed during a period when international tensions were decreasing and public concern over domestic issues was rising. Budgets are manifestations of political priorities, and there is little evidence to suggest that robust military forces will—or ever should—be a priority in times of peace within democratic states. Thus, it is perhaps not undesirable that budgetary considerations play a more prominent role. That said, however, there is a price to be paid for indifference with respect to military issues—a subject that is explored further in later chapters.

Marginalized Military Leaders

Between 1989 and 1996, the Pentagon was "caught in a dilemma between the virtually unguided free fall of the congressional topline (total) appropriations and the attempts of the Joint Chiefs of Staff to carry out an organized retreat to some new respectable and sustainable force posture" (Sullivan 1993, 32). In reality, however, Colin Powell and then Les Aspin led the retreat, and the Joint Chiefs were reluctant, and largely inconsequential, followers. The services chiefs played only a minimal role in the development of a new military strategy or a conventional force structure to support it during this period. As one chief reportedly observed, "The planning for the defense build-down was a case of someone determining in advance what was needed, and then seeing that the result was produced" (Snider 1993a, 18).

The army fared the worst in these budget battles. Kanter writes that "each service seeks to minimize its share of the budget reduction and the 'stronger service' is the more successful in achieving that objective" (1975, 65). By this measure, the army was the least politically effective of the three services. But why is it that the military leaders of the individual services, and army leaders in particular, played a relatively inconsequential role in the decisionmaking process? And why is it that the army continues to feel such pressure for additional cutbacks? Before answering these questions, it is worthwhile to step back for a moment to put them into perspective.

One can make a compelling case that military leaders should be more involved in the development of military policy and an equally compelling case that they should be less involved. The principle of civilian control of the military requires that civilian leaders ultimately make decisions about the size and resources dedicated to the armed forces with or without the support of military leaders. This begs the question, however, of the extent to which military leaders should influence these decisions, particularly given their unique expertise in the maintenance and use of military power. This book does not address this issue. But it is clear that military leaders, with the exception of Colin Powell, played a marginal role in downsizing decisions.

There are a number of reasons to suppose that military leaders would have played a more influential role than they in fact did in the downsizing decisionmaking process. From a political standpoint, for one, it is important for civilian leaders to have the explicit endorsement of the Joint Chiefs for military policies, and traditionally they have gone out of their way to get it. As Arnold Kanter writes, "To the extent that the services publicly support the administration's defense programs, the political risks and burdens of administration policy choices are diffused, and the attacks of domestic political critics are constrained" (1975, 49). The fact that the Joint Chiefs gave their lukewarm support to the Base Force and Bottom-Up Review plans immediately following their release to Congress, for instance, gave political cover to the Bush and Clinton administrations. This should have given the Joint Chiefs added leverage.

Additionally, because both Congress and the executive branch have authority over military policy, the services are able to exploit the separation of powers by appealing to alternative superiors (Congress or the administration) to advance or reverse certain policies. This phenomenon may have been at work, for example, when Congressman Skelton conducted special hearings about the size of the army prior to the Clinton administration's release of the Bottom-Up Review. It also helps to explain the Marine Corps' exceptional success in protecting its budget and force structure in the post–Cold War era by drumming up the support of key constituencies on Capitol Hill.[72]

Finally, senior military leaders wield significant influence through their ability to "manipulate uncertainty." Because public and congressional opinion is sensitive to the possibility of potential threats to national security, "reservations expressed by the military chiefs ... supply the services with leverage that is distinctive when compared with other federal agencies" (Lucas and Dawson 1974, 66). As a consequence, the political costs of a certain course of action may be prohibitive once a senior military official has raised the possibility of "unacceptable risks." Between 1990 and 1995, the service chiefs continuously warned Congress that proposed cuts would "fracture" the armed forces, undermine readiness, and jeopardize national security. Ultimately, however, after such cuts were announced by the administration, the service chiefs openly, if not enthusiastically, gave their support.

There are three plausible explanations for why the military services in general, and the army in particular, played such a marginal role in the downsizing decisionmaking process. First, the army's Cold War mission, its composition, the specific actions taken by its leadership, and its unique organizational culture have made it particularly susceptible to cutbacks. Prior to 1989, the army's size, force structure, equipment, and doctrine were oriented, to a far greater extent than the other services, toward deterring or fighting a conventional war in central Europe. With the fading of the Cold War, so too went the logic behind an army of eighteen divisions and 780,000 soldiers. Given the changes in the strategic landscape, it was appropriate for the army to be cut more deeply than the other services. In addition, the force projection strategy on which the Base Force and the BUR were purportedly founded put the army, the least independent and mobile of the four services, at an inherent disadvantage (despite the fact that Vuono and Sullivan argued that the army's capabilities were ideally situated for the uncertainties of the post–Cold War period).

Also, several inherent characteristics of the modern army help explain its inability to influence the decisionmaking process. The military services have distinctly different institutional priorities. Although the navy, air force, and army all measure their political effectiveness in terms of the absolute and relative size of their budgets, each has a markedly different way of gauging its institutional well-being (Kanter 1975, 5). This, in turn, affects their priorities and the way each service views cutbacks in personnel, force structure, and modernization. Carl Builder of RAND observes that the navy measures its well-being first in the number of carriers and then by the aggregate number of ships it has and that the air force is most concerned with the quality of its technology and the number of wings of fighter aircraft it maintains. The army, like the marine corps, measures its health in terms of the quality and number of people within its ranks (1989, 22). Thus, personnel cuts are more painful for the army and the marine corps than for the other services, and their actions during the downsizing debate reflected their different organizational priorities.

To make matters worse, the army is the most manpower-intensive of the services, with a significantly larger percentage of its budget devoted to personnel. Thus, growing budgetary pressures inevitably required the army to cut deeply where it hurt the most. Additionally, unlike the other services, the active army competes for resources with extraordinarily influential and politically astute National Guard and reserve forces. As post–Cold War cutbacks progressed, reserve and National Guard leaders lobbied heavily for an expanded role in national defense, at the expense of the active force (Kitfield 1992a). These forces coalesced against the army's efforts to protect its share of the budget and its active duty endstrength.[73]

Apart from the political and strategic environment, it also seems that the actions of the army's senior leaders may have been partially to blame for the magnitude of the cuts the army suffered. A 1992 RAND report persuasively argues that the army's political effectiveness may have been undermined by its staunch commitment to maintaining force structure as long as possible, some say to the detriment of its credibility and leverage in the force planning process (Lewis et al. 1992). As one senior general recalls: "The problem was . . . our cultural institution says hang on until you're pushed over the cliff and someone stomps on your fingers and you have to turn loose. . . . We've got to preempt and make the smart decision for the year 1998 as opposed to hanging on to everything and then in the final analysis, losing [in the] near term and long term at the same time."[74] Indeed in hindsight, while Vuono's concerns were understandable, he may have done the army a disservice by expending valuable political capital with the administration and congressional lawmakers through his vehement resistant to endstrength reductions greater than thirty-five thousand per year. In addition, the fact that the army was one of the more forward-thinking of the services in acknowledging the need for force reductions may, ironically, have also put it at a disadvantage as the army's internal studies provided Powell, the Joint Staff, and OSD a number against which to apportion further reductions.[75]

It also appears likely that the army's failure to articulate a clear and compelling vision of its role in the post–Cold War era, particularly as downsizing has continued, has hindered its political effectiveness on Capitol Hill and within the Pentagon.[76] In June 1990, the air force published *Global Reach-Global Power* and in October 1993 the navy and Marine Corps followed suit with *Power from the Sea*. These white papers laid out their respective service visions for the post–Cold War era, emphasizing their unique warfighting capabilities, accenting the importance of their comparative advantage in advanced technologies to the overall defense effort, and providing a framework for justifying future resources. In contrast, the army did not publish a white paper until 1994, and even then its contents were oriented more toward describing the changing strategic landscape than explaining the army's vision or justifying the resources needed to support that vision (*Decisive Victory: America's Power Projection Army* 1994). Similarly, the army leadership's vision, as articulated in various manuals, speeches, articles, and congressional testimony, is of a versatile, deployable, expandable army capable of decisive victory (*Force XXI Operations* 1994; Sullivan and Coroalles 1995). While perhaps more logical and intellectually rigorous than those of the other services, the army's message is also more complex, difficult to articulate, and inaccessible. As a consequence, the army has fallen short in creating a strategic framework for guiding defense planners, inside and outside the Pentagon, and has failed to provide a basis for determining minimally acceptable force levels. The simple, seductive approaches of the other services ultimately may have been more effective, and the army has suffered in the budget battles as a consequence.[77]

Aside from a lack of vision, the army may have had less influence in downsizing decisions as a result of its organizational culture. The navy and air force have traditionally had very clear institutional agendas—often in conflict with the overall defense strategy—which they use to guide their institutions and garner additional resources. The army, however, has been the most likely to reject this approach and seek interservice cooperation and OSD approval, despite the benefits that independent institutional strategies offer (Builder 1989, 57–65). Sullivan's 1995 agreement to support an additional cut of twenty thousand in endstrength to support modernization (a deal on which the other services subsequently reneged) is the most striking example of this phenomenon.[78]

In addition, the army has a reputation for being the least effective of all the services in "working the Hill" for its programs and issues (Kitfield 1992b). Here, too, it seems, the army's culture is a large part of the explanation. A recent study identifies several cultural dimensions that undergird the army's long history of political ineptitude in its relationship with Congress. Among other things, the author identifies the army's propensity to reward performance in the field army over outstanding performance in the Pentagon or Washington. Also at work is the army's discomfort with self-promotion: "The army's value of teamwork and its recognition of its own dependency on others in winning on the battlefield is inculcated into its junior officers and works against service advocacy on the Hill." (Scroggs 1996, 474) Finally, the army, to a greater degree than the other services, sees itself as the nation's loyal obedient servant. Consequently, senior officers convey a more dutiful "can-do" attitude with respect to civilian directives, even if these actions are antithetical to the army's institutional interests. Certainly the army's actions contrasted with those of the navy and marine corps in the months prior to the release of the Bottom-Up Review follow this pattern.

In addition to the specific characteristics of the army, there are also attributes common to all the military services that have minimized their role in military policy in the postwar period.[79] First, since the end of World War II, interservice rivalries have allowed no room for a truly unified strategy and have attenuated the influence of military leaders (relative to civilians) in the force planning process (Lynn 1985).[80] One might speculate that interservice rivalries are likely to intensify in a period of declining resources. During negotiations over the Base Force and the Bottom-Up Review, for example, none of the service chiefs was willing to sit down in the presence of the others and discuss potential trade-offs across military capabilities (Jaffe 1994). Consequently, the service chiefs never presented *unified* resistance to the Base Force or the Bottom-Up Review.

The conservative bias military leaders bring to the formulation of defense policy may make it particularly difficult for them to contribute constructively to discussions about dramatic downsizing. This bias ensured that the military "requirements" identified by the services would be politically and fiscally unacceptable to civilian policymakers. Moreover, there exists among senior military officers the general perception that to discuss significant force reductions is to acknowledge that they are plausible, thereby increasing the likelihood that they will become a reality. Thus, senior leaders in the army and the other services were unwilling to discuss some of the more dramatic proposals being considered during discussions leading up to the Base Force and Bottom-Up Review.[81] A service chief's influence is also somewhat limited by his own political vulnerability. While military leaders may withhold their endorsement of a proposed defense policy in negotiations with an administration to gain concessions, they must do so sparingly in order to ensure the continued support of civilian leaders. Moreover, if cutbacks are inevitable, a service chief is likely to get more concessions from participation than by nonparticipation (Kanter 1975, 50). This, for example, may explain Vuono's decision to accept and publicly endorse the army force levels proposed in the Base Force, despite the reservations he had expressed earlier.

Because of their own internal constituencies, the service chiefs are also constrained in their ability to participate meaningfully in negotiations over significant reductions in the size or the budgets of their respective services. As a consequence, they were marginalized in the decisionmaking process:

> A service chief will dissent, almost as a matter of routine if . . . asked to endorse a position which threatens a core mission of that service: Recommendations to reduce the number of army divisions, the number of aircraft carriers, or the funding for the follow-on manned bomber have virtual guarantees of dissent from the service chief affected. To maintain the morale and to stimulate the loyalty of these subordinates, the Chief must be prepared to [disagree], whatever his personal views and the pressures for JCS unanimity notwithstanding. (Kanter 1975, 29)

Thus, whether or not the army's chief thought a ten-division army plausible or the navy's chief personally supported a ten-carrier navy is of little consequence; their internal constituencies demanded that they fight the good fight for the things their services valued the most. This phenomenon affected other senior military leaders as well. "Every prospective Chief of Staff . . . is [also] subject to organizational constraints on his discretion and behavior" (Kanter 1975, 98). As the net effect of these attributes, senior military leaders, with the exception of the Chairman of the Joint Chiefs of Staff (JCS), played a peripheral role in the downsizing decisionmaking process, at least in part because they were unable to participate seriously in discussions of substantial reductions.

Finally, the unprecedented influence of JCS chairman Colin Powell and his support for significant cutbacks mitigated the influence of other senior military leaders. Political and budgetary pressures would have required dramatic reductions regardless of who was serving in the key policymaking positions during this period. But with Powell, a well-respected senior army officer, leading the fight for the Base Force and eventually supporting the Bottom-Up Review these proposals gained instant credibility. Powell clearly believed that it was in the best interest of the military services to take the initiative with Base Force cutbacks, but there is no doubt that Powell's influence came at the expense of the Joint Chiefs. One might also speculate that because Powell was an army general, he had added credibility in debating the future size of the army. Powell's unprecedented role in the development of the Base Force was clear when he effectively circumvented the Planning, Programming, and Budgeting System and overrode the objections of the Joint Chiefs by making his case directly to the Secretary of Defense and the President.

Powell was the quintessential Washington insider. Having spent much of the previous decade at the highest levels of the national security structure, he was extraordinarily well-versed in the politics of the policymaking process and knew many of the key players. In addition, Powell had Cheney's support throughout this process. The two shared not only responsibility for restructuring the post–Cold War defense apparatus but also the same supporters and critics. Thus, "one could not see daylight between them" (Hammond 1994, 167).[82] Additionally, Powell had a vision. One can quarrel with the accuracy of that vision, but its clarity and force were formidable. By presenting a plan that was dramatic enough to be taken seriously but prudent enough to gain the core support of defense conservatives, Powell seized the initiative and did not relinquish it until the Base Force was a reality. Finally, the 1986 Goldwater-Nichols Act gave Powell unprecedented authority and freedom of action, permitting him to make his case directly to the President and Secretary of Defense on numerous occasions without the approval, or even the knowledge, of the Joint Chiefs (Lewis et al. 1992).[83]

Conclusion

Between 1990 and 1996, the army underwent a 40 percent reduction in its budget and a 35 percent cut in its endstrength. Budget cuts have resulted in a plans/resources mismatch that exists across all the services, but particularly within the army, and which worsens by the day.[84] Moreover, the incremental nature of budgetary and personnel cuts have made it difficult for army leaders to plan effectively for the future. The prolonged uncertainty of downsizing has undermined the vitality of America's army.

It would be easy to blame this situation on the irrationality of the military policymaking process, the absence of foresight among civilian policymakers, and the inadequacies of military leaders. Perhaps all three are to some degree at fault. But there will always be a certain measure of irrationality in the planning of defense policy, particularly during peacetime. Defense preparations have no meaning except in relation to foreign policy, which is often ambiguous, particularly in periods of transition. At such times, the future is often uncertain, both with respect to the nation's own purpose as well as the intentions and capabilities of adversaries (Schilling as cited in Snider 1993a, 73). Thus, strategic consensus will be elusive during such periods and determining "how much is enough" a most difficult proposition. More often than not, policymakers are only able to judge defense reductions as too large or too small after the fact, once they have had the opportunity to view the results in terms of peacetime readiness or wartime effectiveness.

For a number of reasons—some historical, others cultural—the army was not as politically effective as it might have been in the post–Cold War downsizing debate. Given this fact, it is tempting to fault senior officers for the army's current problems and for what may be a foreboding future. While this is fair to a degree, one must also acknowledge that downsizing decisions resulted from forces largely outside the army's control. Even the most clearly articulated vision and vigorous lobbying would have had only a minimal impact against the groundswell of political and budgetary pressures that made dramatic downsizing a fait accompli. And though the army has fared marginally worse than the other services, it has been more effective in defending its resources than some people expected, certainly more so than in the past.

3

Reducing the Ranks
Anatomy of a Decisionmaking Process

> The downsizing of the American military is an untold success story. Like back surgery, the operation has been ... long, complicated, and painful. ... [But] the team of doctors—military leaders, Pentagon executives, and lawmakers—have conducted the operation with great care. Their patient, the American military, has not been crippled or hollowed out as predicted, but will come out of surgery healthy.
> —George C. Wilson, "Although Painful, Latest Drawdown Proving a Success"

Although the army's leaders had minimal control over the magnitude and pace of personnel reductions, they had significantly more influence over the manner in which these cuts were achieved. The army has managed mandated personnel reductions with great precision, compassion, and success. Yet, the downsizing of the U.S. military is not finished. In truth, although personnel reductions in the army have slowed, they continue; the "operation" is not yet complete. In addition, the "team of doctors" responsible for downsizing were primarily senior military, and only to a lesser extent civilian leaders within the army. Congress and the executive branch required that the army downsize in the first place, and both have supervised and assisted the process. But the army's military leaders developed the plan and made the critical decisions concerning who was downsized when, and how. They should be given credit for the success achieved thus far.

This chapter describes the scope of the army's downsizing efforts and the programs put in place to achieve these cuts. It first identifies the army's goals in this process and evaluates its success in achieving them. The chapter also traces how four generations of army leaders struggled to meet the competing demands of internal (the officer corps) and external (OSD and Congress) constituencies while managing these personnel reductions. Finally, it seeks to solve a series of riddles: Why did the army succeed when there were reasons to expect it would fail? What did it do differently than in the past? What factors led it to develop and execute a balanced and compassionate downsizing plan?

I make two principal arguments. First, the army's downsizing objectives were reasonable and balanced—particularly given the political, legislative, and organizational constraints it faced. And, second, the army has been mostly successful in achieving these goals. It is important at this point to state my definition of success: given its mandate to downsize, the army developed an appropriate plan and effectively carried it out. Relative to the army's experience after Vietnam, its recent downsizing activities are indeed an achievement, and senior army leaders appropriately view it as such. This is not meant to suggest, however, that downsizing has not had a devastating effect on the army, an argument I make in chapter 4. This chapter attempts to explain this management achievement. I conclude that the generous support provided by Congress, the lessons that army leaders learned from the post-Vietnam experience, and an analytic capacity developed within the army personnel community over the past two decades explain the army's effectiveness in downsizing.

Army Personnel Management

Military personnel systems are different from civilian ones in that they are "closed," allowing no lateral entry. Civilian organizations may expand rapidly by hiring individuals with varying degrees and types of training or experience. The army, too, can swiftly augment its junior force by recruiting or drafting more soldiers, but because lateral entry is untenable, it cannot expand its middle- to senior-grade officer and noncommissioned officer corps in the same way. The hiring, firing, promoting, and retiring of military personnel are significant activities, therefore, because of their irreversibility as well as their lasting effects. Since World War II, the army has created several institutions and administrative systems for guiding personnel decisions.

The Army Personnel Community

There are four main floors in the Pentagon, and on each floor there are five concentric pentagonal-shaped rings labeled A though E. The rings are connected by twelve corridors that lead from a grass-covered courtyard enclosed within the A Ring outward to the E Ring. The offices of senior civilian and military leaders in the army, navy, and air force are located on the second, third, and fourth floors, respectively. Generally, the more powerful the individual, the farther his or her office is located from the center, with the most senior officials situated on the E Ring overlooking Arlington Cemetery or the Potomac River. Since World War II, two of the three institutions created to manage army personnel policy have been located within this labyrinth.

The first, the Office of the Assistant Secretary of the Army for Manpower and Reserve Affairs (ASA/M&RA), is located on the second floor of the E Ring, between corridors five and six. The responsibilities of the Assistant Secretary (who has civilian rank equal to a four-star general) have grown over the last several decades with the expansion of civilian involvement in defense policy and the increased emphasis on morale, welfare, and equal opportunity accompanying the creation of the all-volunteer force (Birtle 1988, 21). Among other things, the Assistant Secretary has oversight responsibility for personnel policy, reporting on these matters directly to the Secretary of the Army.

Less than a hundred meters southwest along the E Ring, around a bend between corridors six and seven, is the Office of the Deputy Chief of Staff for Personnel (ODCSPER). Although the latter is almost within eyesight of the Assistant Secretary's office, the level of cooperation between the two offices has varied substantially over the years, depending on the personalities and the personal (or political) agendas of the senior officials within them. The Deputy Chief of Staff for Personnel, usually a three-star general, oversees the planning and implementation of army personnel policy. The Deputy Chief reports directly to the army Chief of Staff in the military chain and to the Assistant Secretary in the civilian chain of command. The office's two major directorates are squeezed into a pie-shaped wedge between corridors six and seven. The Personnel Management Directorate, located in the B Ring, is responsible for policy regarding the recruiting, distribution, and promotion of enlisted soldiers and officers. In the C Ring, the Manpower Directorate conducts analysis on budgeting, compensation, and manpower policy. The disparate responsibilities of the two ensure that the policy recommendations made by the B Ring, which are frequently based on subjective analysis, often conflict with those of the C Ring, which are based on "hard data." The predictable tension between the advocates of "art" and "science" has important implications for personnel policy.

Six stops south of the Pentagon along the Washington Metro's yellow line are two pink, slightly surreal-looking, twelve-story buildings, home to the U.S. Total Army Personnel Command (PERSCOM)—the third key institution in the army personnel community. PERSCOM is commanded by a two-star general who reports directly to the Deputy Chief of Staff for Personnel. PERSCOM implements the officer, enlisted, and civilian personnel policies made by the Office of the Deputy Chief of Staff and approved by the Assistant Secretary for Manpower and Reserve Affairs. It links the corporate army that makes personnel policy in the Pentagon to the muddy boots army most affected by it.

Officer Management

One hundred fourteen pages of legislation mandate the way in which the four services manage their active officer corps, yet no legislative guidance exists concerning the administration of their enlisted forces. The 1980 Defense Officer Personnel Management Act (DOPMA) is the most recent attempt on the part of Congress to establish universal guidelines concerning the recruitment, promotion, and separation of active duty military officers. One of DOPMA's major provisions places a ceiling on the number of offi-

Diagram 3.1. Organization of the Army Personnel Community

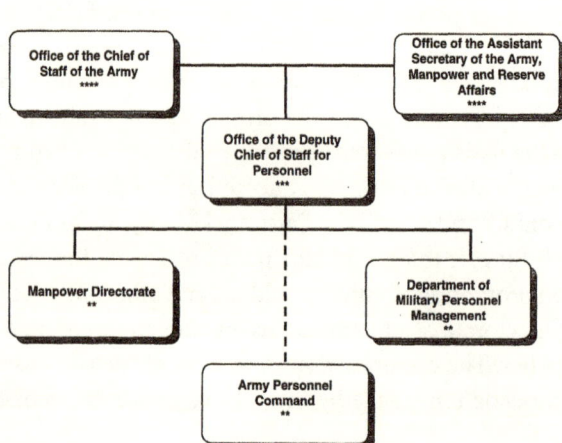

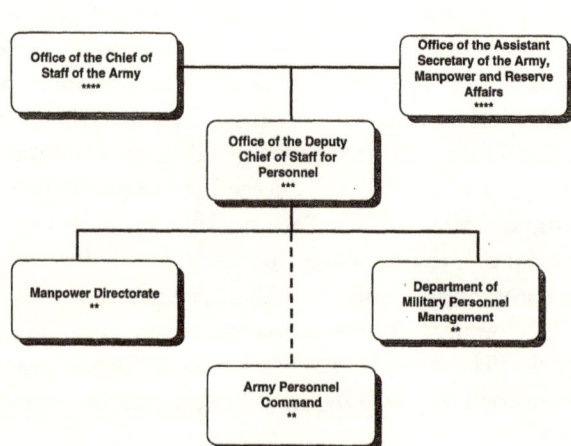

cers authorized in grades O–4 (major) through O–6 (colonel), depending on the overall size of the officer corps (which is set by Congress and tied directly to the overall endstrength of the army). The so-called DOPMA Field Grade Tables were designed to: (1) allow the services to meet their requirements for officers in various grades and levels of experience; (2) provide career opportunity to attract and retain high-quality officers; and (3) provide consistent career opportunity across the services (*Officer Management Legislation: Why Needed?* 1990, 4). DOPMA is also the most recent manifestation of the U.S. military's up-or-out promotion system, in which the large majority of officers who are not promoted to a certain rank are forced to resign. This law, which also stipulates procedures for the appointment, separation, promotion, and retirement of officers, imposed significant constraints on the army's downsizing efforts.

Officer reductions are also influenced by the way in which the army determines its officer requirements. The size and shape of the officer corps are largely, though not wholly, functions of the size and shape of the army it leads, although national strategy, organizational design and structure, doctrine and operational concepts, and technology all play important roles (Strand 1993, 64; Thie and Brown 1994, 12). The number and type of officers "required" to support the army's force structure may be loosely categorized as a combination of direct and derived demands. Direct demand for officers to serve in combat units and the units that immediately support them—the army's teeth—are spelled out in documents called Tables of Organization and Equipment, or TOEs. Derived demands, such as requirements for supporting forces, infrastructure, and overhead in military departments—the army's tail—are identified in the Tables of Distribution and Allowances, or TDAs (Thie and Brown 1994, 13). More than half of the officer corps, primarily the field grade ranks, generally serves in TDA assignments.[1]

In contrast to TDA assignments, TOE officer requirements are developed through a centralized, rational, and disciplined process based primarily on doctrine and overall organizational design. If, for example, army planners determine that ten divisions are needed to satisfy the national military strategy, the number of officers required to support this structure is simply the aggregate of the officer requirements for each type of division. The officer requirements for TDA units follow no such formula, but depend on the type and intensity of work necessary to execute a unit's mission and are largely at the discretion of a handful of senior generals who oversee the army's major commands (*Army Command, Leadership, and Management* 1994–95, 11–24).[2]

As a consequence, TDA "requirements" have steadily grown as a percentage of overall officer authorizations over the last decade. As one senior army civilian remarked, "The TDA is an undisciplined beast—one that no one has yet been able to tame."[3] Additionally, the overall requirements for officers have grown as the result of a number of congressional mandates. Since 1987, Congress has mandated that military officers be assigned in certain numbers to a variety of assignments, including "joint" or interservice billets, positions in reserve units, and the Special Operations Command; these requirements are also classified as TDA authorizations.[4] As a consequence, long before downsizing began, a growing gap existed between the demand for officers (requirements) and the supply (actual inventory). In order to reconcile this shortfall, the army relies on an annual officer distribution plan (ODP), which allocates these shortages across its major commands.

Finally, the army's Officer Personnel Management System (OPMS) also influenced its approach to downsizing. Conceived in 1971, OPMS is the army's means for procuring officers in the right skill areas, developing their professional capacities through schooling and assignments, and promoting and allocating (and when necessary separating) them to satisfy the army's needs. To fulfill these objectives, most officers are given a "dual designation" and assigned not only a basic branch but also a functional area.[5] Thus, in the course of a career an officer is likely to serve not only in his or her primary branch but also in a functional area and myriad military schooling assignments. This process is complicated further by the fact that officers must serve in specific jobs within a certain time frame to remain competitive for promotion and to satisfy mandated professional development requirements. Army leaders planned and implemented downsizing within the context of these systems.

Downsizing in Retrospect

Human resources may be seen in terms of three dimensions: quantity, quality, and composition (Dyer 1983, 268). The challenge in downsizing, of course, is reducing the first without sacrificing the second and third. This task is complicated by the fact that the army, like all public organizations, must balance between the demands of internal and external constituencies. Consequently, between 1990 and 1995 the army's leaders engaged in a variation of what political scientists describe as a "two-level game" as they attempted to develop a downsizing plan that satisfied both constituencies. On one level, they participated in the aforementioned debate with Congress and the administration over the magnitude and pace of cuts in force structure and endstrength. On the other level, they marketed the army's reduction plan to other generals and to the rank and file. This chapter examines the second level—how the army's personnel community developed, implemented, and then communicated its downsizing plan to the officer corps.

Reductions in the number of army units, or in "force structure," largely, though not entirely, drove decisions regarding the downsizing of personnel. With the elimination of units, authorizations or "spaces" for military personnel disappeared and so too did the need for "faces" or people to fill these positions. These decisions were (and are) made largely outside the personnel community by senior military and civilian leaders based on the recommendations of the army's Deputy Chief of Staff for Operations. As a result of these cuts in structure, the army's personnel community was given the task of making critical decisions concerning reductions in personnel.

The scope of the army's downsizing efforts is daunting. The army began 1990 with a corps of line officers roughly 70,000 strong. It ended 1995 (with downsizing toward a force of 495,000 97.5 percent complete) with this group 30 percent smaller, at a strength of almost 50,000. The overall size of the officer corps (including special branches) fell by roughly the same percentage (see diagram 3.2). These statistics, however, are misleading: more

Diagram 3.2. The Downsizing of the Army Officer Corps, 1990–1995

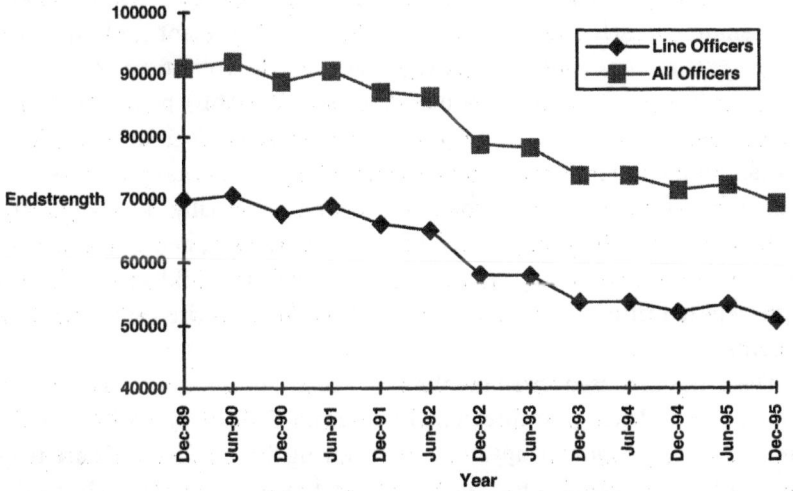

SOURCE: Office of the Deputy Chief of Staff for Personnel

than 40,000 officers departed the army during this period—the overall strength of the corps was supplemented annually with roughly 4,000 newly commissioned lieutenants—and an unknown percentage of those who left would have done so through natural attrition regardless of downsizing.

Under DOPMA, the army is required to maintain a continuous flow of officers through the promotion system. Junior officers are commissioned in a cohort, or year group, which grows smaller as it advances or flows through the ranks toward retirement. Officers generally leave the army at various stages of their career by choice or as victims of "up or out" or mandatory retirement. The army controls the magnitude and rate of this flow by manipulating accessions, separations, and promotions. In cases in which the actual inventory surpasses the projected inventory, the year group is "overstrength" for the downsized force. Downsizing programs have generally been directed toward this "excess."

Given this background, the mechanics of the recent downsizing have been relatively straightforward. The army reduced the intake of new officers and targeted an array of voluntary and involuntary downsizing programs at different components of the existing officer inventory. Some of these programs already existed and were simply amended, while others were created specifically to achieve the army's downsizing objectives. Three voluntary programs targeted different components of the officer corps. The Voluntary Early Release/Retirement Program (VERRP) permitted both junior officers (lieutenants and captains) to resign from the army prior to fulfilling their active duty service obligations and senior officers (lieutenant colonels and colonels) to retire at their present rank, waiving existing retirement eligibility criteria. Second, the Voluntary Separation Incentive/Special Separation Bonus Program (VSI/SSB) passed by Congress in 1991, provided the army with the resources and legislative freedom to offer junior and mid-career officers (captains and majors) generous separation benefits to encourage voluntary separation. Finally, the Temporary Early Retirement Program, passed by Congress in 1992, helped the armed services avoid involuntary separations by permitting field grade officers with between fifteen and twenty years of service to retire early with full benefits.

The army also used three involuntary separation programs during the same period. Although it threatened numerous Reductions in Force, only one RIF of 244 majors in 1992 occurred during this period. RIFs are performed by centralized selection boards and traditionally have been directed at junior and mid-career officers. The army also used Selective Early

Retirement Boards (SERBs) sporadically through the late 1980s and heavily from 1990 to 1995 to meet downsizing objectives. SERBs are centralized boards charged with selecting "retirement eligible" officers (majors, lieutenant colonels, and colonels) for involuntary separation. Lieutenant Retention Boards (LTRBs), centralized boards designed to select officers for involuntary separation during their third year of service, were also used extensively during this period. The number of officers separated through each program between 1990 and 1995 is included in table 3.1 and a more complete description of each program is provided in the appendix to this chapter.

The army developed and used these programs in accordance with a very clear set of organizational principles. These principles, established by the army's leadership in 1990, set the tone for the downsizing decisions made over the next six years. No Army Chief of Staff covets the distinction of overseeing a substantial downsizing. General Carl E. Vuono, who was Chief from June 1987 to June 1991, was no exception. By 1989, political changes at home and abroad made it clear that large force reductions were probable, though the future size of the army remained uncertain. The personnel decisions made over the next several years were guided by Vuono's six imperatives—maintaining or improving doctrine, force mix, training, leadership development, modernization, and quality—that he established early in his tenure.[6]

Although the priority Vuono placed on each of these areas was said to be equal, in reality he placed a premium on avoiding a decline in readiness and

TABLE 3.1
Summary of Officer Downsizing Programs

Downsizing Programs	1990	1991	1992	1993	1994	1995	Total End 1995
Involuntary							
Reduction in Force	0	0	244	0	0	0	244
Lieutenant Retention Bd.	0	0	705	526	450	0	1,681
Selective Early Retirement Bd.	419	0	1,739	552	693	409	3,812
Voluntary							
Vol. Early Release/Ret.	643	769	1,308	497	611	258	4,086
Vol. Sep. Incentive/ Special Sep. Bonus	0	0	4,640	2,011	1,220	1,079	8,950
Early Retirement	0	0	0	89	550	732	1,371
Total	1,062	769	8,636	3,675	3,524	2,478	20,144

SOURCE: U.S. Army, Office of the Deputy Chief of Staff for Personnel, as of the end of FY 1995.
NOTE: Data by fiscal year; includes both line officers and specialty branches.

maintaining training and leadership development opportunities.[7] Within the context of these overarching priorities, Vuono and his staff (particularly Lieutenant General Allen Ono, Deputy Chief of Staff for Personnel, and Brigadier General Theodore Stroup, Director of the Military Personnel Management Directorate) articulated a more specific set of principles to guide personnel reductions over the next five years. These four principles—protecting quality, shaping the force, sustaining personnel readiness, and demonstrating care and compassion—were the criteria by which most downsizing decisions were made.[8]

The preservation of a quality force meant continuing to recruit and retain high-quality individuals in the enlisted and officer ranks. In the decades following Vietnam, the army made notable gains in the quality of its officer corps and enlisted force, and its leaders were eager to preserve this progress throughout this tumultuous period (Halloran 1984, 17). They were committed to designing voluntary separation programs that encouraged "lesser quality" officers to depart, regardless of whether they had regular army (RA) or other than regular army (OTRA) commissions.[9] Likewise, they promised to maintain officer promotion, command, and professional development opportunities (Kitfield 1993a).

Army leaders also placed a premium on shaping the force early in the downsizing process. "Shaping" has several components and may be gauged in a variety of ways. Downsizing, of course, generally goes hand in hand with fundamental changes in the army's mission that require dramatic changes in its structure and personnel requirements. Decisions at this level are made by senior military and civilian leaders within the army and the Department of Defense, and they directly affect the size and shape of the army and the officer corps. More conventionally, shaping means reducing the officer corps in a way that best fits the officer inventory requirements (in terms of skill and grade) for a given force structure. The army personnel community is primarily responsible for shaping at this level. For several reasons, however, this is easier said than done. As noted previously, most officers have a branch designation as well as a functional area, and they may serve in assignments in either. Moreover, many assignments are neither branch nor functional-area specific and may be filled by officers from a variety of backgrounds. The result is an extraordinarily dynamic model in which an array of actual officer inventories (combinations of grades and skill sets) could conceivably satisfy a given force structure.

In addition, the army's traditional selection processes, whether for promotion, schooling, or separation, are primarily quality-based rather than skill-based. This makes shaping all the more difficult. Selection boards, comprising senior officers from a variety of backgrounds, evaluate the quality of an officer's performance with only minimal regard for his or her branch, functional area, or specific skills.[10] As one colonel observed: "We select the best athlete, rather than the best infielder."[11] This makes it difficult to protect or promote officers in needed specialties. Finally, shaping requires the balancing cuts across all officer grades. In 1990, the army, to a larger degree than the other services, had an overabundance of officers in the field grade ranks (major to colonel) due to historically high retention rates and its failure to balance officer cuts appropriately after Vietnam.[12] Among other things, this imbalance slowed promotion rates and reduced professional development opportunities for junior officers. Thus, for the army in particular, shaping meant distributing cuts across the senior grades.

Of all the downsizing principles, the army's leadership may have placed the greatest emphasis on the need for maintaining a trained and ready force. Since the late 1970s, when a host of personnel problems—low-quality recruits, poor retention rates, and undermanning—contributed to "hollowness," the army's leaders have worshipped at the altar of readiness.[13] Readiness is defined by DOD as: "The ability of forces to deploy quickly and perform in wartime as they were designed to" (CBO 1994c, 1). All four services gauge readiness at the operational level in terms of the status of resources in four interdependent areas: personnel, training, equipment and supplies, and equipment condition. Under the current readiness evaluation system, personnel readiness is the most objectively measured of the four categories. At the unit level, commanders assess personnel readiness by comparing the number, grade, and skill qualifications of the individuals assigned to them with their unit's authorizations. Personnel readiness may be gauged in the aggregate as well by comparing the army-wide authorizations across grades with the operating inventory in those grades; substantial shortfalls in either have obvious consequences for the army's wartime and peacetime effectiveness.

Finally, the army's leaders were sincerely committed to conducting personnel reductions with great care and compassion. This emphasis appears to have several antecedents. Post-Vietnam RIFs left a bitter taste in the mouths of not only those who left the army but also of those who remained. Junior officers, in particular, many of whom were decorated veterans, were callously dismissed with pink slips, scant separation pay, and meager transition assistance. Senior leaders, who had witnessed this debacle as junior officers, vowed not to repeat it. In addition, unlike the post-Vietnam army, the enlisted and officer corps of 1990 consisted completely of volunteers. This made compassion and care even more important, particularly toward those with more than six years of service who had presumably committed to a military career.

In addition to these explicit principles, several additional concerns guided downsizing decisions. Even in today's relatively well-integrated army, issues of race and gender remain sensitive. Army leaders, perhaps protective of the army's reputation as one of the most colorblind of America's institutions, feared that African Americans would be separated in disproportionate numbers (Ellis 1992, 72);[14] likewise, they feared the army's female population would be disaffected by downsizing. The army also sought to maintain, or perhaps even improve, promotion opportunity (the percentage promoted) and timing (the speed of promotion) to achieve DOPMA goals during and after downsizing.[15] Improved promotion rates have already been mentioned as a means for maintaining high-quality officers and as a by-product of "shaping the force" but were also viewed as an end in themselves. In the latter half of the 1980s, high retention rates, combined with the aftereffects of a promotion boom in the early 1980s, reduced promotion opportunity and stretched out promotion timing well beyond DOPMA objectives (Rostker et al. 1993, 29). Downsizing was viewed as an opportunity to remedy this situation.

The army faced a monumental task. It was charged with cutting the size of its officer corps by more than 30 percent in five short years. To complicate matters further, its final downsizing target was incrementally lowered throughout this period. In 1990, the army established a clear set of principles to guide this decisionmaking process. In retrospect, it is important to step back and ask the following questions: Were these principles appropriate? How successful has the army been in achieving its objectives? What might it have done better? While acknowledging minor shortcomings, those in the army who participated in the process are almost uniform in their agreement that downsizing has been a smashing success. As one senior civilian leader observed, "This is a case study of a successful program. I don't see what could have been done better."[16] Are the army's leaders too fulsome in their praise?

In some respects, the guidance from the Office of the Secretary of Defense gave army leaders relatively little flexibility in developing their downsizing plan. During 1989, the army established its guiding principles and an outline of its downsizing plan (designed for personnel cuts significantly smaller in magnitude than those eventually realized). By August 1990, however, OSD directed that the services maintain (and if possible improve) the quality of their forces and the proper skill mix, protect readiness, and treat personnel in a fair and equitable fashion (*An Assessment of Service Manpower Reduction Plans* 1990). Further, OSD monitored the success of the services in achieving these objectives. The army was constrained as well by DOPMA legislation (albeit with some waivers) and its own rigid officer management system, selection board process, and officer evaluation system.

Despite these constraints, each military department had some autonomy in planning and implementing officer cuts. The air force, for example, relied far more heavily on reducing accessions than involuntary separations, explicitly protecting its senior officer corps.[17] The navy, on the other hand, made no attempt to distinguish among the officers who applied for voluntary separation in terms of "quality," maintaining that the entire corps was of exceptional quality.[18] When implementing cuts, the army chose to devote much more resources to transition assistance than the other services. Despite common constraints, each service had the flexibility to downsize in a way that best satisfied its individual needs and missions. Given this flexibility, how appropriate were the army's downsizing objectives and how successful has it been in achieving them?

Judging the appropriateness of the army's downsizing objectives is more complicated than it might appear. The logic behind each of the four primary objectives—protecting quality, shaping the force, sustaining personnel readiness, and demonstrating care and compassion—is persuasive. An officer corps of exceptional quality is obviously crucial to a dynamic and effective military organization, even more so given the uncertain challenges of the post–Cold War era. Maintaining promotion opportunities and enhancing professional development opportunities as a means for retaining top performers seems reasonable, too, especially since downsizing organizations often lose their most valued performers.

Similarly, there is an obvious and compelling need for shaping the officer corps by precisely identifying the individuals with the specific skills and expertise needed in a downsized organization and for distributing officer cuts across the entire officer corps. Undoubtedly, a drastic reduction in accessions would have been the path of least internal resistance, but this alternative would have created several problems. Protecting the career force, at the expense of accessions would have reduced promotion opportunities and slowed the pace of advancement across the entire officer corps. This would have had implications for overall officer professional development opportunities as well as morale, retention, and recruitment. Second, if the Army procured fewer officers than necessary to maintain a steady-state flow through the promotion system, it would likely suffer a shortage of qualified senior officers beyond the year 2000.[19] Third, uneven cuts threatened to violate OSD guidance and the DOPMA grade tables. Balanced cuts, while painful, were necessary.

Sustaining personnel readiness is also a reasonable objective. Personnel readiness in the aggregate is a telling indicator of the alignment between cuts in force structure and cuts in personnel, two activities that should ideally go hand in hand. Thus, personnel readiness allows the army to gauge how effectively it is managing this aspect of downsizing. In addition, at the unit level, reasonably high levels of personnel readiness are necessary for effective unit training and operation. And, personnel readiness obviously has significant implications for the army's wartime capabilities. Finally, a caring and compassionate approach to downsizing is justified on moral as well as practical grounds. From a moral perspective, it has traditionally been understood that the army and the nation have a special responsibility to those who loyally serve. And, as noted earlier, fair and compassionate treatment of downsizing victims affects the attitudes and performance of those who remain and influences an organization's ability to recruit new members in the future.

The army's two implicit objectives—protecting minority representation and improving promotion opportunity—are more controversial. Its concern that minorities and women not be disadvantaged was a reflection of the controversy over race and gender in America that lies well outside the scope of this study. Several general observations, however, warrant mention. Some argue that selection decisions (for promotion or separation) should be based solely on performance and that race and gender should not be considered; others maintain that measures should be taken to guard against institutional discrimination and to compensate for past inequalities. The army's selection system moderately reflected the second view, and hence a structure already existed to factor race and gender into the downsizing decisionmaking process.[20] Moreover, whether or not one is sympathetic to the notion of affirmative action, there can be no doubt that the army was under tremendous political pressure to ensure that minorities and women not be disadvantaged by downsizing. To have done otherwise would likely have jeopardized the army's political effectiveness in other areas. Thus, on political grounds alone, protecting minority and female representation was an important objective.

Improving promotion opportunity during downsizing was also a contentious goal, as the price of improved promotion rates is ultimately paid through the involuntary separations of officers from the senior and middle ranks.[21] Certainly, OSD expressed its desire that the army use downsizing as an opportunity to rectify existing promotion stagnation and achieve DOPMA promotion guidelines (*An Assessment of Service Manpower Reduction Plans* 1990, 9). And, prudent management practices required that cuts be balanced across the entire officer corps. But, DOPMA only *recommends* adherence to its promotion timetables. The army's leaders were eager, perhaps too eager, to use personnel reductions as an opportunity to get their "house in order" by meeting DOPMA promotion guidelines. Additionally, army leaders clearly linked stable promotion opportunity with retaining quality officers, believing that marginal changes would have deleterious effects on retention, an unproved proposition at best. By 1994, the army's commitment to improving promotion rates was beginning to be questioned by critics inside and outside the organization.

While each of these downsizing goals appears justified when considered individually, the army's success in satisfying them collectively has been complicated by the fact that they sometimes conflict. For example, shaping the officer corps inevitably requires involuntary separations of middle-grade and senior officers, an inherently painful act. Shaping may run counter to the notion of protecting quality, as well. For instance, it may require retaining an officer in one specialty area (say a computer specialist) who is a mediocre performer at the expense of an officer in another specialty (an infantry officer, for example) who is an outstanding performer. The same possibility exists when attempting to protect diversity. Thus, the true test of the army's effectiveness in downsizing is its ability to strike a reasonable balance across these objectives by achieving moderate success in each without sacrificing the others.

Quality

There is compelling evidence that the army has been surprisingly successful in retaining its "best and brightest" officers if one accepts its method for assessing such officers. Quality is judged by selection boards on the basis of an officer's performance (as measured by evaluation reports), qualifications (as exhibited through critical assignments, schooling, and awards and decorations), and, to a far lesser extent, the army's requirements (branch and functional area).²² The selection process is highly subjective, imprecise, and unpredictable. A range of factors—luck, timing, and the composition of the board—all come into play in the process. But short of returning to the decentralized and highly politicized promotion procedures of the past, there are few, if any, plausible alternatives. To paraphrase Winston Churchill, the army's current selection process is the worst system there is, except for all the other forms that have been tried and have failed (Partington 1992, 202).²³

The army's downsizing programs put a new wrinkle in the selection process, however, by requiring boards to choose officers of "lesser quality" for involuntary separation. This difficult task was made even more so by the fact that many of the officers selected would have qualified for promotion, or at the very least retention, a few years earlier.²⁴ Despite this fact, the boards reported that they were able to distinguish the least competitive performance files from among those considered.²⁵ Thus, if one accepts the legitimacy of the selection process, the officers who were involuntarily separated were the "right ones" from the army's point of view.²⁶

It was the army's voluntary downsizing programs that threatened most to siphon off top-quality officers. There was great apprehension that the VSI/SSB specifically would desiccate the officer corps by inducing the best captains and majors to leave. The centralized nature of the officer management system makes it possible to demonstrate that this has probably not been the case.²⁷ Assignment officers within the Army Personnel Command maintain the performance files of all line officers. These individuals were tasked with assessing and then dividing the performance files of all officers eligible for the VSI/SSB into four categories (on the basis of a normal distribution)—*A*bove center, center-*P*lus, center-*M*inus, and *B*elow center. Roughly 20 percent of the cohort were rated at the top or the bottom, with 80 percent in the two categories in between.²⁸

According to PERSCOM's assessments of all eligible performance files, roughly 70 percent of the officers who volunteered were from the lower 40 percent (M or B files) of the eligible population in each of the four years. In 1994, 71 percent of the eligible officers who volunteered to depart the army through the VSI/SSB were ranked in the lowest third (B or M files) of their cohort; additionally, only 6 percent (20 of 336 eligible) of those ranked as particularly strong performers took advantage of the program (see table 3.2). Similarly, in 1995, almost 70 percent of the volunteers were taken from the lowest third of the group, and 5 percent were taken from among the strongest performers (data from 1992 and 1993 show similar results). Thus, we may conclude that the large majority of the roughly ten thousand officers who left the army through the VSI/SSB between 1992 and 1995 were those with the weakest performance files. One can only speculate why this was the case, but it is certain that this is one of the few occasions on which officers had a true understanding of where they stood in relation to their peers.

Interestingly, this finding runs counter to views expressed on a number of occasions in the *Army Times* as well as to the commonly held perceptions in the field army (Philpott 1993). This is not to say that some extraordinarily talented people did not depart the army through this program; undoubtedly, some of its brightest stars have gone elsewhere.[29] On average, however, the overall quality of the officer corps was enhanced through the VSI/SSB, as the officers who left were generally from the bottom third of their cohort.[30] Perhaps more important, those who stayed did so after choosing not to take advantage of a generous separation plan. There can be no doubt of their commitment to continued military service.

Shaping the Force

The army's success in shaping the force may be evaluated on two levels: how well it matched its stated officer requirements with the needs of a downsized force structure and how effectively its personnel community, given these re-

TABLE 3.2
Officer "Quality" and the VSI/SSB (1994–1995)

PERSCOM	1994[a]				1995[b]			
	# Eligible	# of Takers	% of Eligible	% of Total	# Eligible	# of Takers	% of Eligible	% of Total
A Files	336	20	6	3	300	16	5	3
(% of total)	(12)				(12)			
P Files	1,469	178	12	26	1,361	152	11	29
(% of total)	(54)				(54)			
M Files	690	316	46	46	718	258	36	49
(% of total)	(25)				(28)			
B Files	225	178	79	26	165	98	65	19
(% of total)	(8)				(7)			
Total	2,720	692	25	100	2,544	524	21	100

SOURCE: U.S. Army Total Personnel Command, Officer Distribution Division.
[a]Eligible population consisted primarily of captains commissioned in 1985.
[b]Eligible population consisted primarily of captains commissioned in 1986.

quirements, shaped the existing officer inventory to match the downsized force structure. It appears to have done reasonably well in the latter and less well in the former. There are some concerns that certain specialties—foreign area specialists, for example—were disproportionately separated through involuntary programs in spite of the attention the army leadership devoted to this issue.[31] However, personnel planners designed voluntary and involuntary programs with mechanisms to ensure that the army retained officers with the necessary skills, and these mechanisms were mostly successful. The VSI/SSB program, for example, was limited to those branches that were overstrength, and the program was immediately terminated in each branch as soon as the appropriate number of officers volunteered to leave. Likewise, the Secretary of the Army instructed SERBs to identify critically short specialties and separate officers with skills in these areas only if their files clearly warranted it. After reviewing all eligible files, for example, the 1992 SERB retained a number of lieutenant colonels with military intelligence or special operations backgrounds who were lower on the order of merit list than others who were retired. This decision illustrates the army's commitment to shaping the force, occasionally even at the expense of "quality."[32]

With regard to the first question, critics inside and outside the army argue that it has been slow to rethink its fundamental structure in the post–Cold War period. Today's army, they maintain, is simply a smaller version of its Cold War predecessors. This issue, while interesting, is outside the scope of this discussion. It is clear that cuts in force structure have been somewhat unbalanced. Specifically, cuts in TDA units, the army's infrastructure, have lagged well behind reductions in TOE units, the army's fighting force. Officer authorizations under the TDA have grown as a percentage of the overall officer requirements in the active duty force (see table 3.3). In other words, the army has a relatively greater demand for officers in its tail than in its teeth. There are explanations for this shift. Some senior army leaders complain that TDA cuts have proceeded more slowly than reductions in TOE structure due to organizational politics.[33] Additionally, one might expect that there is a minimal level of TDA structure necessary to support the active army, regardless of its size. The army, for example, requires a minimum number of hospitals, training areas, and educational facilities regardless of whether the force is eight hundred thousand, four hundred thousand, or two hundred thousand strong. And, as already noted, TDA requirements for officers have grown as a consequence of congressional mandates since 1987.

These changes in the structure of the army, and in the requirements for officers, are also reflected in the composition of the officer corps. TDA units are substantially more "officer-rich" than TOE units, and field grade officers (majors and above) are more heavily distributed in TDA units. As a consequence of this lag, there is a relatively larger requirement for officers in TDA units (the army's tail) than TOE units (the army's teeth). Predictably, the personnel community sought to fill this new force structure, and two changes in the composition of the officer corps have resulted. First, the officer corps has become slightly more senior. This change is illustrated by a decline in the ratio of company grade officers (lieutenants and captains) to field grade officers, from 1.8:1 in 1990 to 1.5:1 in 1995 (see diagram 3.5 in the appendix to this chapter). Field grade officers (majors through colonels) comprise a significantly larger percentage of the officer corps than they did prior to downsizing.

Additionally, the army's enlisted to officer (E/O) ratio has decreased from 6.1:1 in 1990 to 5.2:1 in 1995 (see diagram 3.5). This means that officers are a larger percentage of the army as a whole. From a historical perspective, neither finding should be surprising, as the rank distribution of the regular officer corps tends to be inflated during periods of retrenchment (Lang 1964, 72). Similarly, the E/O ratio has declined significantly following every conflict in the postwar period (Luttwak 1985, 289–305). These changes occurred despite the fact that the army aggressively used the SERB to cull its senior ranks.

TABLE 3.3
Changes in the Distribution of Officer Authorizations (1987–1997)

	Fiscal Year 1987 (Endstrength of 780,000)				Fiscal Year 1997 (Endstrength of 475,000)[a]				
	TOE	TDA	Total Officers	% in TDA	TOE	TDA	Total Oficers	% in TDA	Relative Δ in TDA
First Lieutenant	14,037	2,297	16,334	14	7,928	1,455	9,383	16	+2
Captain	14,059	17,641	31,700	56	9,739	11,415	21,154	54	-2
Major	6,015	11,687	17,702	66	4,270	10,382	14,652	71	+5
Lieutenant Colonel	2,229	8,798	11,027	80	1,704	7,559	9,263	82	+2
Colonel	534	4,260	4,794	89	429	3,563	3,992	89	—
General	114	373	487	77	76	291	367	79	+2
Total	36,988	45,056	82,044	55	24,146	34,665	58,811	59	+4

SOURCE: Office of the Deputy Chief of Staff for Personnel.
[a]This endstrength target was directed by Secretary of Defense Perry in April 1995, but is still in contention.

None of these phenomena— the relative growth in TDA structure, declining ratios of enlisted soldiers to officers or of junior officers to senior officers—is by itself necessarily undesirable, though each has been criticized by Congress (Maze 1995, 4). The army defends these changes as the logical outcome of a smaller force structure and the increasing external demands for field grade officers.[34] Moreover, personnel planners deride the use of such ratios for monitoring an exceptionally complex officer requirements process. Even for a complex, high-tech army, however, common sense dictates that civilian policymakers should question a military organization in which there is an increasing majority of officers in the tail rather than in the teeth, one officer for every five enlisted soldiers, and three field grade officers for every two company grade officers. Part of the explanation may lie in the army's failure to fundamentally alter the composition of its force structure at the end of the Cold War. This trend may be attributed to lags in cuts of TDA force structure. Some of the explanation rests with burgeoning external requirements for officers that are outside the army's control. And part of the answer is found in the fundamentally flawed officer requirements process described earlier. Each of these areas will require some attention when downsizing comes to an end.

Personnel Readiness

When Congress, OSD, and military leaders discuss personnel readiness, they are generally referring to the enlisted force rather than the officer corps, despite the fact that the readiness of the officer corps is equally important to military effectiveness. As already noted, personnel readiness may be measured by the extent to which authorized positions (spaces) are filled with persons of the correct grade and appropriate occupational skill (faces). In the aggregate, this may be roughly measured by comparing the army-wide authorizations across grades with the available inventory of officers in those grades; substantial shortfalls have obvious consequences for army-wide readiness.

During downsizing, maintaining personnel readiness required that force structure be reduced at the same rate as personnel, thus allowing the services to maintain high aggregate levels of personnel readiness. Although the army suffered some short-term personnel readiness problems in some units, at the aggregate level, army-wide readiness (as measured by the percentage of authorized positions filled) remained relatively constant.[35] For the officer corps, the same aggregate measure may be used. Overall, the army has suffered a slight decline in its level of officer manning or "fill" during downsizing (see diagram 3.3). In particular, the army suffers from a substantial shortage of majors—the available inventory is approximately three-fourths of the authorized requirements. On the basis of the army's officer distribution plan described earlier, some "lower priority" units consequently receive only 65 percent of their authorized allocation of officers.

Officer shortages are a chronic problem worsened by downsizing. There are several explanations. Force structure cuts have generally lagged behind cuts in personnel, thereby placing increasing pressure on the personnel system to fill relatively more spaces with fewer faces. Additionally, delays in cuts of the officer-rich TDA force structure and increasing congressionally mandated requirements for officers exacerbated existing officer shortages between 1990 and 1995. All things considered, the army has been relatively effective in maintaining officer manning during this tumultuous period, though officer shortages will continue to challenge personnel planners in the years ahead. The officer shortage problem is, of course, closely tied to the problems observed earlier. The solution to this dilemma will require thoughtful consideration and unprecedented action when stability returns to officer personnel management. While Congress must seriously evaluate

Diagram 3.3. Percentage of Line Officer Positions Filled, 1989–1995

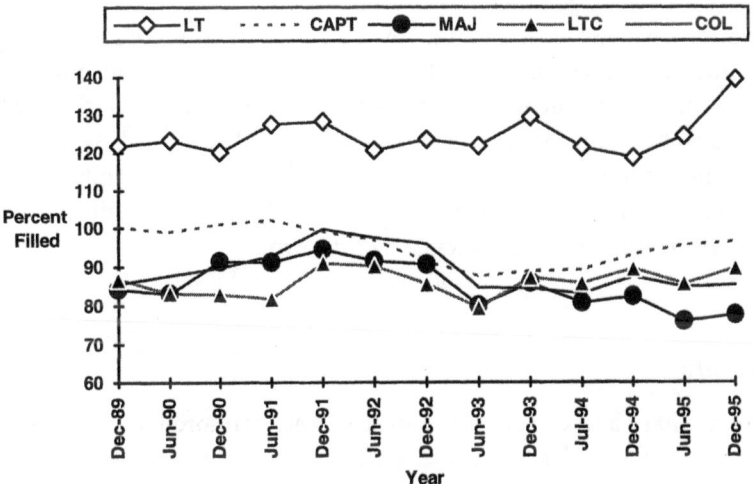

SOURCE: U.S. Army, Office of the Deputy Chief of Staff for Personnel.

and modify the laws governing officer management, the army must make a concerted attempt to rationalize its officer requirements process, even though this may require dramatic cuts in TDA units.

Care and Compassion

The army's leadership demonstrated its commitment to care and compassion in three notable areas. First, it placed extraordinary emphasis on minimizing involuntary reductions, even though involuntary programs are significantly less expensive than voluntary programs and pose less risk to the quality of the officer corps.[36] The army energetically lobbied for the VSI/SSB and the early retirement option, and enthusiastically marketed these alternatives to the officer corps. When involuntary separation programs were necessary, the army implemented them compassionately. For example, every effort was made to treat the officers chosen for involuntary separation with dignity by informing them in confidence of their selection and by providing them with ample time and resources to ease their transition to civilian life. This is indicative of the spirit that pervaded the entire downsizing effort.[37]

The army also devoted significantly more resources to transition assistance than the other services. The Army Career and Alumni Program (ACAP), which provides counselling, job assistance, and a variety of other services to departing soldiers, is an example of the priority placed on assisting those leaving.[38] A recent study by the Human Resources Research Organization found that the army's transition program significantly improved job placement rate, income, and relative financial condition of those who took advantage of it (Sadacca et al. 1995, 65–66).[39] In short, ACAP not only assists former service members in getting jobs but provides a symbolic message to officers and enlisted members alike—both those who left and those who stayed—that the army takes care of its own.

Diversity

While military and civilian policymakers were extraordinarily concerned after the Gulf War that minorities (African Americans in particular) and women would be disproportionately affected by downsizing, their worst fears never materialized. Despite the fact that blacks and women have suffered from institutional discrimination in the past, there is little evidence to suggest either group was disadvantaged by personnel cuts. To the contrary, both groups served in larger proportions in the active army officer corps in 1995 than in 1990. Table 3.4 illustrates the proportional changes in the number of blacks and women across grades in the officers corps between September 1990 and September 1994 (the years during which the army made the biggest cuts). The overall representation of blacks in the officer corps increased slightly. While there was a slight decrease in the representation of black officers in the junior ranks, this appears to be a consequence of a decreasing propensity among college-bound African Americans to consider the military (Tice 1994a, 18). African American representation in the grades of major and lieutenant colonel increased appreciably.

Likewise, the proportion of women across the officer ranks grew during downsizing, especially in the ranks of major, lieutenant colonel, and colonel. One explanation for this trend is that black and female officers did not take advantage of voluntary separation programs at the same rates as their contemporaries, signaling perhaps that the army does indeed offer more opportunity for these groups than does society more generally. In addition, blacks and women serve disproportionately in branches found primarily in TDA units where officer authorizations have been reduced more

TABLE 3.4
Downsizing's Effects on Diversity (1990–1994)

	Black Officers/All Officers			Female Officers/All Officers		
	September	September	Percent	September	September	Percent
Second Lieutenant	1332/11298 (11.79%)	927/9206 (10.07%)	-1.72	1969/11298 (17.43%)	1652/9206 (17.94%)	0.51
First Lieutenant	1654/12907 (12.81%)	1135/8900 (12.75%)	-0.6	2316/12907 (17.94%)	1637/8900 (18.39%)	0.45
Captain	4590/32913 (13.95%)	3258/26349 (12.36%)	-1.59	4940/32913 (15.01%)	3970/26349 (15.07%)	0.06
Major	1633/17183 (9.50%)	1812/14512 (12.49%)	2.99	1856/17183 (10.80%)	1976/14512 (13.62%)	2.82
Lieutenant Colonel	551/10439 (5.28%)	762/9185 (8.30%)	3.02	695/10439 (6.66%)	892/9185 (9.71%)	3.05
Colonel	206/4452 (4.63%)	185/3805 (4.86%)	0.23	133/4452 (2.99%)	205/3805 (5.39%)	2.40
General	27/407 (6.63%)	22/335 (6.57%)	-0.06	3/407 (.74%)	3/335 (.90%)	0.16
Totals[a]	9993/89599 (11.15%)	8101/72292 (11.21%)	0.06	11912/89599 (13.29%)	10335/72292 (14.3%)	1.01

SOURCE: Office of the Army Deputy Chief of Staff for Personnel, Human Resources Directorate.
[a]Totals include both officers managed by the Officer Personnel Management Directorate and those in special branches.

slowly (see table 3.3). Finally, the retention "goals" established for all SERBs and RIF boards reduced the possibility that blacks and women would be slighted.

This analysis is not meant to suggest that the army, or the downsizing process, was completely free of bias or controversy over gender and race.[40] Despite the army's well-publicized success in the area of integration, defense policymakers continue to debate how it and the other services should incorporate issues of race and gender into the selection process. In the army, blacks and women clearly lack role models and are underrepresented in the senior ranks (Graham 1995, A1). Surveys of service members indicate that many minorities and women do not believe they have the same opportunities as white males and that many white males believe undeserving minorities and women benefit from "quotas" (Hudson 1995, 8). In the case of downsizing, minorities did occasionally suffer disproportionately from involuntary separation programs, though there is no indication that this was a consequence of bias.[41] Overall, however, the absence of uneven losses on the part of black and female officers is evidence of the army's continued progress in this area.

Promotion and Command Opportunity

In addition to maintaining professional development opportunities, the Army's leadership emphasized maintaining or improving promotion opportunity and timing during downsizing. Balanced cuts across the entire officer corps have been marginally successful in achieving this goal, though promotion opportunity and timing still fall short of DOPMA guidelines.[42] Under DOPMA, the 1980s was a decade of boom and bust in army promotion policy. The Reagan administration's decision to expand and modernize the force also led to authorizations to increase the size of the officer corps. Under DOPMA rules, the growth in endstrength led to a corresponding increase in the number of allowable field grade officers; a promotion boom resulted as the army hurried to move more junior officers into newly authorized spaces.[43] These early decisions led to a promotion bust in the late 1980s (see diagram 3.6 in the appendix to this chapter), as the promotion system once again achieved equilibrium and the retention rates of field grade officers proved to be higher than expected (Rostker et al. 1993, 29). Army leaders believed that downsizing provided the opportunity to correct this imbalance and possibly achieve DOPMA objectives.

Overall, the army made modest gains in this area between 1990 and 1995. There was a noticeable rise in promotion opportunity for colonels, captains, and particularly majors in the latter years of personnel reductions (see diagram 3.6). Promotion opportunity to lieutenant colonel remained roughly stable at the desired DOPMA objective of 70 percent. During this same period, there were modest changes in promotion timing (the average amount of time before officers of a certain rank are promoted to the next higher rank). Timing for lieutenant colonels, in particular, decreased by a year, from seventeen years and six months to sixteen years and six months (see diagram 3.7 in the appendix to this chapter). In addition, early promotion, or "below-the-zone" (BZ) promotion, to the ranks of major, lieutenant colonel, or colonel increased dramatically during the late 1980s, and this trend has been maintained throughout the 1990s.[44]

The percentage of officers chosen to serve as battalion commanders remained relatively constant throughout this period for officers in combat, combat support, and combat service support branches (see diagram 3.8 in the appendix to this chapter). It would seem, therefore, that the army has fulfilled the promises made to the officer corps in this area. In some respects, however, the statistics are misleading. Beginning in 1992, the army began to use the same centralized selection process previously used to pick battalion commanders to select lieutenant colonels for "garrison command" as well.[45] Thus, while the opportunity of being selected for "command" has remained relatively constant, the likelihood of being selected for battalion command—as traditionally defined—has declined significantly. Moreover, between 1991 and 1996, the percentage of TOE commands was reduced substantially (24 percent), while the number of TDA commands declined by a mere 1 percent.[46] The Army's "Commanders" now serve in relatively larger proportions in the army's tail. All in all, the army for the most part satisfied its commitments regarding promotion and command opportunity during downsizing. The subtle changes that have taken place particularly with regard to command and below-the-zone promotion opportunity are discussed more fully in chapter 4.

Decisionmaking in the Office of the Deputy Chief of Staff for Personnel

How were the decisions that led to these favorable outcomes made? Although the Army Chief of Staff ultimately made most of the final downsizing decisions, the Office of the Deputy Chief of Staff for Personnel considered, developed, and decided many policy questions before presenting recommendations to the Chief of Staff. Likewise, while each of the three primary actors in the army personnel community—the Office of the Assistant Secretary of the Army for Manpower and Reserve Affairs, the Office of the Deputy Chief of Staff for Personnel, and the Army Personnel Command—played a crucial role in downsizing, ODCSPER was at the core of downsizing decisionmaking. To comprehend why the army downsized as it did, how it balanced and achieved competing downsizing objectives, it is important to understand what happened there.

That the downsizing process is such a recent phenomenon makes it both easier and more difficult to evaluate. Many of the key players still hold positions in and around the army, and many of the decisions are fresh in their memories. At the same time, these insights are colored by a variation of Miles's law—where these individuals remember themselves to have stood on various issues depends not only on where they sat then, but also on where they sit now.[47] Recognizing such limitations, this discussion seeks to convey the essence of the downsizing decisionmaking process between 1990 and 1996 by focusing on key events, the most critical and controversial downsizing programs, and the most influential personalities. During this period, there were four distinctly different phases of the downsizing process, each with its own management challenges and generals overseeing it. By tracing downsizing policy during the tenures of the four consecutive Deputy Chiefs of Staff for Personnel—Lieutenant Generals Allen Ono, Bill Reno, Tom Carney, and Ted Stroup—it is possible to identify the factors that contributed most to the army's success.

Laying the Foundation: Ono

Lieutenant General Allen Ono served as the Deputy Chief of Staff for Personnel from June 1987 to July 1990. His tenure is most notable for the guiding principles that were put into place. As a colonel in the army Recruiting Command from 1979 to 1980, Ono's career was strongly influenced by his immediate boss, Major General Maxwell Thurman. Known as one of the army's toughest, most dispassionate leaders, Thurman was infamous for the intensity and analytic rigor he brought to every job and problem. Like a kiln, he either hardened or shattered the people who worked for him. Those who survived were left with an unmistakable imprint, more distinct on some than on others. This imprint was visible in the way in which Ono, and his Director of the Military Personnel Directorate, Brigadier General Theodore Stroup (another Thurman protégé), developed the initial downsizing plan.[48]

At its starkest, downsizing is a combination of three interdependent processes —communicating its logic and the method, separating the organization's least valuable employees, and assisting their transition to careers outside the organization. There was consensus from the beginning that the way in which the army's leaders communicated the downsizing plan to the rank and file was important but less agreement on what the content of and conduit for that message should be. Ono and Stroup took the lead in communicating the downsizing plan to the field army. The primary objective of their communication strategy was to reduce uncertainty and generate support for the downsizing plan around the army. Reports from the field in 1989, however, suggested that the official messages, briefings, and *Army Times* articles being used were failing to achieve these objectives.[49]

In early 1990, the PERSCOM commander, Major General Robert Ord III, proposed a variation of chain teaching—a process used in army basic training in which the unit commander teaches the next level down, and those leaders teach the next level, and so on, until the entire unit receives the lesson. The chain teaching concept flowed from the principle that it was a "commander's army," and that the army's leadership had to get the commanders involved if downsizing was to be successful.[50] Chief of Staff Vuono embraced this initiative and continually reaffirmed the importance of clear, frequent, and honest communication with army leaders at every level.[51] A chain teaching briefing was developed and then presented to senior commanders around the army for their review. A version that reflected their critiques was distributed to commanders throughout the army in the latter half of 1990 and was revised and redistributed annually thereafter to update the army on the downsizing plan.[52]

Involuntarily separating the "least valuable" employees, particularly from among the senior ranks, is a sobering activity for any organization. The army's implementation of Selective Early Retirement Boards between 1990 and 1995 was a manifestation of its downsizing principles in action. The army began to consider using SERBs to reduce "overstrength" components of the officer corps as early as 1984, but opponents of this measure successfully argued against it.[53] In 1988, however, the army established a precedent by convening a SERB for line officers. Within two years, the SERBs were a well-practiced, though increasingly unpopular, management tool.[54] The use of SERBs went a long way toward permitting the army leadership to "shape the force" by distributing cuts across the entire officer corps. From the very beginning, an aggressive SERB policy had the support of senior officers within the personnel community. Army leaders also viewed SERBs as a means for improving promotion opportunity and timing. As one participant recalls: "It had everything to do with keeping the force moving and promises to the younger people."[55]

For Vuono and other senior leaders, the SERB process was particularly difficult because the officers being separated were their contemporaries—officers with whom they had served earlier in their careers. As one analyst recollects: "It was emotional and gut-wrenching. No one wanted to do it. The very thought that you'd take men and women who had served the army faithfully and say, 'You're outta here,' was hateful to the senior leadership. But the coldhearted reality of it was, we had no choice."[56]

The army made every effort not to stigmatize those being separated (although arguably the secrecy surrounding the effort did just that by seeming to suggest that the officers selected for early retirement had something to be embarrassed about).[57] Personnel planners carefully screened the SERB lists to ensure that none of the officers selected had been awarded the Medal of Honor or Distinguished Service Cross (the nation's two highest awards for valor), believing that to separate recognized war heroes would be the ultimate display of disrespect.[58] Generals were tasked with informing the officers in their command who had been selected for early retirement. The Deputy Chief of Staff for Personnel signed each SERB letter personally. As the size of the impending personnel reductions became apparent, the army received authority from Congress to expand the SERB program to balance cuts across the officer corps and minimize the need for Reductions in Force of less senior officers. SERBs were used extensively from 1990 through 1995. In this period, 3,812 army officers (mostly lieutenant colonels and colonels), more than one-fourth of the total officer populations in these two grades, were involuntarily "retired."

The army devoted substantial energy to assisting individuals who were separated make the transition to civilian life. In 1990, it created the Army Career and Alumni Program (ACAP) for this purpose, and this was one of the few occasions when army civilians overrode military leaders on the specifics of downsizing policy. Kim Wincup, Assistant Secretary of the Army for Manpower and Reserve Affairs from 1988 to 1992, championed a comprehensive transition and job assistance program. Senior uniformed leaders resisted this idea, fearing that transition assistance would encourage the wrong people—those with the most talent—to leave the army. Field commanders opposed the program as unacceptably disruptive because it required them to release soldiers periodically in order for them to attend counseling and training sessions months prior to their departure.[59]

The civilian perspective prevailed. With the backing of Wincup, a task force was formed in March 1990 to outline the components of the program. The program was designed to integrate relocation services, enhance the army's image among soldiers and the larger public, send the message that "the army takes care of its own", and avoid the negative effects of downsizing—uncertainty, loss of control, and reduced productivity.[60] By May 1994, ACAP employed approximately 600 military and civilian employees at 62 locations in 27 states and 4 countries to assist departing soldiers with pre-separation counseling, workshops, job bank facilities, and an employer network.[61]

Building a Plan: Reno

Vuono selected Lieutenant General William H. Reno to replace Ono in July 1990. In his previous position as Director of Army Program Analysis and Evaluation, Reno had argued against limiting the pace of personnel reductions to thirty-five thousand annually, maintaining that this number had no rigorous analytic basis, was inordinately expensive, and stretched out the pain of downsizing.[62] Despite these recommendations, Vuono settled on thirty-five thousand a year and a clear set of downsizing objectives. Reno was tasked with building a personnel downsizing plan that satisfied these conditions.[63]

Reno's willingness to serve as the Army Staff's gadfly was one of his distinguishing characteristics along with his sharp analytical mind and extraordinarily long work hours. He had a reputation for being one of the brightest, most dedicated generals in the army, and by all indications it was well-deserved. Like Ono, he spent three years as a colonel working directly for Thurman, in this case when Lieutenant General Thurman was the Deputy Chief of Staff for Personnel from 1981 to 1983. During this time, Reno had a front row seat to many of the dramatic, analytically oriented reforms of the army personnel community undertaken by Thurman. Not surprisingly, this experience also affected his approach as Deputy Chief of Staff for Personnel.

Theoretically, building the army's personnel downsizing plan should have been relatively straightforward. Reno's counterpart in the Office of the Deputy Chief of Staff for Operations (DCSOPS) would identify the TOE or

TDA units to be eliminated or cut significantly, and Reno would simply develop the personnel policies needed to reduce the appropriate number and type of soldiers. Two factors, however, confounded Reno's efforts from the very beginning. First, a range of thorny domestic and international political issues precluded the army from making timely public announcements about force structure cuts, even after such decisions had been made.[64] Second, by early 1990, it was already clear that the reduction of both TOE and TDA force structure was lagging behind cuts in personnel. The delays in cutting force structure may have stemmed at least partially from disagreement among army leaders about where such cuts should be made. Reno confirms this: "We could never get . . . the army's leadership to agree on where force structure cuts should be made."[65]

Not surprisingly, cuts in TDA force structure were particularly slow to materialize. In 1990, Vuono initiated the Vanguard Study to address this problem, but its recommendations encountered tremendous resistance throughout the army (Demma 1994b, 14). As a consequence, TDA cuts were sporadic and generally distributed evenly across commands. "In the final analysis," recalls a former Director of the Army's Manpower Directorate, "nobody wanted their ox gored and the easiest thing to do was simply distribute cuts evenly across the entire TDA—salami slice it."[66]

To a far greater extent than by delays in force structure cuts, however, Reno's responsibilities were complicated by Saddam Hussein's invasion of Kuwait on August 2, 1990. For the remainder of 1990, Reno oversaw two enormously complicated and difficult enterprises—preparing the Army for an operational mobilization while at the same time planning an extensive personnel reduction. Although the downsizing programs scheduled for 1991 were canceled, the army's leadership remained committed to achieving mandated endstrength reductions in subsequent years (Demma 1994b, 13). Reno's typical eighty-hour work weeks, combined with the magnitude of the tasks at hand, resulted in a frenetic level of activity in the Office of the Deputy Chief of Staff for Personnel during and after the Gulf War.

As a consequence of the war, the army did not meet the FY 1991 endstrength objectives set by Congress and exceeded DOPMA grade tables for officers.[67] By March 1991, the army's active duty endstrength was 744,000, thirty thousand over its projected downsizing target (diagram 3.4).[68] In the months after Desert Storm, the army reduced its active duty endstrength more quickly than expected, to 610,000 by September 1992. Voluntary separation programs were used extensively to decrease the officer and enlisted endstrength during this period. But the rapid reductions in personnel were not matched by corresponding reductions in force structure, exacerbating personnel shortfalls and creating a short-term decline in readiness.[69]

In the twelve months between the conclusion of Desert Storm in March 1991 and Reno's retirement in March 1992, his office made a series of policy recommendations and decisions that guided personnel reductions over the next several years. The army developed its downsizing plan on the assumption that 535,000 would be its final endstrength, and that if the number went below that, the plan would require adjustment and perhaps fundamental rethinking.[70] For the officer corps, in particular, this target was critical because the 535,000 downsizing plan subjected each year group to the possibility of Reduction in Force no more than once, thereby allowing the army to achieve mandated reductions while still promising relatively secure career opportunities for those who remained.[71]

Reno established an unusual command climate within the Office of the Deputy Chief of Staff for Personnel during his tenure similar in many respects to the atmosphere created under Thurman. Unlike other major commands, ODCSPER has access to the performance records of every officer in the army and the final say on where each officer is assigned. In the Thurman tradition, Reno and Stroup exploited this situation by "recruiting" a generation of high-performing officers (many of whom had quantitative

Diagram 3.4. Impact of the Gulf War on Downsizing

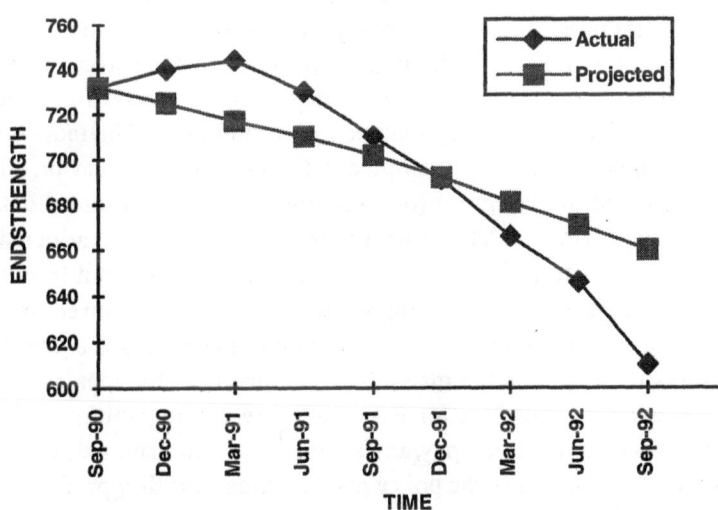

SOURCE: Office of the Deputy Chief of Staff for Personnel.

backgrounds) from around the army. Reno also reinstated the Program Analysis and Evaluation "integrating" cell within ODCSPER to provide him with an overview of the issues being handled by the individual directorates.[72] Finally, Reno, like Thurman, emphasized "running the rabbit down every rabbit hole to get the facts."[73] In other words, Reno created an environment in which rigorous and exhaustive analysis, on each and every alternative, preceded all policy decisions.

Over the last two decades, the Office of the Deputy Chief of Staff for Personnel has relied increasingly on the output of models and automated personnel management systems to set personnel policy. This is indicative of a general movement toward rigorous analytic capacity that has occurred within the army throughout the twentieth century, but most notably since the advent of systems analysis in the Pentagon in the 1960s (Hewes 1975; Hough 1989).[74] This analytic capacity played an important role in the downsizing decisionmaking process, particularly as it became clear that substantial involuntary separations would be necessary to meet mandated cuts. For the officer corps, the questions upon which the models focused were relatively straightforward: What year groups are overstrength and how much should they be reduced? How much should the army reduce accessions? What impact would separations of one group have on the attrition rates of the others? And, how would downsizing decisions affect the officer corps' quality, readiness, demographic makeup, and promotion opportunity?

Reno periodically charged three analytic cells within ODCSPER, and several others outside it, with analyzing these questions. Within the office, the Manpower Directorate, the Personnel Management Directorate (each of which had analytic cells), and Reno's new Program Analysis and Evaluation division had overlapping analytic responsibilities.[75] The models used were all similar in that they attempted to forecast human behavior, relying primarily on officer retention (or continuation) rates—historical data on the rate at which officers left the army for disparate reasons at various stages of their careers—to project future retention rates. With output from these models, analysts were able to compare the projected officer inventory with impending army requirements. Theoretically, this comparison allowed policymakers to determine the magnitude and targets of the separation programs needed to "shape" the force for the future. Although the models varied in complexity, methodology, and assumptions concerning continuation rates, they differed less in the policy recommendations they produced.[76]

Many of those who worked in ODCSPER during this period recall a unique blend of energy, intellectual openness, and creative tension. "Free-for-alls," in which generals, senior civilians, colonels, lieutenant colonels, and majors would sit together in Reno's office brainstorming about various aspects of the downsizing plan, were commonplace. Anyone with a good idea, one person recalls, was encouraged to voice it: "If you disagreed with one of the generals, you were expected to speak out." In addition, the senior leaders were intimately involved in the analysis. Reno and Stroup had analytic backgrounds: "Both understood the numbers and knew where they came from."[77] Reno, in particular, would often manipulate the models himself prior to making a decision.

Reno frequently tasked several analytic cells with analyzing the same problem independently. Each group would then be called upon to present its findings and recommendations. After these briefings, Reno would compare and contrast the outcomes, often requesting more iterations or the inclusion of other variables. Not surprisingly, this practice created noticeable tension between the analytic cells within ODCSPER as well as stressful relations with those outside it. As one participant recalls: "There was tension by design. It often digressed into political squabbling as egos became involved, but generally the tension was healthy."[78] This approach served several purposes in forcing communication among various analytic groups that otherwise rarely interacted, creating a level of competition that ultimately enhanced the quality of analysis, and allowing key decisionmakers to tap quickly into the entire analytic community prior to making a decision.

In retrospect, the analytic effort dedicated to the downsizing decision-making process was extraordinary; clearly, it was important and necessary to have a great deal of precision when identifying where and how the army should implement its cuts. There is some question, however, whether the Office of the Deputy Chief of Staff for Personnel, particularly under Reno, was overly reliant on the output of its models and on the analysts who designed and manipulated them. Nevertheless, by March 1992, Reno the engineer and consummate analyst had built a well-conceived downsizing plan. Lieutenant General Thomas Carney, an infantry commander and "soldier's soldier," was charged with implementing it.

Implementation: Carney

Tom Carney was selected by Chief of Staff Gordon Sullivan to serve as Reno's replacement for a reason. Substantial personnel cuts were taking a toll on morale, particularly in the officer corps, and Sullivan wanted an exdivision commander—well-known and respected by the officer corps—to be the army's front man on downsizing.[79] Several aspects of Carney's twenty-five months as Deputy Chief of Staff for Personnel deserve special attention. First, his operating style was distinctly different from Reno's, offering an interesting comparison. Additionally, the Voluntary Separation Incentive Program, one of the most innovative and successful downsizing programs, was instituted under his direction. Finally, during his tenure, the Bottom-Up Review was promulgated by the Secretary of Defense, and the army was required to modify its downsizing plan to achieve even lower end-strengths.

Carney's career followed a unique course. He had served primarily in "troop assignments" prior to being assigned as a colonel in 1984 to serve as Executive Officer to the Vice Chief of Staff of the Army, Max Thurman. Although he spent significant portions of his career under Thurman's tutelage, Carney is an exception in that he seems not to have emulated Thurman's operating style. He became DCSPER after alternating between "troop" and "personnel" assignments (including a two-year stint as a division commander). Unlike many of his predecessors, he was as intimately familiar with the army's personnel community as he was with the muddy boots army.

Carney, perhaps to an even greater extent than the generals who preceded him, agonized over downsizing. He had a distinctive people-oriented approach to the development and implementation of downsizing policy. As a former staff officer recalls: "He would always ask us, given that we have to make cuts, how can we best satisfy the needs of the soldiers?"[80] His intuitive approach to decisionmaking differed dramatically from Reno's analytic style:

> He was no data hound. He'd bring in the experts, listen to what they had to say, apply his experience and his judgment—which was a field commander's perspective—and if it felt good, he went with it.... I'd say, "here are the options and here is what the analysis supports," and he'd say, "Independent of the analysis, I'd like to go in this direction."[81]

Carney also delegated responsibility more freely and rarely involved himself in the specifics of how subordinates carried out their tasks. According to staff officers, "He liked to get lots of information, but gave very little feedback, and the adversarialism and the free-for-alls encouraged by Reno were shut down under Carney. Decisions were made in a very tight and controlled way."[82]

These differences in the operating styles of Reno and Carney in particular are important for explaining the army's overall success in its downsizing efforts. Reno was numbers-oriented; Carney was people-oriented. Reno made decisions on the basis of exhaustive analysis; Carney made them based on intuition. Reno immersed himself in the details of policy alternatives; Carney focused on the general direction of, and perceptions about, downsizing. In some respects, each man was ideal for the phase of downsizing for which he was responsible. In planning, Reno could be counted on to force the army's leadership to consider all the alternatives and probable consequences. In implementation, Carney could be trusted to put a caring and compassionate face on downsizing and to be sensitive to the perceptions and concerns of the muddy boots army.

Beginning in 1990, army leaders worked diligently to convince Congress and OSD that downsizing was predominantly an army problem, and lobbied extensively for much needed-changes to DOPMA.[83] The magnitude of the army's personnel reduction in comparison to that of the other services, combined with its overabundance of field grade officers, created unique management challenges. In its original form, DOPMA offered the services limited flexibility. Once a Regular Army officer had passed the six-year point, he could not be separated unless passed over for promotion twice; and if an officer was promoted to lieutenant colonel, a twenty-year career was assured. The services were also limited to offering voluntary early outs, discharging officers in their first five years of service, or lowering promotion rates (thereby increasing the number of individuals passed over twice for promotion) as reduction options. In short, it was impossible to downsize the officer corps without sacrificing one or more of the army's downsizing principles, and the army forcefully made this case to Congress (Rostker et al. 1993, 29).

Congress had always been uneasy about the notion of involuntarily separating Regular Army officers. Eventually, lawmakers heeded the army's requests and expanded the authority of the services to separate involuntarily "tenured" Regular Army officers through SERBs and RIF boards. After the Gulf War, however, Congress was again reluctant on this score. During congressional hearings, members voiced reservations about the prospect of RIFing tens of thousands of Desert Storm veterans.[84] In 1992, Congress partially remedied this situation by authorizing the use of the Voluntary Separation Incentive and the Special Separation Bonus, thereby minimizing the need for involuntary separations.

The army supported these proposals, but with several caveats. First, it wanted to maintain control over the skills, level of experience, and "quality" of those who departed.[85] Second, it was convinced that the voluntary programs would not generate sufficient volunteers, particularly among officers with fifteen to nineteen years of service. Thus, it wanted the authority to use involuntary separations (the stick) in conjunction with voluntary programs (the carrot). Consistent with this concern, the army proposed the Selective Early Annuity, a voluntary retirement option that would allow it to avoid more draconian involuntary programs against this group of officers.[86]

The Voluntary Separation Incentive Program provided a stream of payments equal to 2.5 percent of a service member's annual base pay, multiplied by the number of years of his or her service; the payments were to be made in equal installments for twice the number of years a person had served. The Special Separation Bonus incentive program provided a lump-sum payment of 15 percent of a soldier's annual base pay, multiplied by his or her years of service.[87] Between 1992 and 1995, the army used the VSI/SSB to encourage voluntary separation, primarily among officers with between six and fourteen years of service, to avoid repeating the notorious RIFs of captains and majors that beset the army after Vietnam.[88]

To ensure that the VSI/SSB would not encourage the army's best and brightest junior and mid-career officers to resign, Carney tasked Major General Gerald Putman, Commander of the U.S. Army Personnel Command, with implementing the program in a way that minimized this possibility.[89] Personnel assignment officers within PERSCOM's Officer Personnel Management Directorate (OPMD) were of critical importance to Putman's efforts to retain the army's most promising officers.[90] Putman gave them clear and unequivocal guidance: the voluntary incentive programs were the carrot, but they would only be successful if wielded in tandem with the threat of RIFs—the stick. Putman was brutally frank with those who worked for him, and under his watchful eye PERSCOM adopted an equally candid persona. Traditionally, PERSCOM assignment officers had not been permitted to give specific assessments of how likely an officer was to be promoted or RIFed, or stood in relation to his or her peers.[91] Putman modified this policy, directing assignment officers to evaluate the performance files of the officers for whom they were responsible and to convey to these officers their assessment regarding their vulnerability to the RIF. The intent was to encourage officers likely to be RIFed to depart by choice and with dignity. Generous separation benefits sweetened the option.

The army's centralized officer management system simplified the mechanics of this process.[92] Once an aggregate number of officers within a cohort had been targeted for the voluntary incentive programs, the Officer Distribution Division within PERSCOM determined how many officers in each branch were in "excess of army requirements."[93] Based on this evaluation, each branch was given a goal for the number of officers it should encourage to volunteer. Armed with this number, each branch developed a rough order-of-merit list (OML) of the officers eligible for the VSI/SSB. Assignment officers then targeted those officers with the least competitive performance files for the voluntary separation programs.

Meticulous preparation—the creation of checklists, rehearsals, and exhaustive briefings—preceded any contact with officers in the field. Each branch mailed all eligible officers a personalized letter explaining the program and informing them that they would be contacted shortly by their assignment officer to discuss their options. Assignment officers then called individual officers to encourage them to consider the voluntary option; the calls were carefully logged, and follow-up calls were made periodically throughout the program. Each branch and division maintained a detailed tally of the number (and performance assessments) of those who volunteered. The army repeated this process annually from 1992 to 1995 and successfully avoided all but one RIF. As shown previously, it was also successful in encouraging the least competitive officers to volunteer while retaining the majority of what it deemed to be the "best and brightest."

Carney's last six months as Deputy Chief of Staff for Personnel were particularly turbulent ones for the army.[94] The incoming Clinton administration brought with it good news and bad for the army's downsizing effort. After taking office, Secretary of Defense Les Aspin approved the use of the Temporary Early Retirement Authority, which the Army used with increasing frequency between 1993 and 1995.[95] In September 1993, Aspin directed the army to reduce its numbers by an additional forty thousand, to an end-strength of 495,000, in accordance with the outcome of the Bottom-Up Review. In the short run, this had only minimal effects on the downsizing plan. The programs already in place were simply extended until 1997 and adjusted to accommodate the needs of a force of 495,000. However, the long-term effects of this change are less certain. The drawdown plan was initially conceived for a force of 535,000, and individual officer cohorts were targeted for downsizing up to 1994 with this in mind. At substantially lower force levels (given current retention rates), these groups may once again be "too large" in the future and create a "bubble" in the officer inventory not unlike that seen after Vietnam. Even more significant, this change has had a notable impact on the attitudes and behavior of officers in the muddy boots army.

Reconstitution: Stroup

In many ways, Lieutenant General Theodore Stroup's appointment as Deputy Chief of Staff for Personnel in September 1994 was a homecoming. He had served in the Office of the Deputy Chief of Staff for Personnel as the Director of Military Personnel Management (DMPM) from 1989 to 1992, after Vuono had assigned him to the Pentagon as a newly minted brigadier general to be the principal architect of the downsizing plan.[96] As DCSPER several years later he was tasked with overseeing the completion of the efforts he had begun. Like his three predecessors, Stroup's career had been significantly influenced by four years of mentorship under Thurman, an experience evident in Stroup's own operating style.

Sullivan selected Stroup to serve as DCSPER to reestablish stability in personnel management and make the necessary alterations in the personnel system for a substantially smaller active army.[97] Three factors make it difficult to evaluate Stroup's tenure. First, by the time Stroup returned to ODCSPER, the implementation of the cuts to 495,000 was almost complete. Both 1994 and 1995 were routine years as no formal downsizing briefing was given to the Chief of Staff or Secretary of the Army.[98] Second, in some respects, long-range personnel planning has been placed on hold in anticipation of additional cuts by OSD or Congress in 1996 and 1997. Third, Stroup only retired in winter 1996. This makes his leadership difficult to analyze, as the fragments of this complicated and evolutionary decisionmaking process can only be brought into focus with the benefit of time.

These points notwithstanding, several issues of particular import between 1994 and 1996 deserve brief attention. By 1994, a small but expanding group of senior civilian and military leaders was beginning to question whether the benefits of the Selective Early Retirement Boards were worth their undesirable impact in terms of low morale, mistrust, and heightened uncertainty on the army's culture.[99] The SERBs had always been an unsettling idea to the army's leadership (civilian and military), but as surveys from the field revealed their deleterious effects, opposition to them grew.[100] Based on guidance from the Army Secretariat, Selective Early Retirement Boards were canceled for fiscal year 1996. This turnabout is interesting not only from a policy perspective, but also as an example of civilian intervention having a notable effect on army downsizing policy. Among other things, critics argue that the army had become overly dependent on SERBs, particularly in light of the array of other instruments provided by Congress, and that too much emphasis was being placed on improving promotion opportunity and timing. As one general remarked: "We tried to adhere to closely to DOPMA, and we are now stuck in a cycle we cannot escape."[101] Moreover, critics note that the continuation rates on which the required number of SERBs is calculated have become increasingly volatile and unreliable as downsizing has progressed.[102]

Growing officer shortages also gained attention during Stroup's tenure. To a certain extent, the increasing shortages of field grade officers have been self-imposed, as the army's reduction in force structure (particularly TDA) has lagged behind reductions in personnel. However, this dilemma also results from the growing number of external requirements imposed by Congress. As a consequence, the army went from having control over 77 percent of its officer requirements in 1987, to 70 percent in 1995.[103] Predictably, these two factors have created increasing shortages, particularly of field grade officers, and difficult management challenges for the Deputy Chief of Staff for Personnel, as the distribution of these shortfalls across major commands has become an increasingly contentious issue.[104] While such problems have been exacerbated by downsizing, they are mild in comparison to those that have arisen in the past and are perhaps the predictable outcomes of dramatic organizational change. By the aforementioned measures—protecting quality, shaping the force, sustaining personnel readiness, and demonstrating care and compassion—the army's downsizing efforts have been mostly successful. What are common threads running through this experience that explain this success?

Congress, Cognitive Learning, and Culture

The army's effective management of downsizing was not an accident but resulted from a combination of several key factors. First, Congress provided the military departments the needed flexibility and necessary resources to downsize in a balanced and compassionate way. Second, the officer reductions in the aftermath of Vietnam traumatized the army's current generation of leadership and thus profoundly influenced the planning and implementation of the post–Cold War officer cuts. Third, over the last decade, the army personnel community has developed an analytic mindset and capacity that has significantly influenced the manner in which it responded to its downsizing mandate. As a result, the army downsized with precision as well as compassion, on the basis of rigorous analysis overlaid with common sense.

A Conscientious Congress

The role of Congress in assisting the army's downsizing efforts cannot be overstated. As a senior staff member on the House Armed Services Committee observes, "Congress gave the services a lot of flexibility and resources and simply asked to be kept up to date on how they were going to downsize and what groups they were going to target."[105] This statement, though self-serving, is nevertheless valid. While Congress was unrelenting in its pressure for deep and rapid personnel cuts and substantial budgetary savings, it was exceptionally cooperative in allowing the army flexibility and providing it with the resources to downsize effectively. Had Congress not waived the constraints imposed by DOPMA, the army would have been forced to cut too deeply into accessions and its junior officer ranks to meet mandated endstrengths. Moreover, these waivers permitted the army to consider both Regular Army officers and Other than Regular Army (OTRA) officers for various separation programs, thereby avoiding the discriminatory treatment accorded OTRA officers in the aftermath of Vietnam. Even more important, Congress provided funding for voluntary separation incentives in 1992 and the authority to expand early retirement in 1993. This helped the army minimize involuntary separations and give soldiers and officers reasonable and legitimate alternatives.

The cooperative relationship between Congress and the Department of Defense resulted from several factors. First, Congress had a genuine interest in sustaining the successes in recruitment, training, and retention in the all-volunteer force achieved over the previous two decades. Congress played an important role in building the all-volunteer force, and it was equally attentive to its responsibilities in reducing it (Blechman 1990). Second, the Gulf War produced a sense of obligation in Congress to those who fought, and this completely and undeniably changed the politics of downsizing. Prior to Desert Storm, voluntary incentive programs had been proposed but were by no means assured; in the aftermath of the war, members of Congress expressed grave reservations over the prospect of RIFs. The involuntarily separation of Desert Storm veterans not only seemed wrong but politically unacceptable. Finally, the Department of Defense, and the army in particular, made a persuasive analytic case for DOPMA relief, legislative flexibility, and financial support for voluntary incentive programs. The army's success in this area is in notable contrast to its ineffectiveness in resisting endstrength and budgetary cutbacks.

The Ghosts of Vietnam

"That men do not learn very much from the lessons of history," Aldous Huxley wrote, "is the most important of all lessons that history has to teach" (1959, 242). Numerous scholars have argued over the extent to which this observation applies to the Vietnam War. It is clear from the army's most recent downsizing experience that the events following Vietnam left a distinct and enduring impression on the officers who lived through it and affected the manner in which they downsized the U.S. Army.

Social scientists have for decades studied the manner in which decisionmakers learn from the past, the kinds of events from which they learn the most, and the types of lessons that are commonly learned. Many seem to agree that what decisionmakers learn from key events in history is an important factor in determining the images that shape their interpretation of a situation and the ultimate decisions they make (Neustadt and May 1986). Moreover, the amount of "learning" from an event varies with the degree to which it involved an individual's time, energy, and ego, and events that occur at a relatively early stage in one's life appear to have the most discernible influence on a person's life (Jervis 1976, 240–51). This case study offers evidence to support each of these propositions.

The colonels and generals of the 1990s were lieutenants, captains, majors, and lieutenant colonels during and immediately following the Vietnam War. This generation of leadership experienced first-hand the deep cuts in the size of the officer corps as it went from a high of 172,000 in 1969 to 100,000 by 1975, a 36 percent decrease (Lester 1974, 8–10). The size of this cut meant that those officers who remained in the army during this period knew others who left, voluntarily or involuntarily, as a consequence of downsizing. Vuono, for example, commanded an artillery brigade in 1975, and was charged with informing several captains in his unit that they had been RIFed.[106] Between 1973 and 1976, four of the eight generals discussed in these pages—Sullivan, Stroup, Ord, and Putman—worked in the Military Personnel Center (PERSCOM's predecessor) after serving tours in Vietnam. Each was deeply involved in implementing some aspect of officer reductions.[107]

Not only did the army's post–Cold War leadership observe and participate in the officer reductions, they also endured the consequences—the departure of numerous outstanding officers, low morale, and reduced personnel readiness—of poor personnel management decisions made during this period. They observed that the distinction the army made between officers with Regular Army and Reserve (other than Regular Army) commissions was unfair and unwise, and they ensured that this mistake was not repeated.[108] Reserve officers suffered the majority of the cuts between 1969 and 1975 despite the fact that they served in combat in Vietnam as frequently and with the same distinction as regulars, and the overall quality of the officer corps suffered accordingly (Dunnigan and Macedonia 1993, 102)[109] Moreover, these cuts were heavily weighted against junior officers, and very few senior officers were culled from the ranks (Gabriel and Savage 1978, 160).

The generals and colonels of the 1990s also observed and were victims of a conscious, though perhaps unavoidable, reduction in promotion opportunity and slowdown in timing, and eyewitnesses to the corresponding effects on morale and retention.[110] The army's rapid expansion during the Vietnam War had created a windfall in rapid and generous promotions. After the war, however, personnel planners were subjected not only to the officer corps' unrealistic promotion expectations but also to legislative constraints that forbade the "shaping" of Regular Army year groups with five to twenty years of service.[111] Discontent in the officer corps was exacerbated by a failed attempt in the early 1970s by Army Chief of Staff Creighton Abrams to introduce a new Officer Evaluation Report to replace the existing one that had become inflated to the point where most officers were receiving perfect ratings during the Vietnam War (Famiglietti, 1972, 1). The officer corps' lack of confidence in the new report resulted in its swift inflation as well, to the point that it too was replaced, in 1975 (Famiglietti, 1974, 1; Sorley 1992a, 356–57). Morale fell sharply among the officers who remained in the army after Vietnam and witnessed the brutal manner in which the army managed the RIF process. The army informed officers of their imminent separation by means of pink slips sent through official channels, gave them ninety days to depart, and provided minimal separation pay and little transition assistance.[112] The designers of the army's most recent downsizing were determined to avoid or mitigate these effects.

Finally, the Army's leaders in the 1990s observed how the decisionmaking of their predecessors two decades earlier had led to a gap between the existing force structure and the available personnel, resulting in a significant decline in personnel readiness. In March 1974, to the surprise of his staff and other senior army leaders, Abrams revealed his intention to build a sixteen-division Army, an expansion he achieved in part by relying more heavily on the Reserves.[113] Abrams's short-term objective was to stabilize the army's endstrength at 785,000. In the long term, it was to ensure that political leaders could not again commit the army to combat without calling up the Reserves (Sorley 1992b, 360–65). This decision, while perhaps defensible politically, significantly undermined personnel readiness. Resource constraints undoubtedly contributed most to the "hollow army" of the mid- and late-1970s, but the difficulties of fully manning a sixteen-division force were also partly to blame. This lesson was not lost on subsequent generations of army leadership.

In retrospect, the consequences of the downsizing decisions made in the aftermath of Vietnam are evident. Morale suffered, personnel readiness declined, and some of the best and brightest of the junior officers left the army (Dunnigan and Macedonia 1993, 102).[114] The army's post-Cold War leadership took stock of the "lessons" from this earlier day and in a number of instances made significantly different choices. In the 1990s, the army treated Regular Army officers and Reserve officers the same, and balanced the cuts across the senior and junior grades. Unlike earlier decisionmakers, the army's leadership publicly committed to maintaining or improving promotion, command, and professional development opportunities.[115] And, the army took active measures to retain its highest-quality officers. In addition, though a new Officer Evaluation Report was available as officer reductions began, Vuono and Sullivan chose not to implement it until the uncertainty associated with personnel reductions subsided. Army leaders also displayed a uniform commitment to executing officer cuts with sensitivity, care, and compassion. Finally, in contrast to Abrams's approach, Vuono and Sullivan explicitly committed to trading force structure for readiness; a smaller, ready army was the first priority.[116]

One of the key aspects of modern professional militaries is their systematic distillation and application of "lessons learned" from past experiences to improve upon the quality of future performance (Crowell 1993, 232). Certainly the army's leaders in the 1990s were conscious of and attentive to the lessons of the downsizing debacle following the Vietnam War. The extent, however, to which these experiences, consciously or unconsciously, affected their decisionmaking process is not clear. Indeed, it is unlikely that the individuals who made these decisions know themselves. "Placing someone against historical events and personal experience is uncertain work. . . . Inferences are but hypotheses, not even easily substantiated let alone proved" (Neustadt and May 1986, 181). With this in mind, it is perhaps enough to say that the post–Cold War officer reductions have been significantly more successful than those of the 1970s. The lessons learned from the mistakes of an earlier generation are surely part of the explanation.

Army Culture à la Thurman

The army's culture is the final piece of the puzzle. Most organizations have not one culture, but several, and the U.S. Army is no exception (Wilson 1989, 92).[117] Like the post-Vietnam experience, these army cultures—the enduring assumptions, values, and beliefs shared by the members of an organization—played an important role in downsizing decisions (Lorsch 1986, 95). The "heroic leader" culture, which springs from the heroic traditions of the American fighting man, is most pervasive in the active duty army and to a certain extent affects every facet of army life (Janowitz 1960, 35). It is within the bounds of this overarching culture that all others exist.

In the past several decades, however, an analytic culture, reflecting a scientific and rational approach to decisionmaking, has become increasingly prominent in a variety of army organizations, most notably in the personnel community (Hough 1989).[118] James Q. Wilson observes that an organization's culture often evolves as a consequence of a "founder who imposes his or her will on the first generation of operators in a way that profoundly affects succeeding generations" (1989, 96). General Maxwell Thurman fulfilled this role in the army personnel community. Thurman's legacy is the analytic culture he inculcated by creating analytic institutions, introducing an unprecedented level of rigor and analysis into the personnel decisionmaking process, and mentoring several generations of officers who carried on this tradition when they became generals. The extent to which Thurman's legacy will endure is uncertain. It is clear, however, that this analytic mindset profoundly affected the downsizing process, undoubtedly explaining in part the army's success.

Throughout the twentieth century the army has been torn between traditionalists and rationalists—those seeking to bring industrial management techniques and statistical and fiscal controls to its management (Hewes 1975, 370). As early as 1909, Frederick Taylor, one of the century's first management gurus, found avid proponents within the officer corps for his "scientific management" approach to human relations (Segal 1989, 48). The trend toward bureaucratic rationalization within the military departments continued to find favor through the 1960s, and was accelerated by Defense Secretary Robert McNamara's systems analysis approach to defense planning (Lucas and Dawson 1974, 90). The army adapted to the McNamara revolution through its Office of the Assistant Vice Chief of Staff where it attempted to integrate its planning, resource, and budgeting systems and to present a unified and compelling voice to the Office of the Secretary of Defense and Congress. In the vanguard of the army's transition toward more analytic decisionmaking in the late 1960s and early 1970s was General William E. DePuy, Vice Chief of Staff from 1969 to 1973 (McIntire 1992).[119] One of DePuy's protégés was Colonel Max Thurman.

Thurman created an analytic capacity within the army personnel community by building analytic organizations and decisionmaking processes. He conceived of analytic cells in the Army Recruiting Command, at West Point, and within the Office of the Deputy Chief of Staff for Personnel, and institutionalized the infamous Functional Area Analysis (FAA), a process by which the army's resource systems—personnel, logistics, research and development, recruiting, and so forth—were regularly integrated.[120] Thurman also established ties with civilian contractors, scholars, and research institutes, including the RAND Corporation. He often incorporated the analysis from these institutions into the army planning process, and requested their assistance in developing a new generation of sophisticated personnel models. To cultivate this kind of expertise within the army itself, Thurman sent a generation of junior officers to civilian graduate schools, to train with industry, and into fellowships at RAND, and he subsequently integrated these officers into key positions in the army's analytic community.[121]

Thurman's legacy also included the several generations of army leaders he influenced profoundly. Each of the four Deputy Chiefs of Staff for Personnel during the downsizing worked directly for Thurman (see table 3.5). Ono had been Thurman's Chief of Staff at Recruiting Command, and Deputy Chief of Staff for Personnel when Thurman was Vice Chief of Staff. Reno served for almost three years as Thurman's "right-hand man" when Thurman was Deputy Chief of Staff and Vice Chief. Carney worked directly for Thurman in the mid-1970s as an analyst at the Army's Training and Doctrine Command (TRADOC) and later as his executive officer when he was Vice Chief. Stroup also served as Thurman's executive officer when he was the Vice Chief and then followed him when he became TRADOC commander.

Thurman recruited bright young officers from around the army. He mentored the strongest performers, took them with him as he was promoted, and made certain that they served in the jobs that would enable

TABLE 3.5
The Thurman Legacy

Thurman	1975–1977 DCSRM TRADOC	1979–1981 Cdr, Rec Command	1981–1983 DCSPER	1983–1987 VCSA	1987–1989 Cdr, TRADOC	1990–1992 Panama/ Retired	1992–1994	1994–
Ono		Chief[a] of Staff			DCSPER	Retired		
Reno			Exec.[a] Officer	Exec.[a] Officer	Cdr, Rec Command	DCSPER	Retired	
Carney	Analyst[a]			Exec.[a] Officer	Cdr, Rec Command		DCSPER	Retired
Stroup				Exec.[a] Officer	DCSRM[a] TRADOC	DMPM		DCSPER

SOURCE: U.S. Army, General Officer Management Office, July 1995.
[a] Positions in which Thurman's protégés worked for him directly. The other assignments noted are key positions in the personnel community or ones that Thurman held himself.

them to remain competitive for advancement.[122] It is no accident that Ono, Reno, Carney, and Stroup were all promoted to lieutenant general and served as DCSPER; it is an extraordinary occurrence, however, particularly when one considers the probability of any colonel (let alone four colonels) being promoted to that rank.[123] Each worked for one of the most powerful four-star generals in the post–World War II army.[124] Each had been groomed for senior leadership at the highest levels of that organization. And all, to a greater or lesser degree, perpetuated this analytic culture.

There is compelling evidence that the analytic culture created by Thurman had a substantial effect on the style and substance of the downsizing decisionmaking process. Reno's creation of an independent analytic cell within ODCSPER, the overall confidence placed in personnel models, the propensity of Reno and Stroup, in particular, "to chase the rabbit down every rabbit hole to get the facts" are all characteristics of an analytic culture. This robust analytic capacity also had substantive policy implications. The army's leadership was able to consider many downsizing alternatives and to speculate with some confidence on the outcomes that various decisions would have on minority representation, quality, promotion rates, and the like. Moreover, this capacity allowed the army to target those components of the officer corps that were most expendable and gave it the instruments to make its case to OSD and Congress for DOPMA waivers, more resources, and voluntary separation incentives.

As commander of the Army Training and Doctrine Command, Thurman was deeply involved as the army began to make decisions concerning the means for achieving the first round of mandated officer reductions in January 1988. Over the next several years, however, it became clear that personnel cuts would be much deeper than anyone had initially imagined. As things turned out, Thurman, who fell ill soon after his retirement in 1990, played only a minimal advisory role in the downsizing decisionmaking process.[125] In retrospect, however, it was unnecessary for Thurman to be present for his influence to be felt. The analytic culture he had inculcated in the army's personnel community assured that downsizing policies would be developed, evaluated, and ultimately determined in a way that fulfilled the army's objectives.

While the army's reliance on rigorous analysis in this case contributed to sound decisionmaking, blind faith in scientific management can be more destructive than productive for several reasons. First, overreliance on rational decisionmaking may have dysfunctional effects on organizational effectiveness.[126] Specifically, some contend that bureaucratic rationalism undermines cohesion, esprit, commitment, and leadership behavior, thereby hampering the ability of the armed forces to perform their wartime missions (Johns 1984, 27). Second, an overreliance on analytic tools may ultimately lead to poor management decisions. Modeling in personnel policy in particular has significant limitations. Most personnel models are static in the sense that they are incapable of portraying dynamic near-term and long-term impacts of dramatic changes or shocks to the personnel system because they are calibrated in terms of retention rates for the system as it existed in the past. These assumptions fail to account for the effects that a dramatic disturbance like downsizing might have on short-term and long-term retention rates (*Defense Officer Personnel Management Act* 1980, 29–30).

The army's penchant for placing undue faith in models and modelers, at the expense of wise and balanced policy decisions, is well-documented. In the area of personnel in particular, the growing emphasis on analysis since the early 1970s is indicative of a larger trend toward a more bureaucratic, mechanistic, and impersonal approach to managing people (Segal 1989, 50–53). Carl Builder's unflattering description of the army's style of analysis is admittedly somewhat reminiscent of the atmosphere within the Office of the Deputy Chief of Staff for Personnel between 1990 and 1995, particularly during the tenure of Bill Reno:

> Detail and scope are prized. . . . If enough factors are taken into account, in enough detail by competent mathematicians, the analytical results are deemed to carry weight. Much of the army analysis appears to be aimed at

getting the right answer (often a number) rather than illuminating the alternatives in the face of recognized uncertainties.... army analysts tend to associate themselves with models (or particular analytical techniques) rather than the problems to which their models are applied. (1986, 11)

Despite the accuracy of this description, however, the army's leadership never lost sight of its downsizing principles, particularly the emphasis on care and compassion, established in the earliest days of the downsizing planning process. It is true that the Office of the Deputy Chief of Staff for Personnel at times devoted excessive energy to modeling and placed extraordinary confidence in these analytic efforts. And there were clearly some individuals within the ODCSPER as well as at the highest levels of the army who advocated cutting deeper to save money for modernization, who believed that the voluntary incentive programs were too generous and risked losing the most promising junior officers, who argued that the army should cut even more deeply into its senior ranks to improve promotion opportunity and timing for the junior officer corps, who asserted that involuntary separations should continue during the Gulf War (a policy followed by the navy), and who believed that the Army Career and Alumni Program was an unaffordable luxury in a period of diminishing resources. Solely on the basis of cost-benefit analysis, these positions were compelling. A combination of forces, however, tempered the personnel community's inherently rational approach to personnel policy, ensuring that policy decisions were informed by but never the products of cost-benefit analysis or personnel models alone.

First, the exhaustive analysis of the Office of the Deputy Chief of Staff for Personnel helped the army's leadership frame and understand downsizing alternatives, but ultimately the army Chief of Staff approved the final downsizing plan. The decisions of Vuono, and later Sullivan, often included a more holistic set of considerations. Second, Congress and the Office of the Assistant Secretary of the Army kept a watchful eye on downsizing plans. On the few occasions in which either actively opposed the positions proposed by ODCSPER, it was generally to weigh in on the side of "human factors" they perceived were being overlooked.

Third, despite the growing prominence of an analytic culture in the army personnel community, there remains a healthy mix of advocates of art and science, and a small minority of senior officers who are able to incorporate both effectively into the decisionmaking process. The tension between the advocates of these two approaches ensured that an appropriate blend of rigorous analysis, intuition, common sense, and compassion were incorporated into most major downsizing decisions. It was to the army's advantage that for every Bill Reno there was a Tom Carney and vice versa. There is a continuing need for some of both throughout the army. Moreover, though the likes of the leaders discussed in this chapter are branded by some in the army as technocrats, the contribution of these tough-minded analytic thinkers to downsizing specifically and decisionmaking more generally is beyond dispute. Finally, the post-Vietnam experience weighed heavily on the hearts and minds of all involved, including personnel planners. This tempered the decisionmaking process, ensuring that human factors figured into every decision. The outcome was a reasonably balanced approach to decisionmaking—"scientific management," yes, but with a heart.

Conclusion

For the most part, the army did what it set out to do. Its downsizing goals were appropriate. Its leaders staked out a suitable middle ground between long-term and short-term concerns over readiness and quality, as well as between the sometimes conflicting needs of individual soldiers and the institution. To the extent that personnel management problems remain, some of the blame lies in the army's failure to reduce its TDA force structure as rapidly and efficiently as its TOE structure. Some of these problems also may be attributed to burgeoning external officer requirements that are outside the army's control. And, some may be attributed to the army's failure to reform its officer management system. In fairness, however, they pale in comparison to the management dilemmas that resulted from large-scale personnel cuts in the past.

To pass judgment on the army's management of downsizing, one must place it in context. Public organizations are often perceived as being slow, inefficient, and overly centralized and bureaucratized, while commercial organizations, faced with the rigors of the marketplace, are seen as the paragons of efficiency. However, in many cases even private companies have been ineffective in downsizing, and those that have been successful (particularly when cuts have been deep) are few. Many have managed the downsizing process poorly, suffering declines in productivity, increased costs, and the loss of their finest performers. In contrast, few organizations can boast the success the army has enjoyed in its most recent downsizing, and never has the army been as precise, as compassionate, or as effective in managing significant personnel cuts. With its recent efforts, the army broke a cycle of failure that has plagued it for much of the past century.

From its experience we might also glean several lessons useful to other managers faced with the daunting task of downsizing. Among other things, the army's experience suggests that downsizing is extraordinarily difficult for managers in any organization, but particularly so for public managers unable to control the magnitude or pace of personnel cuts. This not only complicates planning and implementation but undermines the credibility of institutional leaders, eroding the trust and faith placed in them by members of the organization. Second, it is clear from the army's downsizing efforts that personalities, bureaucratic politics, organizational culture, and institutional history all dramatically influence an organization's conduct of and reaction to downsizing. This suggests that "cookie-cutter" approaches to managing downsizing are unrealistic and unwise. Each organization must forge its own way, based on its unique needs and objectives. This is by no means a profound finding, but it should be instructive to organizational scholars who appear at times to be overly reliant on checklists, buzzwords, and diagrams, and who pronounce, one, and only one, set of "best practices" in downsizing.

Despite the findings of this chapter, it would be premature to conclude that the army's downsizing is an unequivocal success. Final judgment must wait, of course, until the process is complete. In addition, in order to fully grasp the process and the effects of downsizing, one must also view it through a different lens—far from the Pentagon—from the perspective of the majority of the officer corps who experienced it in the muddy boots army. This is the purpose of the next chapter.

Appendix: Personnel Downsizing Programs

Voluntary Separation Programs

Voluntary Early Release/Retirement Program (VERRP). This program is targeted at retirement-eligible lieutenant colonels, colonels, and company grade officers (captains and lieutenants) who have been passed over for promotion or have minimal time left on their initial active duty service obligation (ADSO). The 1991 National Defense Authorization Act authorized the Secretary of the Army to waive one year of the DOPMA-imposed requirement that field grade officers remain in a certain grade for three years before being permitted to retire at that grade. In addition, company grade officers were permitted to resign within one year of their ADSO. The army used this program continuously between 1990 and 1995. The Office of the Assistant Secretary of the Army (Manpower and Reserve Affairs) delegated approval authority for this program to the commander of PERSCOM, except in special cases.

Voluntary Separation Incentive/Special Separation Bonus Program (VSI/-SSB). The 1992 Defense Authorization Act provided the Secretary of Defense with the authority to use two voluntary separation programs. The Voluntary Separation Incentive (VSI) featured a stream of annual payments for a period twice the length of time served at the time of separation. The Special Separation Bonus (SSB) provided authority for a lump-sum separation incentive. The army used these programs from 1992 to 1995 to target officers who had been passed over once for promotion, officers in surplus skills and specialties, and officers in preestablished RIF zones. Approval authority for the VSI/SSB was delegated to the commander of PERSCOM and all waivers or exception to policy were approved by the Assistant Secretary of the Army (Manpower and Reserve Affairs).

Temporary Early Retirement Authority (TERA). The Congress approved the Temporary Early Retirement Authority (TERA) in the 1992 Defense Authorization Act. The purpose of the program was to minimize the necessity of field grade RIFs. Despite congressional approval, the Department of Defense under the Bush administration forbade the use of TERA. Soon after the Clinton administration came into office, TERA was released to the individual service secretaries. The army used the program between 1993 and 1995 to target captains and majors who had already been passed over for promotion once, majors in overstrength year groups (RIF-eligible) prior to consideration for lieutenant colonel, and captains with more than fifteen years of service in excess specialties. The commander of PERSCOM was delegated approval authority for this program except for special cases.

Involuntary Separation Programs

Reduction In Force (RIF). DOPMA provided tenure for Regular Army (RA) officers, forbidding involuntary separation after five years of active duty service (RA officers could, of course, be separated for disciplinary reasons and as victims of up-or-out or SERBs). The 1991 Defense Authorization Act, however, lifted this constraint and gave the Secretary of the Army Regular Army RIF authority, to be used only after implementation of all other reduction options. RIFs were conducted by centralized army selection boards. The RIF target population included RA officers not eligible for retirement and not on a promotion list, and it was limited to 30 percent of those in an eligible group. The army threatened to conduct RIFs in each year between 1992 and 1995. They were canceled every year except 1992, however, when 277 majors were involuntarily separated.

Selective Early Retirement Boards (SERBs). Selective Early Retirement authority is provided in DOPMA which permits the use of SERBs for colonels with four years in that grade (and not on the promotion list) and lieutenant colonels who have been passed over for promotion twice. Additionally, the legislation requires that no more than 30 percent of any group considered for selective early retirement may be selected, and that once considered, officers cannot be considered again for five years. Selection Early Retirement Boards are organized and executed in the same manner as other centralized selection processes. The army held its first SERBs for special branches under this authority in 1985 and 1987. The first for line officers was held in 1986, but Army Secretary John O. Marsh did not approve the results. A SERB for line officers was held again in 1988 and the precedent was established.

The 1991 National Defense Authorization Act expanded the authority of the Army to use SERBs for colonels with two or more years in grade and all lieutenant colonels with eighteen or more years of active service. In addition, it removed the five-year protection clause, thus exposing numerous officers to consecutive SERB consideration. This expanded SERB authority (E-SERB) was used between 1992 and 1995.

Lieutenant Retention Boards (LTRBs). This program targets Regular Army officers in their third year of service to determine if they will be retained on active duty. It is provided for by the 1990 DOPMA legislation but its implementation was initially forbidden by DOD. The Office of the Secretary of Defense eventually lifted this ban and the program was used to separate Regular Army officer and Other than Regular Army officers (on active duty) between 1992 and 1995. Lieutenant Retention Boards are organized and executed in the same manner as other centralized army selection processes. No Lieutenant Retention Board was held in 1995, as that year group was the first to be properly "sized" at accession.

Sources: Military Personnel: End Strength, Separations, Transition Programs, and Downsizing Strategy, 1993, Annex J to Adjusting to the Drawdown, Report (Washington, D.C.: Defense Conversion Commission).

Diagram 3.5. Enlisted to Officer (E/O) and Company to Field Grade (CG/FG) Ratios during Downsizing

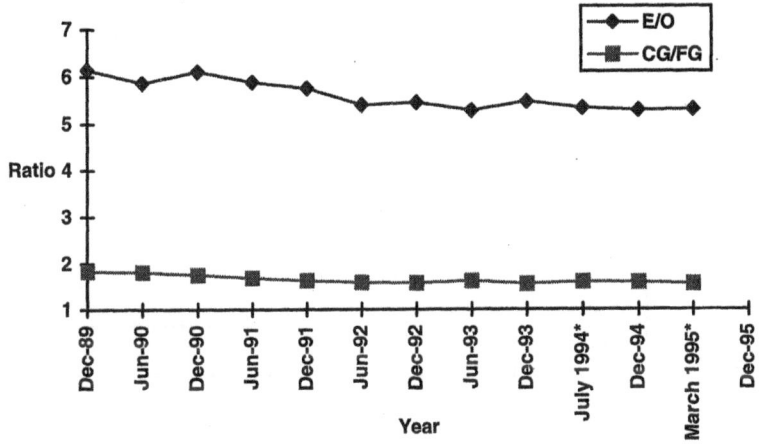

SOURCE: Office of the Deputy Chief of Staff for Personnel

Diagram 3.6. Promotion Opportunity during Downsizing, 1985–1995

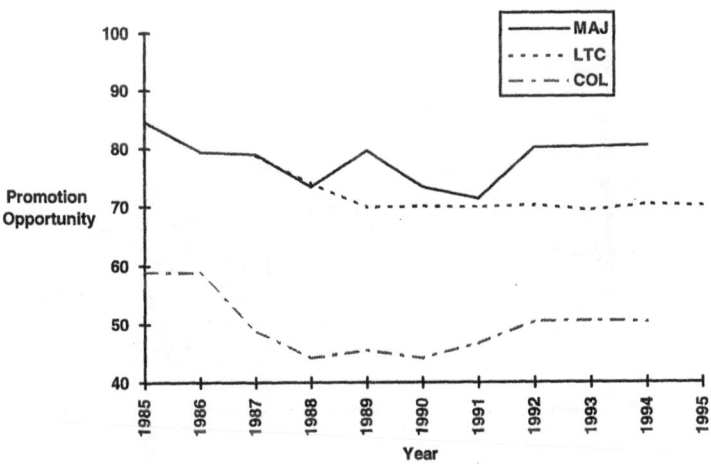

SOURCE: Office of the Deputy Chief of Staff for Personnel

Diagram 3.7. Changes in Promotion Timing during Downsizing, 1985–1995

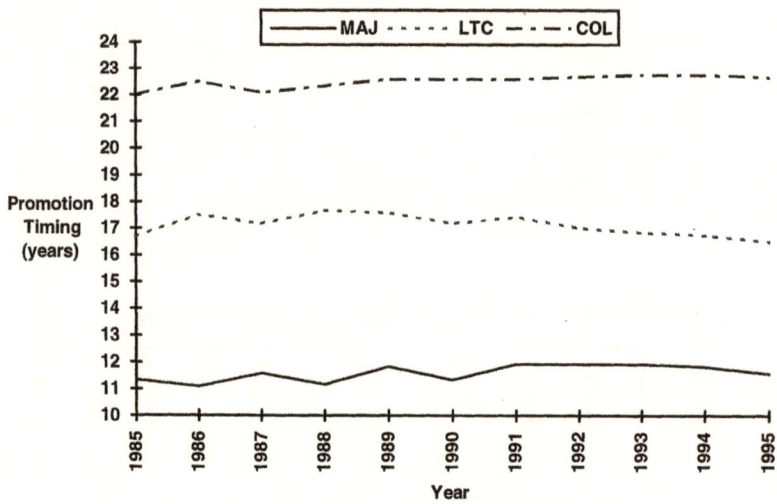

SOURCE: Office of the Deputy Chief of Staff for Personnel; Rostker et al. (1993), 102.

Diagram 3.8. Battalion Command Opportunity during Downsizing, 1991–1996

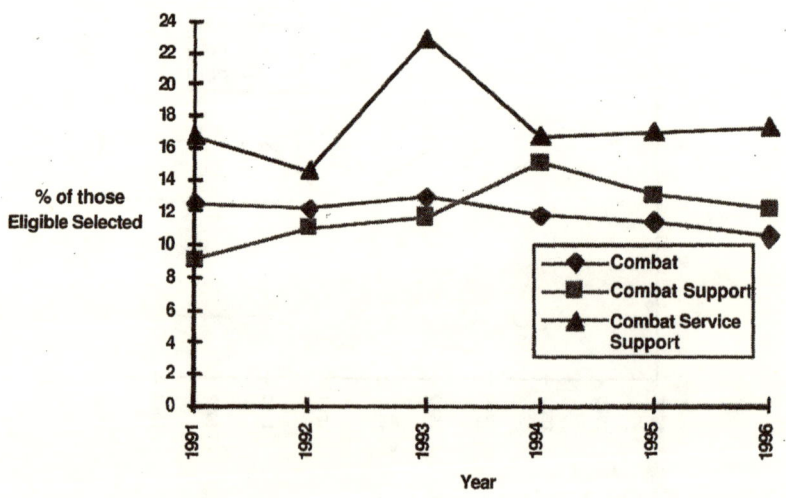

SOURCE: PERSCOM, Leadership Development Branch.

4

Lean and Mean
Changing Attitudes and Behaviors in the Muddy Boots Army

> Well, Mr. Secretary, you people up here are like the captain of an aircraft carrier. You're up on the deck, with the wind in your face, enjoying the splendid view.... All you have to do is tell the helmsman ... "hard rudder left" and then "hard rudder right," and you think you are making some dramatic changes. Meanwhile, all the rest of us poor slobs are down in the hold getting seasick as hell.
> —Chief of Staff Creighton Abrams to Defense Secretary Schlesinger, as quoted in Lewis Sorley, *Thunderbolt*

How has downsizing affected the soldiers and the officers who remain in the post–Cold War army? The perceptions, attitudes, and behavior of these individuals are as important to the effectiveness and institutional health of the army as any of the factors discussed thus far. Military historians have for centuries observed that such "intangibles" as leadership, loyalty, cohesion, and esprit de corps profoundly influence military effectiveness and ultimately the outcomes of wars.[1] Yet policymakers often overlook these considerations, as we have seen over the last two decades when rational, market economic models came to dominate personnel planning.

Scholars, too, often exclude noneconomic considerations from their studies of military personnel and organizations. This omission both reflects and reinforces the assumption that these intangibles are of secondary consideration simply because they are less amenable to quantification. At the very least, this tendency overlooks a crucial component of military effectiveness and precludes a more complex and accurate understanding of the motivations and behavior of military personnel. But far worse, this tendency—which some critics have labeled the "materialist bias"—undermines military effectiveness and ultimately leads to failure in combat. As Luttwak writes, "What is extraordinary about the habitual neglect of all these intangibles by the American military establishment is merely that it persists virtually unremarked, notwithstanding all the failures in war that gross overemphasis on material inputs has caused ever since Korea" (1985, 145).

This chapter is about the intangibles. The magnitude and prolonged uncertainty of downsizing, both of which were largely outside of the army's control, have compromised the institutional health of the officer corps in ways not fully understood. Downsizing has changed attitudes. Officer morale, career expectations, and organizational commitment have fallen dramatically. Downsizing has changed behavior. Competition and careerism within the officer corps are on the rise, and initiative and cooperation are in decline. Downsizing has altered the career patterns and career choices of officers, particularly junior officers, in unrecognized and undesirable ways. In short, the post–Cold War army is not only leaner but also meaner—unhappy, more selfish and competitive, and less committed and cooperative. The army's leadership has been slow to acknowledge and even slower to address these alarming trends.

Some will mistakenly say that the problems identified here are nothing new. It is true that the organizational pathologies discussed in this chapter have existed and been debated in the army since at least World War II. Nor are they exclusively the consequence of downsizing. But they have become much more pronounced, dangerously so, because of it. Some of the effects of downsizing will fade when stability returns to army personnel policy. Others, however, will persist, and some of these pathologies have already altered the officer corps in ways that will effect it well into the next century. This chapter highlights the consequences of downsizing that are most damaging and enduring.

The findings elaborated in this chapter should matter to four audiences. First, they should matter to professional soldiers who have suffered the harmful effects of downsizing, and whose story remains mostly untold. They should matter to military and civilian army leaders who have been slow to recognize and even slower to react to the deleterious consequences of prolonged personnel cuts. They should matter to civilian leaders in Congress and the administration who are likely to consider additional army personnel cuts in the years ahead. Finally, they should matter to members of the public concerned about the esprit, professionalism, and effectiveness of the U.S. Army.

The chapter is divided into six parts. The first discusses how the army evaluates the effects of downsizing and examines the strengths and the limitations of these approaches. The second section describes the three primary sources of uncertainty and anxiety that are at the root of the army's problems. The next three sections, which are the heart of the chapter, argue that downsizing has unfavorably altered officer attitudes, behavior, and career choices. In short, downsizing has undermined the professionalism of the army officer corps. The final section presents a brief synopsis of these findings. The implications of these changes and some recommendations for how military and civilian leaders should address them are taken up in chapter 5.

The Soft Side of Downsizing

Like civilian studies of downsizing in the private sector, the army's attempts to evaluate the impact of personnel cuts have been limited, narrow, and largely quantitative. These studies often use data from surveys of survivors of downsizing to gain insight into the changes in organization, communication patterns, and attitudes and behavior that result from it. Few have applied more qualitative approaches, such as individual and group interviews, to explore the impact of downsizing in ways not easily captured through quantitative means. In fact, these approaches may be seen as complementary, more informative when used together, each applying a different lens to view the same organizational phenomenon. This chapter uses survey data periodically to portray the general effects of downsizing on attitudes across the officers corps and a qualitative lens more heavily to bring perceptions, attitudes, and behavior into sharp focus.

The army's efforts to evaluate the effects of downsizing have been sporadic, fragmented, and incomplete. The U.S. Army Research Institute for the Behavioral and Social Sciences (ARI) has conducted two sets of surveys since 1987 that indirectly consider the effects of downsizing.[2] The survey data indicate that there is increasing anxiety among officers about diminishing promotion and career opportunities, and future manpower and budget reductions. Additionally, surveys taken since 1989 document significant declines in officer morale, career expectations, and willingness to recommend a military career to others (Harris 1994).

In 1994, the army Inspector General concluded that downsizing had engendered the belief that the army had broken faith with the officer corps, fostered a less-forgiving work environment, and contributed to selfish, rather than selfless, service.[3] During the same period, the Strategic Fellows, a small group of colonels assigned to the Army War College, found that junior officers equated success with "survival to retirement," were "living one assignment at a time" with service to self growing in importance, and believed the officer evaluation system was becoming ineffective.[4]

The findings from these two studies were presented to the army's senior leaders but never formally documented, and neither was released outside of the army. Despite these telling indications of organizational malaise, the Army has publicly acknowledged only recently the dramatic effects of downsizing on the attitudes, behavior, and career expectations of the officer corps.[5] Further, the army has taken no formal action to address these problems. Some senior army leaders even refuse to admit that such pathologies exist, or have any connection to downsizing. One three-star general remarked in summer 1995: "Downsizing was difficult, but now that it's almost over, things are returning to normal. In many ways, things are better for the officer corps now than before downsizing."[6] In the officer corps, however, there is the perception that downsizing is not over, that "things" are not better. Although officer cuts have slowed to a trickle, they will soon begin again in earnest given the proposed cuts in the recently released Quadrennial Defense Review. Clearly, the uncertainty about the magnitude and duration of future reductions, coupled with the effects of the cuts that have occurred thus far, have taken a devastating toll on the officer corps.

But a number of questions remain unanswered. For example, are the attitudes, perceptions, and beliefs described by the army's research unique to a certain segment of the officers corps or are they universal? How serious and widespread are these effects of downsizing? What are the implications of these effects for organizational effectiveness, or in military parlance, fighting power? What, if anything, can and should be done? This chapter offers insight into all of these questions.

Perceptions may shape reality even when they are inaccurate. People behave on the basis of things they believe to be the case, whether their perceptions are correct or not (Dawkins 1979, 317). Therefore, this chapter addresses the questions of what officers perceive is happening in the downsizing army and how these perceptions affect their attitudes and behavior, and, ultimately, organizational effectiveness. Huntington writes that the most fruitful approach for understanding the military mind "is to analyze ... the attitudes, values, [and] views of the military man" (1957, 60). But those who study military organizations have struggled with attributing a unified set of views to the members of organizations as diverse as the military services. Such broad generalizations "often [take] the form of caricatures with all that word implies about exaggeration and loss of detail ... as the great diversity of views ... are transformed into a monolithic voice" (Builder 1989, 8). This chapter is more like an impressionist painting than a caricature. The individual brush strokes—the perceptions and experiences of individual officers—are clearly visible for the reader to scrutinize and draw from them his or her own conclusions.[7] However, I also offer an interpretation of the overall picture—what these individual perceptions mean for the vitality and health of the U.S. Army.

My conclusions about the prevailing professional climate in the post–Cold War army are based on in-depth interviews conducted with over one hundred and thirty junior, mid-career, and senior officers on five active duty army posts in the United States in summer 1995.[8] Three of the five posts—Fort Sill, Oklahoma, Fort Leavenworth, Kansas, and Carlisle Barracks, Pennsylvania—are the locations of army schools. From these locations, one would expect to gain more objective and representative insights into the views held by officers army-wide than from army posts where circumstances may vary greatly or unit or individual loyalties abide (*Study on Military Professionalism* 1970, iv).[9] The other posts—Schofield Barracks, Hawaii, and Fort Hood, Texas—are home to combat divisions from which units were heavily deployed over the last several years.[10] The officers interviewed represent a broad spectrum of experience, grades, and skills.[11] Their views are undoubtedly indicative of those held by the majority of the officer corps.[12]

A Downsized, Down-and-Out Army

Most observers agree that the attitudes and behavior of the officer corps have changed dramatically in the post–Cold War era. At the root of these changes are three sources of anxiety and uncertainty that make an army career increasingly unattractive and stressful (diagram 4.1). First, the budgetary pressures that precipitated dramatic personnel cuts have also led to reduced retirement and health benefits and heightened anxiety that these benefits will erode further (Maze 1995, 3). The erosion of benefits has been

Diagram 4.1. Sources of Uncertainty and Anxiety in a Downsizing Army

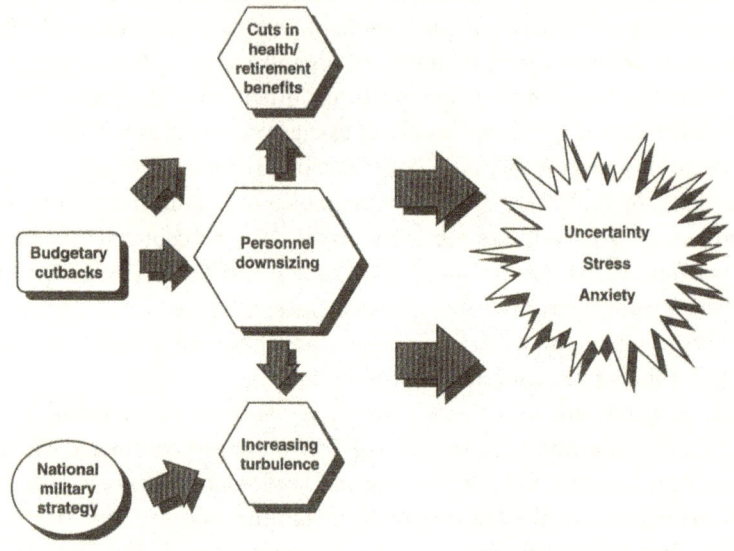

a chronic concern among career military members since the advent of the all-volunteer force in 1973. Based on the recommendations of the 1970 Gates Commission, military compensation was redesigned to be comparable with that in the civilian sector. As military salaries have become more competitive, however, the case for additional entitlements such as housing, retirement, health benefits, and so on for military personnel has become more difficult to make politically, and particularly since the end of the Cold War (Moskos and Wood 1988b, 20; Snyder 1994). As one officer remarked:

> We're seeing, in the five years I've been on active duty, the benefits are just disappearing. I mean, they're going away.... So I'm saying to myself: "Do I want to stay in 20 years and retire?" It's easy to look ahead and speculate that you're not going to have anything when you do. (Captain, Fort Hood)

The attractiveness of a military career has also been undermined by the uncertainty caused by downsizing. Prolonged personnel reductions have made officers apprehensive about their prospects for a military career. First, officers fear they will fall prey to future cuts. Second, even without more cuts, officers are less certain they have what it takes to be "successful" in a downsized army. And, third, even those officers most confident of their abilities are less certain about the most desirable career paths for advancement. In the first case, officers no longer trust the promises of military and civilian leaders that downsizing will soon come to an end, and continual changes in the announced "final" endstrength of the army are a great source of consternation and cynicism:

> They drag us all into the auditorium and say, "We're going to cut the army to this number and we will not go below this number." Six months later they'd drag us back to the auditorium and say, "OK, it's this number now." Six months later they do it again. And, now the Defense Secretary is talking about twenty thousand more people.[13]

Officers also believe that at the same time opportunities are diminishing, the quality of the officer corps is rising. As a consequence, officers think it is harder to "get ahead," and they are more skeptical that they can have secure, productive, successful careers. To a certain extent, downsizing has turned traditional officer paradigms on their head. As a consequence, officers are less confident of how career decisions made today will affect their potential for advancement in the future:

> From my foxhole, the drawdown causes just uncertainty. I can't say right now today whether I'll be here twenty years from now. I don't know how big the army's going to be. I don't know what the army will look like.... So I'm just not sure. I ride it out day by day, do the best I can, and don't really know where I'll be in the future. (Captain, Fort Hood)

Increased turbulence is also an indirect consequence of downsizing. Today's army is doing more with less, forcing officers to work longer and harder, be away from home more often, and change assignments and locations more frequently. This has created stress, anxiety, and uncertainty with predictable effects on the attitudes of the officer corps. A smaller army, combined with a national commitment to an expanding range of unprecedented, nontraditional military missions, has stretched the organization to full capacity as all ten existing divisions deploy more often, with less warning, and must constantly maintain a high state of readiness. In the downsized army, there has also been an increase in the number of training deployments: the army's combat training centers continue to train forty-four battalions each year (the same number annually trained during the Cold War), despite the fact that the number of combat battalions has decreased by almost a third.[14] At the same time, U.S. forces have been deployed around the world—to Iraq, Turkey, Saudi Arabia, Rwanda, Somalia, Haiti, Macedonia, Bosnia, for example—with increasing frequency. Additionally, the officer supply/demand gap described in chapter 3 has strained the officer corps further by forcing officers to rotate through assignments more quickly to satisfy both professional development needs as well as the army's expanding officer requirements. In today's army, most officers currently change duty stations, or locations, every two years.[15] And turbulence results from the fact that officers change jobs more regularly, regardless of where they are located.[16]

Through the Fat, Past the Muscle, and into the Bone

The effects of downsizing on officer attitudes—morale, career expectations, and organizational commitment—are as predictable as they are damaging. Morale within the officer corps has greatly declined as a result of downsizing, as have career expectations. The officer corps as a whole is less committed to the army and the military profession than it was before downsizing began.

Terms such as morale, career expectations, and organizational commitment are ambiguous, interdependent, and mean different things to different people. *Webster's Unabridged Dictionary* defines morale as "a state of individual and psychological well-being and buoyancy." It is based, among other things, on "pride in the achievements and aims of the group, faith in its leadership and ultimate success, a sense of fruitful participation in the work, and a devotion and loyalty to the members of the group." In this dis-

Diagram 4.2. Changing Attitudes in a Downsizing Army

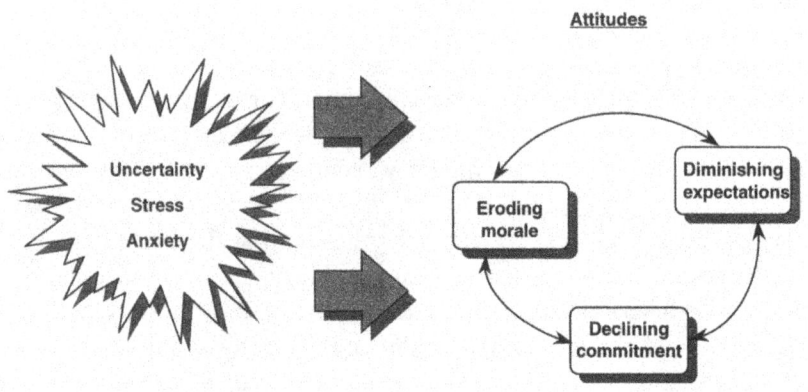

cussion, morale refers to the "buoyancy" of spirit of officers, or esprit de corps, and the faith they have in the army's leadership and in the army's ability to achieve its organizational aims. Career expectations are what officers perceive may reasonably be anticipated in terms of promotions, security, etc. from a career in the post–Cold War army. In particular, career expectations are a reflection of how officers define success and how the corps collectively perceives the probability of being successful. Commitment describes the obligation that officers feel toward the army, the military profession, and one another. Clearly, morale, career expectations, and commitment are closely linked, with a decline in one possibly contributing to a decline in the others.

Morale

Ardant du Picq, in his 1880 classic, *Battle Studies*, wrote that "army organizations and tactical formations on paper are always determined from the mechanical point of view, neglecting the essential coefficient, that of morale. They are almost always wrong" (Fitton 1990, 194). The quality of the "essential coefficient" within the U.S. Army and its officer corps, though undeniably of import, is manifested in a variety of ways and linked to a number of specific concerns difficult to gauge. The decline in morale in today's army is evident in a flatness of spirit that permeates the officers corps, along with a lack of confidence in the ability of the army to accomplish its wartime mission and a growing disillusionment with respect to military and civilian leaders.

Downsizing has spawned a widely acknowledged "cloud of pessimism" that affects the day-to-day attitudes and interactions of professional soldiers:

> I don't see the positiveness, I don't see that esprit that was there even twelve years ago when I came into the service. I come from a military family, a long line of service. The things that I saw as a kid—the closeness, the officer corps working together—I don't see as much now. I've seen that change every year from the impact of downsizing.... I can tell you that having discussed this with many of my contemporaries, there is not a positive view. (Major, Fort Sill)

An officer from Fort Hood agrees: "Whereas everything used to be positive, now it's more negative.... I think everybody has taken a very pessimistic view of things. I know I have." If this perception is indeed representative, it will have both short-term and long-term consequences.

In the short term, the uncertainty distracts officers, siphoning valuable time and energy from more productive endeavors. One major observed, "Every time a couple of guys get together for a Pepsi or a beer or something, we spend an inordinate amount of time talking about the drawdown—Who has it affected and what units are going away? We wonder every day, When is the next shoe going to fall? When are we going to lose the next twenty thousand?" In effect, the possibility (and, in the minds of many, the certainty) of future cuts, perpetuates the low morale that accompanied the initial reductions. In the long run, declining morale may undermine retention and recruitment.

Rising turbulence and a perceived increase in the workload have also lowered morale. The growing number of operational and training deployments places demands not only on the units that deploy overseas but also on those that assist with their preparation and departure, and often fulfill their training and support requirements in their absence. "Burn-out" appears to be a symptom or a concern of the majority of company grade and field grade officers.[17] The effects of these trends are heightened by the fact that such a large percentage of the members of officer corps and enlisted force are married,[18] increasingly to spouses with career concerns of their own:

> I left my unit in 1989 and disappeared into academe for five years, so I can compare then and now. It's like night and day. I was in the Eighty-second Airborne Division, which is a fast-paced animal, but the pace here in the Twenty-fifth Infantry five years later is approximately twice as fast. . . . Officers are working like dogs. I sleep in my office at least twice a week. There's just too much to do. All the units went away, but the exercises, the post details, and other stuff didn't. You can burn out real fast.
> (Major, Twenty-fifth Infantry Division, Schofield Barracks)

> You can almost count on every year being deployed somewhere, whereas before you had a little more stability. . . . In the old army, you were lucky if you were deployed once in your career. Now, that's the cost of doing business, but it's also affecting morale, and I know it's starting to affect families a lot.
> (Captain, Twenty-fifth Infantry Division, Schofield Barracks)

The morale of the officer corps is also affected by and reflected in its faith and confidence in the army's ability to accomplish its missions. There appears to be almost universal agreement among professional soldiers that the size of the army has been reduced too much, too fast. As a major at Fort Hood colorfully put it: "We've cut through the fat, past the muscle, and we are at the bones right now. You can't cut it anymore." This comment receives nods of affirmation from officers of every rank and branch throughout the U.S. Army. Junior officers, in particular, are skeptical of the national military strategy and of the army's ability to fulfill future missions:

> They talk about us being able to fight two major regional conflicts at one time, and I don't believe for a second we can do that. And, they are now talking about cutting another twenty thousand. (Captain, Fort Sill)

> If we are going to fight two major regional contingencies, I sure as hell want to be on the first one. (Major, Fort Hood)

> No way can we do it with ten divisions, but that is the official policy. (Captain, Twenty-fifth Infantry, Schofield Barracks)

Whether more senior officers disagree with these assessments, or are simply unwilling to voice their opinions publicly, is difficult to determine. (Whether or not the army's present structure and size is sufficient to support the current strategy is outside the scope of this study.) The point here is that many junior officers believe that the army is incapable of accomplishing its potential missions, and that fact has important implications for morale and, in turn, military effectiveness.

Finally, the faith and trust officers have in military and civilian leaders also influences morale. For the effective management of the downsizing process, the officer corps generally gives credit where credit is due. Uniform agreement exists in the field army that the leaders did an outstanding job of planning and implementing personnel reductions. One former battalion commander at the Army War College remarked: "The personnel programs that were developed for our soldiers, noncommissioned officers, and officers were super, remarkable in comparison to what we saw after Vietnam." With few exceptions most officers agree with an assessment made by a captain at Fort Hood: "They set a goal and came out with a plan. It was not just a blind cut as they had done in the past. It was strictly managed by branch, rank, and quantity. And throughout, the army did its best to take care of people." These views are partially captured in diagram 4.3, which shows how officers viewed the quality of the decisions made by the army leadership during downsizing.

The army leadership receives far fewer favorable marks for the way in which it has addressed the indirect consequences of downsizing, and many officers question whether the leadership even realizes that such effects exist. For example, many officers believe that the personnel management system

Diagram 4.3. Confidence in Army Leadership during Downsizing

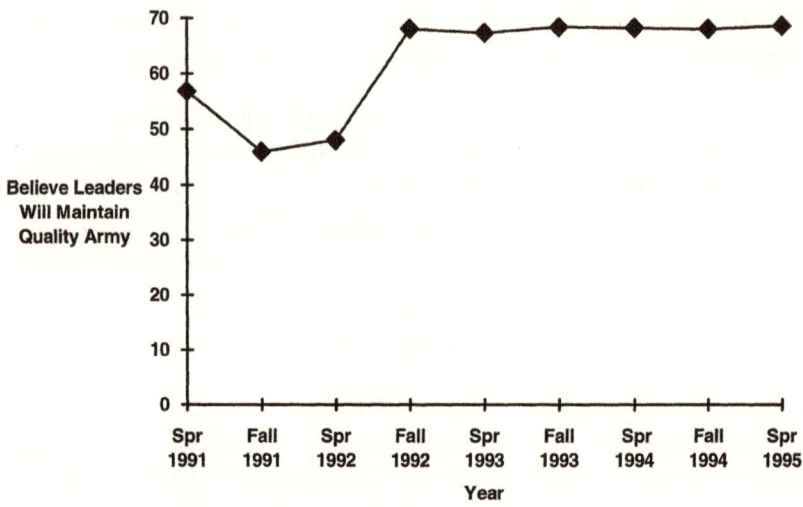

SOURCE: U.S. Army Research Institute for Behavioral and Social Sciences. Data from Semi-Annual Survey of Military Officers, 1991–1995.

has not yet adjusted to the realities of the post–Cold War environment. A major observed, "The army continues to use a rating system, a promotion system, and a schooling system that were designed for an eighteen-division army of the eighties. Now we are a ten-division army, and we're still using the up-or-out mentality, and schooling and promotion systems that are suited for a much bigger force." Officers also lament the army's failure to establish acceptable and credible future career patterns. One student at the Command and General Staff College articulated well the concerns of many of his contemporaries: "The traditional paradigms of officer progression are crushed, they're out the window. But they've been replaced by nothing. This has a big impact on morale."

The officer corps' views on the responsibilities of the leadership in defending army budgets and endstrengths before Congress and the administration are divided. Some believe that the army's leadership is doing the best that can be expected in an unpredictable and hostile political environment, and lay the blame for the current turmoil at the feet of the civilian leadership: "When the civilian leaders tell the army's military leaders to cut, they are going to do it. If they don't, they will simply be replaced. The civilian leadership, not our senior military leaders, have let us down." Others believe that the army's leadership should speak out more forcefully. As one officer remarked: "A lot of people are walking on eggshells on Capitol Hill—and I mean our army leadership. They're too afraid to make the tough calls and stand up and say, no, damn it, this is what the Bottom-Up Review said we could support, and we're going to stick to that."

Views on this issue are grounded in the wider debate over the appropriate relationship between military and civilian leaders. The outcomes of such discussions, however, are incidental to the importance of these perceptions. How officers perceive their military and civilian leaders affects morale. If the army's leaders are viewed as effective in defending the organization's interests before Congress and the administration, (even if they lose "the good fight"), this is likely to boost morale and rally support. Conversely, if officers perceive that their leaders are bowing to political pressures, morale may fall. Army leaders play to both internal and external audiences. Decisions or policies thought to be politically necessary, expedient, or inevitable when directed to the latter, may be debilitating to the former.

Diminishing Expectations

Downsizing has also generated a climate of diminishing expectations within the officer corps. Officers are less confident they will succeed, believe it is harder to succeed, and are less certain of the most promising pathways to success. As a result, the officer corps is undergoing a very painful transformation in the way that it defines success.

Officers believe that downsizing has left fewer opportunities for a larger number of highly qualified officers. Career expectations are, of course, a matter of individual abilities, ambitions, and tastes. But "success" has traditionally been defined as the opportunity to command a battalion and retire as a lieutenant colonel or colonel. There are several explanations for why this has been the case. First, since World War II, promotion to lieutenant colonel has been necessary to ensure eligibility for retirement.[19] Also, the preoccupation with acquiring a command assignment wherever the opportunity exists is deeply ingrained in the army culture, and is driven as much by the desirable career implications of such an assignment as by its obvious correlates with the notion of the "heroic leader" (Dawkins 1979, 144). Finally, command has generally been necessary at every echelon in order to be promoted to the next rank. A young captain summed it up well: "Commanding is succeeding."

It was a good deal easier to "succeed" by this definition in the 1980s than in the 1990s. Commands at every level were more plentiful in an eighteen-division army then they are in a ten-division force. The number of company, battalion, and brigade commands in every branch has been reduced significantly. Perceptions of how command opportunities compare with the past are clouded by the fact that in 1984 the army broadened the definition of command to include myriad TDA (noncombat) assignments and in 1992 broadened it even further to include "garrison commands."[20] As a result of these changes, only a fraction of the officers considered for command will be selected, and only a fraction of those selected will command TOE (combat) battalions and brigades. TDA commands are generally seen as less prestigious, and officers who serve in these positions generally, though not always, suffer for it with promotion boards. Hence, the army faces a predicament in which significantly less than 10 percent of the officer corps will achieve success as previously defined:

> Every artillery lieutenant on active duty wants to command a battalion because the perception is that that is success. That's what we've been told. If 10 percent of all artillery officers succeed, I guess 90 percent must fail. If that is the case, why shouldn't I go and do something where I can be successful?
> (Captain, Fort Sill)

Although the selection rates for promotion and for army schools have remained relatively constant or have improved during the cutbacks, officers believe that the competition has become more intense. As shown in the last chapter, the majority of officers who left the army through its primary voluntary separation program (VSI/SSB) were in the lower third of their cohorts in terms of quality; thus, there is a pool of higher-quality officers, at least among these groups, competing for fewer slots. The perceptions of many officers in the field accord with this reality. Officers are also concerned that a disproportionate number of the "best and brightest" junior officers left the army through the voluntary separation programs. However, there is almost universal agreement that the officer corps is of exceptionally high quality, perhaps of even higher quality than before downsizing. As a consequence, officers are less confident that they can have a successful career:

> I think on average the officer corps probably increased slightly in overall quality. While we lost some on the very high end, no doubt, I think the majority of the losses were from the bottom third or bottom quarter. Overall I think we're at least at the same level of quality, if not a little bit higher.
> (Captain, Fort Sill)

> I think what you saw initially was a lot of sharp people getting out. Then the folks that probably needed to get out left in the following years. Now we're at the point where any time someone gets forced out, you can't believe that guy got forced out.... This reinforces the idea in our minds that the fat's been cut and now we're cutting into the meat.   (Major, Fort Sill)

> We're going to have a good, solid army. But we will not have a great army because we lost the very best guys, who decided that they no longer wanted to take the risk of not making "A-list" and who wanted to have more financial security and more flexibility in their retirement.
> (Lieutenant Colonel, Fort Sill)

Not only do officers believe that it is more difficult to succeed, they are also unsure of how to succeed. The "command expressway"—the sequence of successive command positions within the military hierarchy—remains the most critical and regularly traveled path to success (Dawkins 1979, 144). However, command assignments are increasingly rare, as are the assignments that have traditionally prepared officers for command. Moreover, the growing number of legislated requirements means that officers are assigned more often to billets outside of traditional career patterns. The resulting uncertainty over the best path to the top contributes to lower career expectations:

> The army is a great place. I'm not going to wave the flag and get teary-eyed, but I think the opportunities are still there. I think we're hurting ourselves by not articulating what those opportunities are.... Good grief, give us the new rules. If you laid out for me right now what a real career pattern is supposed to look like ... I'd say drive on. But it's just not there. It's too darn nebulous.
> (Major, Command and General Staff College, Fort Leavenworth)

> I think more and more there's a tremendous concern: Am I doing the right thing? We give them the benefit of what little experience we have, but the uncertainty has increased. There's always been uncertainty of Am I doing the right thing? But now there is more and more.   (Colonel, Fort Leavenworth)

The army appears to be doing its best, officially and unofficially, to alter the perception that battalion command is the mark of a successful career. As the *Commissioned Officer Development and Career Management* pamphlet issued in 1995 states: "About 70 percent of the cohort year group of majors are selected for lieutenant colonel. Of these lieutenant colonels, only 50 percent can reasonably be expected to be promoted to colonel. Thus, attaining the grade of lieutenant colonel is considered to be the hallmark of a successful career" (9). Most officers are now defining success as being promoted to lieutenant colonel. Junior officers are adjusting their expectations, while many senior officers are dealing with the realization that by yesterday's standards and past expectations they have failed. The effects of these diminishing expectations on the retention and recruitment of officer remain to be seen. The following comments accurately convey the views of most officers:

> I told my guys that we have to redefine success. Success now is making it to lieutenant colonel so you can be around long enough to retire.
> (Lieutenant Colonel, Army War College)

> Twenty years without getting booted is a great success. Most people don't even look at battalion command as a reality. And for me, that's unfathomable. I "grew up" in an era when fat majors were retiring after 22 years with a full pension. (Captain, Fort Hood)

> I know a bunch of guys that came out of West Point in '76, '77, '78 and they defined success as battalion command. Many of them didn't make it. They're lieutenant colonels, but they're so bitter because they were "groomed" for battalion command. We see the writing on the wall—if we make it to twenty and lieutenant colonel we've done well.
> (Major, Command and General Staff College, Fort Leavenworth)

Commitment

The post–Cold War officer corps is also less committed to the military as a profession and to the army in particular.[21] This, too, is at least partially a consequence of downsizing. Commitment comes in two forms—the "pure" type and the "social" type (Johns 1984, 5). Pure commitment results from the internalization of group norms and values, and is represented by a sense of calling, while social commitment results from sensitivity to primary groups and is most commonly associated with the type of commitment soldiers in small cohesive combat units express for one another. In contrast to commitment, a calculative orientation is based on a contractual relationship in which the performance of a certain task is exchanged for payment or reward (Johns 1984). These two conflicting orientations might be thought of as a continuum that reflects the range of dedication professional soldiers feel toward the army and their profession. On one end lies the pure commitment and sense of calling of the military professional and at the other extreme the calculative orientation of the mercenary.

Organizational commitment refers to the sense of obligation and selfless service that officers feel toward the military institution and profession. Some officers view commitment in terms consistent with this definition, while others define it as the level of effort and time they put into their professional responsibilities, or the sense of obligation they feel toward their subordinates, their superiors, and their contemporaries. Although these definitions are not unrelated, they are distinct. By the second definition, the officer corps appears strongly committed, and most professional soldiers bristle at the suggestion that they are not devoting themselves completely to the performance of their duties and to the soldiers with whom they serve. There is distressing evidence, however, that organizational commitment may be waning within the officer corps. This assertion is founded on three observations. First, the majority of the officers interviewed for this study say this is so. Most officers today, particularly junior and mid-career officers, acknowledge that their commitment to the organization and profession has been adversely affected by the uncertainty of downsizing:

> As we feel the organization is not committed to us, it's only human nature for us to start losing commitment to the organization.
> (Major, Schofield Barracks)

> The difference between selfless service and selfish service is as wide as the Grand Canyon in the army today. (Major, Fort Hood)

> My commitment to the profession is slipping to commitment to me because I've just got to survive. (Captain, Fort Sill)

A second indicator of a decline in commitment is the astounding number of officers who are preparing to leave the army. Quantitative and anecdotal evidence suggest that career intent—the desire to pursue a military career—has diminished. Survey data from the Army Research Institute, for example, illustrates the change in career intent across all ranks during downsizing, though it fails to capture completely the pessimism that permeates the ranks. Officers at all points in their military careers, it seems, are seriously considering leaving the army. A growing number of field grade officers (majors, lieutenant colonels, and colonels) are presumably preparing their résumés, reevaluating their options, and contemplating retirement several years ahead of their mandatory retirement dates (see diagram 4.4). Likewise, the number of junior officers considering a career change as a consequence of downsizing has increased significantly. While this trend may reflect less desire on the part of some officers to stay in the army, it also

Diagram 4.4. Changes in Career Intent Because of Downsizing

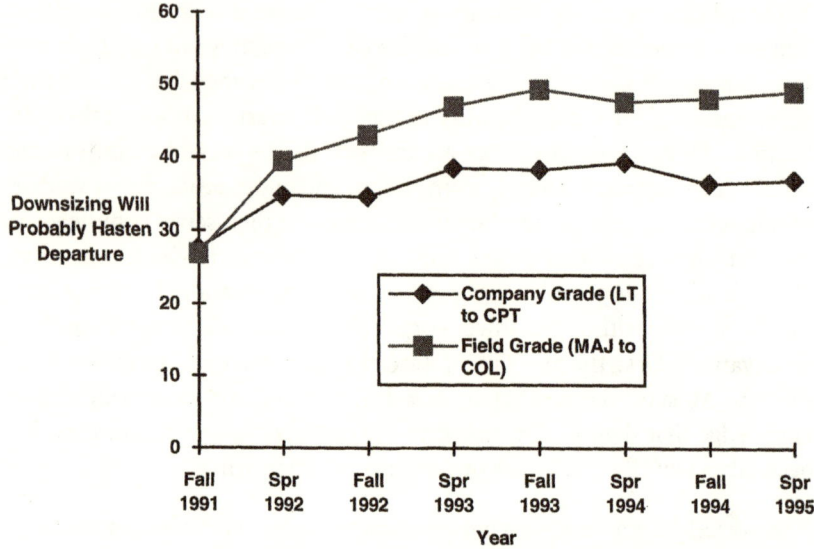

SOURCE: U.S. Army Research Institute for Behavioral and Social Sciences. Data from Semi-Annual Survey of Military Personnel, 1991–1995.

stems from their realization that they might be involuntarily separated. One captain remarked, "Even if you are committed to making the military a career, you can't count on anything."

As a consequence of this trend, one is hard pressed these days to find a young army officer who has not spent at least an afternoon at civilian job fairs designed to assist former military officers in finding employment. Likewise, majors with between twelve and sixteen years of service, who must complete twenty years to be eligible for retirement, are already contemplating their transition to the civilian world.[22] In sum, most officers are, in their words, "taking it one job at a time" and readying themselves for the transition to civilian life, rather than dedicating themselves to the profession of arms:

> You want to talk anxiety? I'm a West Point graduate. I thought I loved the army. I never, ever, thought I would consider leaving. I was at least a twenty-year man. And even I went to a couple of job interviews.
>
> (Captain, Schofield Barracks)
>
> I take it year by year and constantly think about what I have to fall back on if I get out.
> (Major, Fort Sill)

> Last year when the selection list for brigade command was released, a number of students at the War College who were not on the list resigned from the army. In the past, I think people thought there was still something to being in the army, whether you were a brigade commander or not. If the senior leaders—those who you would expect to feel the most loyalty—are getting out, you've got to ask what's going on in the rest of the force.
> (Lieutenant Colonel, Student, Army War College)

> I've got a lot of friends across a lot of different branches, and across the board I can't think of one friend of mine right now that doesn't have one foot in the army and one foot out of the army. (Captain, Schofield Barracks)

Finally, army officers are less willing to recommend a military career to their sons or daughters or close friends, another sign of waning organizational commitment. Survey data from between 1991 and 1995 show a noticeable decline in the willingness of officers to recommend a military career, particularly among field grade officers (diagram 4.5).[23]

Officers are notably reluctant to recommend the military as a career, even though there appears to be almost universal agreement that a short stint as an officer is outstanding preparation for the future. This is a devastating turnabout for an institution that has traditionally relied so heavily on generation after generation of military offspring entering the profession of arms.

> I would not recommend the military to my son or daughter. There's no certainty and there's no guarantee and there are few benefits today compared to what there were 17 years ago when I came into the army. (Major, Fort Hood)

> I've got two boys. Both of them want to go into the military. My recommendation to them is going to be to get in and maybe do four years and get out. . . . I don't think it is the same opportunity that it used to be.
> (Major, Command and General Staff College, Fort Leavenworth)

> One of my last bosses was promoted to general. He advised his own son and his son-in-law, who were considering joining the army as officers, not to do it. His reasoning was that he doesn't know when the downsizing is going to stop, and he's not sure what type of career they would have. And he's a general.
> (Major, Command and General Staff College, Fort Leavenworth)

> I truly love the army. . . . It's been very good to me. I would be very hard pressed, though, to say to my son and daughter, "Go into the army." . . . It is a great life, but understand that at the end of however many years you don't know what's going to be there. It truly depends upon the political situation and Congress. So you have no idea.
> (Lieutenant Colonel, Army War College, Carlisle Barracks)

Diagram 4.5. Willingness of Officers to Recommend a Military Career

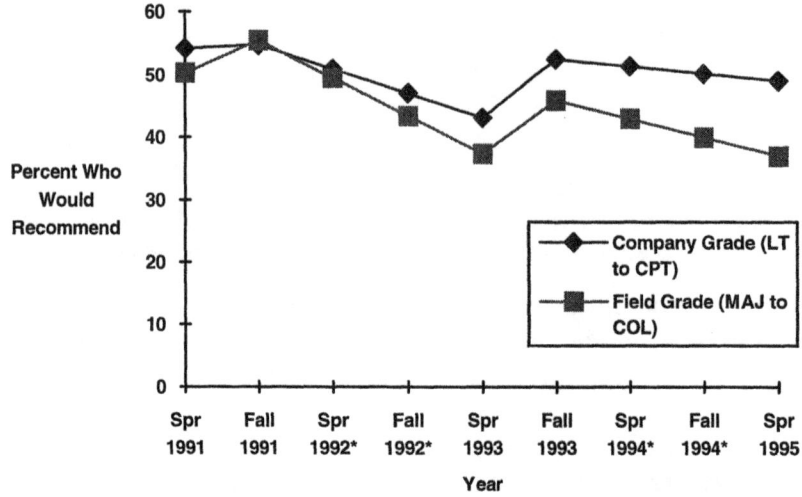

SOURCE: U.S. Army Research Institute for Behavioral and Social Sciences. Data from Semi-Annual Survey of Military Personnel, 1991–1995.
*Question was not asked so data is extrapolated.

Clearly, uncertainty and turbulence in the post–Cold War army have dramatically affected the attitudes of the officer corps. Morale, career expectations, and organizational commitment have declined significantly. These effects, alone, would warrant grave concern. However, perceptions matter most because they influence behavior. The changes in behavior that have arisen in the officer corps as a consequence of downsizing are cause for even greater alarm.

Punched Tickets and Zero Defects

Downsizing has also spawned a careerist outlook within the officer corps and the perception of a "zero-defects," or unforgiving, professional climate. The net effect is that many officers are demonstrating greater commitment to promotion (or job security) than to the army itself and are unwilling to display initiative for fear that honest mistakes will be "career-busters." Although they are discussed separately in the following pages for the purpose of analytical clarity, these two behaviors are closely related and result from the uncertainty created by downsizing (diagram 4.6).

Diagram 4.6. Changing Behavior in a Downsizing Army

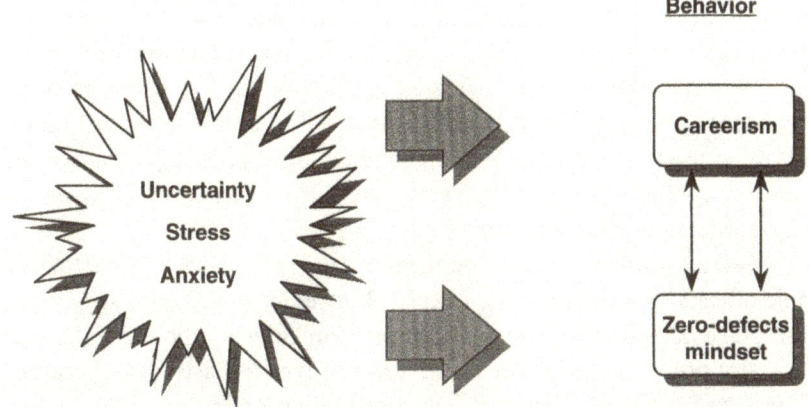

A thorough understanding of these two effects first requires a richer description of the army's officer management system (which is described in detail in chapter 5). Army leaders have argued for decades over the officer management and professional development process. Traditionally, officers have been required to complete a certain set of assignments at each rank prior to being promoted to the next rank. Although *command* is by far the most important entry in an officer's record at each level, other key items include four levels of military schooling, completion of a civilian master's degree, duty on a high-level staff, and, more recently, assignment to a prestigious combat-training center. In short, career development has been grounded in the belief that positions of senior leadership are best filled by broadly trained generalists who have performed admirably at each level of development, but particularly in command.

During the 1970s, critics blamed the lapse in professionalism evident during the Vietnam War on this approach (Hauser 1973; Gabriel and Savage 1978). Although some of the changes recommended at the time by the "military reformers" were realized in 1974 through the implementation of the Officer Personnel Management System (OPMS), the overall system still remains essentially the same (Hauser 1984). Officer careers progress through four basic phases between the rank of lieutenant and colonel, and they are required to serve in certain assignments and complete certain schooling during each phase of development. During each phase, there are a variety of potential assignments, depending on an officer's branch, functional area, and past performance, several of which are viewed as crucial for advancement. Two assignments in particular deserve mention. At the company grade level, the command of a company for at least twelve months is "the essence of leadership development in this stage of an officer's career," and critical for advancement. It is equally important for majors to be selected for the Command and General Staff College and to serve a minimum of twelve months in specific jobs on battalion or brigade staffs that are designated as "branch-qualifying" (*Commissioned Officer Development and Career Management* 1995, 1–10).[24]

These assignments are key "punches" on the metaphorical ticket that enable officers to advance to the next level of responsibility, and strong performance in each is imperative for promotion. Selection boards choose officers for promotion, schooling, and command on the basis of qualifications (measured in terms of physical fitness, military bearing, awards, schooling, and most important, past assignments) and performance (measured in terms of previous officer evaluation reports, or OERs).[25] Performance is by far the most important criterion, and when assessing performance, board members place the greatest emphasis on evaluations made by the officer's "senior raters."[26] It is within the context of this system that careerism and a zero-defect mindset have grown more pronounced.

Careerism

Careerism suggests an overly ambitious condition—the desire to advance one's own position over all other goals and objectives. It is manifested in the tendency for officers and their patrons to gauge and manipulate the assignment system to secure "career-enhancing assignments." Being career-oriented, on the other hand, merely implies dedication to a particular profession and the desire to advance within that profession. Careerism is considered a fatal flaw, while being career-oriented may attest to one's professional commitment and promise. In practice, of course, the line between the two is blurred (Strand 1993, 164). An increase in careerism is clearly evident in the post–Cold War army. While there is uncertainty over ideal career patterns, there is absolutely no doubt that most aspiring officers must do certain jobs in the muddy boots army to remain competitive for promotion. As the availability of these jobs has diminished, the competition for them has become fierce. A rise in competition and political jockeying for these key jobs, increasing officer involvement in assignment policy, and decreasing cooperation within the officer corps are all indications of mounting careerism.

A subtle distinction should be made between careerism as it was described in the post-Vietnam period and in the present climate. In the past, careerism was associated with actions that officers took in order to advance their careers. In this era of downsizing and uncertainty, however, officers are concerned not only with advancement but also survival. There is a crucial difference between self-promotion and self-preservation. Because of the up-or-out system, officers not promoted in the past were always vulnerable to separation. In this era of downsizing, however, they are assured of it. For this reason, advancement and survival are, to a greater degree than in the past, perceived to be the same thing. The result, however, is an alarming rise in careerism:

> The army is building an officer corps of desperation. You've got junior officers—particularly young captains—who know that they are going to have one time at command. And they know that they need to get a masters degree and that command as early as possible, and they need to ace that command because if they don't, they won't go to the Command and General Staff College. . . . So they are desperate. . . . The same thing with majors. Majors are even more desperate than captains because they have an even smaller window of opportunity. (Lieutenant Colonel, Fort Sill)

> It's Darwinism—survival of the fittest. (Major, Fort Hood)

> Dagumit, we're spending an inordinate amount of time making sure we hit the "gates." And I'd be lying to you if I said I didn't think about it. Everybody sitting here does because if we don't make that gate we're done. (Major, Fort Sill)

> The general sat in there and said you don't have to punch this ticket, you just have to do well. But everybody was sitting there going "Ah, bull". (Captain, Fort Sill)

Escalating careerism is also evident in the increasing emphasis officers place on what they need to do to stay "ahead of the pack." Junior officers are more aware of the importance of key assignments. In addition, officers are more sensitive to the need to manipulate their careers to ensure that they complete these assignments within a certain time frame, thus making them eligible for the next sequence of promotion and assignments. Early, or "below-the-zone" (BZ) promotion, in particular, has gained added importance in a downsizing army.[27] As noted in chapter 3, below-the-zone promotion rates for majors, lieutenant colonels and colonels rose on average 3 or 4 percent during the late 1980s. These higher rates have been maintained throughout the current downsizing and since 1990 have bordered on the maximum 10 percent.[28] It is not surprising that during a period when opportunities are decreasing and the relative quality of the officer corps is rising that officers place greater emphasis on the need to stand out to remain competitive for continued advancement. Whether they are right or not is beside the point.[29] More officers are undoubtedly aware of who is and who is not BZ, what one needs to do to become BZ, and what one's options are if not selected BZ:

> BZ has kind of taken on a life of its own. For the last several years personnel officers have been calling officers in the field and saying: "You know, you ought to get into this job and do this and that to stay competitive for BZ." So now a guy is in for five years, and he is punching tickets like crazy so that he can be competitive for BZ consideration.
> (Lieutenant Colonel, Army War College, Carlisle Barracks)

> You get kids who come to you with four or five years in the service and they are talking about selection rates to Command General Staff College and stuff like that. Heck, I didn't know what the selection rates to CGSC were until I was selected. (Lieutenant Colonel, Army War College, Carlisle Barracks)

Decreasing opportunities resulting from downsizing also seem to perpetuate additional "politicking" among officers. As a *Army Times* article observed: "There's a lot of heavy politicking with people showing their resumes all over the place, going to every little event to get noticed" (Anderson 1995, 12). This trend is also obvious in the increased use of what one retired general labeled the labor exchange: "Branch [policies], and the formal personnel system they [are] a part of, constitute only a portion of the process by which assignments are determined and career development proceeds. There is also an informal labor exchange: an elaborate network of relationships through which posting agreements are made and assignments negotiated" (Dawkins 1979, 155). The labor exchange has both a demand side (the desire of senior officers to have capable, loyal people working for them) and a supply side (officers who are hoping to identify someone they know, or know of, who might offer them a job).[30]

The labor exchange was prominent during the Vietnam War when battalion and brigade commanders were often selected on the basis of their reputations and who they knew. In 1974, the army instituted a centralized selection system for officers to command brigades and battalions, doing away with much of the cronyism in officer personnel management that was heavily criticized in the aftermath of Vietnam (Meyer et al. 1995, 164). However, remnants of the informal structure remain, and for assignments other than battalion and brigade command, the labor exchange continues to function, particularly, remarked one colonel, "when a general decides to get involved."³¹ While it is difficult to determine what impact downsizing has had on the "labor exchange," one might speculate that as officers perceive opportunities declining and competition rising, they will be more prone to use informal structures to control their destinies. While careerism has a negative connotation, the labor exchange may serve a valuable function by matching existing talent with demand. In moderation, this phenomenon is analogous to networking in the civilian sector. If taken to the extreme, however, it may undermine the effectiveness of official personnel management practices. The observations of officers in the field army today suggest that the labor exchange is, at the least, very much alive, and perhaps increasingly prominent, in the post–Cold War army.

> I've also seen more people go outside of approved channels because they've been given an assignment that's just bad for their career. And that goes back to the growing perception that each officer has to take care of himself.
> (Captain, Fort Sill)

> I've had guys call me since I've been here trying to figure out what they can do, do I know somebody who can help them, that kind of stuff. They're really concerned because of the increasing competitiveness due to downsizing.
> (Colonel, Former Brigade Commander, Fort Leavenworth)

Increasing competitiveness has undermined cooperation among officers, particularly those who are either vying for, or serving in, key positions (such as company commander or battalion operations officer). A number of officers observe that such behavior often persists despite outstanding leadership climates established by battalion, brigade, and division commanders:

> It's very, very cutthroat, much more than it used to be amongst company level commanders and . . . even worse among majors.
> (Major, Schofield Barracks)

> At Fort Bragg, captains didn't cooperate at all. It's become so competitive . . . I've seen captains do each other in. They would catch someone doing something, not illegal, but a judgment call, and they'd say, "Hey, I'm going to slam him by telling the boss." And they did. . . . It's so disappointing. It makes a unit suffer horribly. . . . Nobody's a team player anymore in the units that I've been in.
> (Captain, Fort Sill)

> I see a lot more competitiveness among majors and a lot less cooperation.
> (Major, Fort Hood)

> I'm not so sure you can tie this directly to downsizing, but neither am I sure that downsizing doesn't have a lot to do with it. . . . [As a chaplain], I've been

on five rotations to JRTC [the Joint Readiness Training Center] with a number of battalion commanders who simply refused to share information and resources.... Some of that stuff is going to happen no matter what. But some of it was doggone contrived.... Man, some of those BZers ... they were the worst.   (Major, Command and General Staff College, Fort Leavenworth)

The controversy among majors over selection for the Command and General Staff College is indicative of the underlying tension and divisiveness that exists in today's army. Approximately half of all majors are selected to attend a nine-month course at the Command and General Staff College at Fort Leavenworth; those not selected are encouraged to complete the course by correspondence. To the casual observer the distinction between the two might seem relatively insignificant. In the officer corps today, however, selection for CGSC means the difference between retention or separation, "good jobs" or "bad jobs," and respect or alienation.

Officially, resident and nonresident graduates of CGSC have fulfilled professional development requirements and are therefore eligible for "branch-qualifying jobs"—the tickets necessary to remain competitive for promotion. However, numerous officers acknowledge that division commanders throughout the army have reserved key jobs only for those officers who are resident graduates of the Command and General Staff College. Thus, there is intense competition for selection to CGSC and tremendous anxiety among those not selected about their future in the army. The effects of these "unofficial" policies on attitudes and behavior are predictable:

> The army policy is everybody gets a fair shot. In reality it is only resident CGSC graduates that get a shot. Nonresidents are not considered. ... I checked in Alaska, in Colorado, in Kansas. I checked the Eighty-second and the Twenty-fourth. All of them had this unwritten policy. It was guidance from the Commanding Generals—nonresidents are not welcome.
> (Major, Nonresident CGSC, Fort Hood)

> The reality is if you don't make Command and General Staff College, you are toast.   (Major, Resident CGSC, Fort Sill)

> People who are not selected for resident CGSC are wondering what's the message. Are they second-class citizens in the army and basically serving in all these other jobs until the army doesn't need them anymore and then they get a SERB notice? By not being forthright, the army is creating a tremendous amount of friction between majors who are resident CGSC graduates, and those who are not.
> (Major, Command and General Staff College, Fort Leavenworth)

I'll tell you straight. A lot of senior guys, from general on down, will tell it to you straight privately.... If you are not selected for resident CGSC, you're living on borrowed time.... That's a fact of life. [Major, Resident CGSC, Fort Sill]

Zero Defects

Closely related to perceptions about increasing careerism is the notion that the army's professional climate has become less forgiving, or "zero-defect." Concern over a zero-defects environment dates back to the Vietnam War when critics faulted the officer corps for its "blatant disregard for principles, but total respect for accomplishing even the most trivial mission with zero-defects" (Gabriel and Savage 1978, 85). There are really two components to this criticism. First, a zero-defects environment has an ethical dimension. The army was, in the words of the *Study on Military Professionalism* (1970), suffering from leadership "engulfed in producing statistical results, fearful of personal failure ... and determined to submit acceptably optimistic reports which reflect faultless completion of a variety of tasks" (14).[32] Zero defects also implies a leadership environment in which it is unacceptable to make mistakes and, by extension, officers are less willing, and less able, to demonstrate creativity and initiative. This second characteristic of a zero-defects environment has traditionally received less emphasis, though arguably the first condition (ethical transgressions) flows logically from the second (an unforgiving command climate).

This point notwithstanding, it is unclear whether or not the moral and ethical climate within the army has suffered significantly as a consequence of downsizing. The aforementioned 1994 study conducted by the Chief of Staff's Strategic Fellows concluded that "the moral climate is sound." The permanency of this sound moral climate, however, should not be taken for granted as the army becomes increasingly competitive and unforgiving. In carrying out the reforms of the mid-1970s, the army made a conscious effort to de-emphasize the use of statistical indicators as measures of performance and to place increasing emphasis on values and ethics throughout the leader development process (Sorley 1992a, 359). Some of the officers interviewed for this study, however, perceive that as the current officer evaluation system searches frantically for "discriminators," undue emphasis is once again being placed on quantitative measures:

Things that people would overlook before are sacred now, like maybe reenlistments in your company.... It doesn't matter if your company or platoon can perform. It is, "Well, you only had a 20 percent reenlistment rate."

(Captain, Schofield Barracks)

In one battery, the commander was bragging that all of his officers got perfect scores on their physical training tests. I knew them well. I was very familiar with their physical abilities, and there is no way on the best morning.... We knew the deal. But how far does that go? A PT score is a small thing, but is it being applied to bigger things we don't know about?

(Captain, Fort Sill)

There is greater emphasis on numbers.... Senior officers now monitor how many people attend family support group meetings, [the] percentage of officers who are members of the Officer's Club, et cetera.

(Captain, Schofield Barracks)

These may well be isolated examples, and undoubtedly some officers had similar concerns before downsizing began. The point is not that there has been a dramatic change, but rather that the officer corps (junior and mid-career officers in particular) perceives itself to be under growing pressure for a variety of reasons. In such an environment, an organization's members feel competing pressures between flawless performance and moral and ethical behavior.

Ethical issues aside, officers today clearly believe that the professional climate within the army is less forgiving and that as a consequence officers are less willing to make decisions independently, seize the initiative, or take risks. One of the root causes of this behavior is inflation in ratings under the current officer evaluation system. This system has been relatively successful since 1979 in retarding ratings inflation, a fate that eventually befalls all officer evaluation systems—though death knells for the current system were being sounded as early as 1985 (Ingraham 1985). The pace of inflation held relatively steady until 1992, at which point it accelerated, first in the ratings of senior officers and then down through the entire system.[33] Advocates on one side argue that the Officer Evaluation Report (OER) should be eliminated, while others simply propose myriad alternatives (Bassford 1988; Bradford and Brown 1973). Regardless of one's views on the appropriate design of the army's performance evaluation system, it is clear that downsizing has accelerated ratings inflation.

The logic behind this accelerated inflation appears to be relatively straightforward: SERBs were heavily used for the first time in 1992, and senior raters sought to "protect" the lieutenant colonels and colonels in their commands by giving them the highest possible ratings. This philosophy eventually carried through the ranks, and today the system is grossly inflated, with it being reported that 70 to 80 percent of captains and majors receive "one blocks," the highest possible evaluation.[34] Inflation of the OER makes the work of selection boards, whether for promotion or separation, more difficult, and ultimately distorts the selection process. Faced with an overabundance of "outstanding" candidates, board members are forced to discover "black marks" in order to narrow their choices (Hauser 1984, 454). One might also posit that as it becomes more difficult to distinguish between officers on the basis of performance, boards members may, consciously or subconsciously, place more weight on an officer's "qualifications." In short, as inflation increases, so, too, does the importance of an officer's assignments. It would seem that an inflated OER system not only perpetuates a less-forgiving environment but also indirectly contributes to the ticket-punching behavior described earlier.

Perhaps most important, the majority of junior and mid-career officers believe that the inflated OER has perpetuated the zero-defects climate in today's army.[35] Evaluation reports are as important for the behavior they promote or discourage as for the performance they evaluate and the potential they identify. As Bassford observes: "Officers are not born sycophants, idiots, or liars; they are men of normal intelligence and morals who quickly figure out where the carrots and sticks of the Army's personnel system lie and adjust behavior accordingly" (1988, 89). Although overstated, this observation is a reminder that the evaluation system should be assessed not only by its ability to distinguish potential among officers but also by the behavior it engenders. The army is purportedly in the business of building bold and audacious leaders, yet the uncertainty bred of downsizing, coupled with an inflated evaluation system, have created junior and mid-career officers less willing to show initiative or to take well-conceived risks. While there is a clearly a distinction to be made between the dangerous risktaker and daring leader, downsizing appears to have inspired fewer of both.

> *Captain 1*: You run your ideas by your bosses to try to get their feedback and then build your plan based on their comments so you know with some confidence that you're within a 80 to 90 percent solution.
>
> *Captain 2*: As a result, we do what the boss wants, instead of doing what we think is right as bosses. It is a survival technique.
>
> (Two Captains, Fort Hood)

It's getting to the point where you don't want to do anything without covering your ass. A lot of that is a function of command, but I would say there is a trend. (Captain, Schofield Barracks)

Prior to this job, I was in the Inspector General's Office. I was shocked by the number of junior officers that would come in and talk to us, because they were afraid to talk to their commanders. They didn't want to let . . . [them] know that this or that is a problem because they were afraid it would reflect on their evaluations. (Major, Fort Hood)

You're going to drop the ball every once in a while. But it's not being allowed. If you take a risk, that ball might slip by your fingers, and it might drop. And if every ball is a glass ball . . . It's killing initiative, it's killing the risk taker. (Captain, Fort Sill)

It's a real nail biter whenever it's OER time. You really do feel the pressure. And it's all tied to downsizing. (Captain, Schofield Barracks)

Officer behavior has been dramatically altered by downsizing. Careerism is on the rise and initiative and independent decisionmaking are in decline. While these things are significant, and potentially very serious, they are mostly the result of the prolonged uncertainty caused by downsizing, combined with outdated officer management practices and deeply embedded norms and career expectations within the officer corps. Even more alarming, however, the uncertainty of downsizing has also altered career choices and career patterns. These changes have consequences that will last well into the next century.

Marketability or Muddy Boots

Downsizing has had subtle but significant effects on career choices, particularly those of junior and mid-career officers. Junior officers have adjusted in one of two ways to the uncertainty and anxiety of downsizing. A substantial number are "hedging their bets" by seeking assignments and educational opportunities that provide them with skills marketable outside the army. The remaining officers, who aspire to a military career, battalion command, and continued advancement, are hedging in a different way by retrenching to the traditional path of army success, seeking positions that keep them closest to "troop assignments" (diagram 4.7).

While these generalizations are obvious simplifications of a diverse set of decisions, interests, concerns, and career choices, they highlight the in-

Diagram 4.7. Changing Career Choices in a Downsizing Army

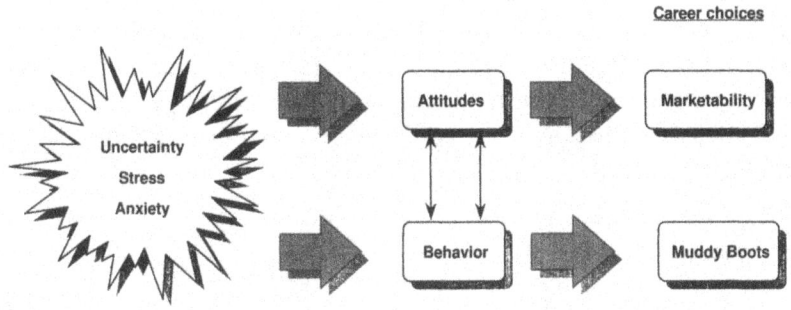

creasing bifurcation of the officer corps in the post–Cold War army. There are also signs that downsizing has reinforced undesirable anti-intellectual tendencies within the army. These issues, introduced here and explained more fully in the next chapter, have been largely overlooked by military leaders, yet they are crucial to the vitality and professionalism of the U.S. Army.

In addition to the professional development sequence mentioned earlier, the Officer Personnel Management System also instituted a policy under which most officers were given a "dual designation." Thus, officers are commissioned into a basic branch and then choose a functional area or secondary specialty between their fifth and sixth years of service (*Commissioned Officer Development and Career Management* 1995, 5).[36] From that point forward, officers spend roughly one-half of their careers as field grade officers in mainstream assignments in their basic branch and the other half working in assignments related to their functional area. In the past, certain functional areas—those with the probability of assignments "close to troops," such as operations or personnel—were chosen by officers who were committed to the traditional command track.[37] At the same time, there was enough flexibility in the system to allow a select few to pursue unconventional, but equally successful, routes to the top. An Arabic-speaking infantry officer, for example, could switch back and forth between assignments as a foreign area officer and assignments in the field army, and if he was a strong performer still have a reasonable expectation of commanding a combat battalion. Likewise, even combat arms officers with personnel or operations specialties would often spend two years out of the field army in civilian graduate school and three to four years teaching at West Point (the alma mater of many of the army's most successful generals), before returning to troop assignments, without notable damage to their careers. This is no longer the case. In the minds of most junior officers, particularly those in combat branches, there are two very clear and distinct choices—marketability or muddy boots.

Marketability

Junior officers generally perceive career opportunities as having been altered by downsizing and are modifying their career choices accordingly. Some junior and mid-career officers are choosing career patterns that provide them with skills marketable in the civilian sector. These individuals have opted for, or are considering, functional areas or other assignments that will give them skills or assure them an opportunity for graduate schooling. Among these officers there is a general recognition that such assignments take them off the "battalion command track" for at least two reasons.

First, "timing" is now more important than ever. Officers who choose such assignments are generally assured of one to two years of graduate school and a three to four year "utilization tour" in which they put their newly acquired skills to use. Unless they are fortunate enough to have commanded a company very early in their careers, this block of time away from the muddy boots army *almost* guarantees that they will be unable to satisfy all the necessary requirements prior to being considered for promotion to lieutenant colonel or selection for battalion command. Chronic concern exists over how selection boards will view assignments away from troops, particularly when choosing the next generation of battalion commanders. In a time when battalions are disappearing more quickly than officers competing to command them, officers are questioning who will be awarded this "golden ring"—those who spend time in academe, research and development, industry, the Pentagon and myriad nontraditional assignments, or those who stay close to the muddy boots? The consensus is that, with rare exceptions, muddy boots career patterns will prevail.

At the same time, officers believe that acquiring "hard skills" may decrease their vulnerability to involuntary separation from the army and most certainly enhance their civilian career prospects outside of it. The assignment officers who oversee the various functional areas report that hard-core specialties—Research, Development and Acquisition, Comptroller, Operations Research, and Systems Automation, for example—have in a sense become "growth industries" as a consequence of downsizing.[38] Many of the officers making these choices appear to view their army service as much an opportunity for additional education and a means for padding their resumes as a career or a way of life. Likewise, many express interest in ROTC and recruiting assignments, despite the potentially negative career implications of such choices. These assignments offer officers educational opportunities and a high quality of life, and may help ease their transition to the civilian sector:

> I'm staying in the army. If my GRE scores are reasonably good, I will be going to a fully funded graduate school starting next summer en route to teach at West Point or training with industry. . . . That makes me marketable when I get out of the Army. . . . Will it reduce my chances for battalion command? Yes. Is it a concern? No. (Captain, Fort Hood)

> I had a battery commander whose functional area was foreign affairs. He was going to learn Farsi. His whole goal, once he got that, was not to advance in the army but to learn Farsi, do his required foreign area stuff, and then get out of the Army and go work for ARAMCO or one of the Arab firms.
> (Captain, Fort Sill)

> I would not have picked a functional area that did not have a masters degree. . . . Now I've got a marketable skill. Whereas with just experience in your primary branch [in this case combat arms], what are you going to do? Are you going to go rattle cages at a correctional facility? Are you going to go out and be a chief of police somewhere and work for $30,000 a year?
> (Major, Fort Hood)

> When I was picking my functional area the brigade executive officer said to me: "Look, I'm an old lieutenant colonel and if I had to do it all over again I would pick a hard skill that you can use on the outside."
> (Captain, Fort Sill)

> *Captain 1*: What I find myself doing is trying to get as much training and as many different types of jobs that I can get, just so that I have a résumé builder if something happens.

> *Captain 2*: Yeah. You think of your army career now as a tool for building a résumé. (Two Captains, Fort Hood)

Muddy Boots

At the same time, other officers are reacting differently to the uncertainty and turbulence of downsizing. These officers aspire to battalion command, an army career, and advancement to the army's highest ranks. Uncertain about the path to the top in today's climate, these officers are choosing what they believe to be and what their assignment officers tell them is the safest route to the top—consecutive assignments in the muddy boots army.

Although there are no clear roadmaps, some rough sketches of a new generation of muddy boots career patterns are beginning to emerge. Successful command has always been, and continues to be, a prerequisite for higher-level assignments. Presently, however, assignments as an observer controller at the National Training Center or the Joint Readiness Training Center are viewed as "hot tickets" for junior officers.[39] Not only do officers in these assignments have the opportunity to become more tactically and technically proficient, they also meet battalion, brigade, and division commanders from around the army who rotate through these training centers, allowing for "networking" army style. For similar reasons, officers seek assignments as instructors or "doctrine developers" at one of the army's combat arms "schoolhouses" where junior officers are taught the basics of their trade. While most of these junior officers recognize that a master's degree is important for promotion to higher grades, they avoid fully funded civilian graduate education at all costs because it, and the subsequent utilization tour, takes them out of the "mainstream." Most will instead complete their master's degree at night sometime during their first decade of service.[40] Captain Mark Redina accurately describes the situation that a growing number of officers face:

> In a desperate effort to ensure job security, officers are forced to seek successive troop assignments. And since, to a far less degree, an advanced civil diploma is also perceived as a promotional discriminator, most officers are forced to squeeze in a master's degree at night school while holding down a challenging job. (1990, 67)

Finally, this group of officers is committed to avoiding assignments like ROTC duty, Recruiting Command, or teaching at West Point, which take them away from the most viable career patterns in the field army.[41] In a sense, this fixation on "troop time" and command is a manifestation of traditional "heroic leader" values at the core of the army's culture (Janowitz

1960, 21). Although the basic branches must market and fill a range of assignments with the officers they manage, they steer their "best" officers to the career pattern outlined above.[42] It is no wonder that those who are committed to being the Army's future leaders adhere so closely to a "muddy boots" career patterns:

> As we've gone down from . . . 780,000 to . . . 495,000, people are asking themselves, can I afford to be that maverick [when it comes to career choices]. If I am a maverick that goes out and does what he thinks is best for the service, will the service think it's best for me?   (Colonel, Fort Leavenworth)

> The going perception in the field—and I went this route also—is that as a senior captain it is a smart move to try to get an observer controller job at one of the CTCs [Combat Training Centers], or you can get back to the schoolhouse to stay with the doctrinal issues and the training environment. . . . All you've got to do is look at the promotion rates and command selection for officers who serve in those positions. They bear this out.   (Major, Fort Sill)

> Taking time out for civilian graduate school is actually a bad thing now. . . . It looks like you went out and screwed off for two years. When you come back the attitude is, "Oh, you want to be a soldier again." Now the only way to still be considered competitive is to get your master's in your spare time and keep taking mainstream jobs—observer controller at the National Training Center, Army Staff, that kind of stuff.   (Captain, Fort Sill)

Both these sets of attitudes have always existed within the officer corps. In the past, officers have had to make decisions that implied trade-offs between marketability and muddy boots at least twice in their careers. This trade-off is first evident in the choices facing officer candidates from ROTC, West Point, and OCS when they select their basic branches.[43] Those who choose combat arms branches are assured a muddy boots existence for at least their first five years of service, while most in combat support or combat service support branches will also be in or close to field units but performing duties with clearer parallels in the civilian workforce. Moreover, officers in combat support or combat service support branches have greater opportunities to serve in positions away from the muddy boots arena later in their careers. The implications of this choice for future civilian employment are self-evident. As one ordnance officer in Hawaii remarked, "I just think the guys in the combat arms are really affected by downsizing. . . . As a tank and automotive material manager, I actually have a skill applicable in the outside world. If you're an infantry officer, it's a harder sell."

Likewise, there has always been the recognition that the choice of a more "civilianized" functional area made advancement along the command expressway more tenuous. As one major in Oklahoma suggested, "It kind of falls back into that category of being conservative. If your functional area is operations or personnel, that's going to increase your chances of getting around troops. Certainly there has always been the understanding that certain functional areas could decrease your chances of getting battalion command because the academic and the specialty requirements pull you away from troops." Despite this understanding, the system was flexible enough in the past to ensure that success on the command expressway and civilian graduate school or certain functional areas were not seen to be mutually exclusive. That flexibility is gone, and there is now only one perceived route to the top in today's downsizing army.

Anti-Intellectualism

The retrenchment to muddy boots career patterns is also consistent with what can only be described as a growing anti-intellectualism within the post–Cold War army. The U.S. Army is and always has been "a fundamentally anti-intellectual organization" (Bassford 1988, 147). This is because intellectual pursuits run counter to the "heroic leader" culture that pervades the army's hierarchy.[44] As Ward Just observes: "There has never been a Clausewitz in the American Army because the writing of *Vom Kriege* took time and serious thought. An Army officer has no time to think, and imaginative reflection is discouraged. Tours of duty are rapid, and designed to thrust a man into as many different situations as can be managed.... It is the theory of a utility infielder" (1970, 109). Anti-intellectualism, however, has become significantly more pronounced as a consequence of downsizing.

First, officers from all branches, but particularly combat arms officers (who traditionally have become generals in far greater numbers), are retrenching to more rigid muddy boots career patterns. This trend has affected the propensity of junior officers to pursue civilian graduate schooling. The notion of full-time graduate schooling for officers has always been a contentious issue within the army. Some argue that the immersion of officers into civilian graduate studies gives them a better appreciation of the society they serve, tempers absolutism, and avoids intellectual isolation. Others maintain that civilian education is exorbitantly expensive and diverts attention from an officer's primary purpose—the proficient use of military force. Regardless of one's position on this issue, it is clear that officers today believe that full-time civilian graduate schooling jeopardizes future promotion and command opportunities, and senior officers often advise them against this option. The effects of this perception are evident in the fact that in recent years the number of officers who volunteered (or the army convinced) to attend civilian schools has dropped precipitously and a substantial portion of the funds budgeted for this purpose has been unused (*The Science and Engineering Requirements* 1996, 21).

Officers with the rank of major are also less likely to apply for an additional year of study at the School of Advanced Military Studies (SAMS) at Fort Leavenworth. The SAMS program was created in 1983 to permit a selected number of the army's brightest officers to study the theory and application of the "operational art" of war. The purpose of the course was to teach officers "how to think about military operations, not necessarily what to think" (Dunnigan and Macedonia 1993, 139).[45] SAMS graduates became known throughout the army as "Jedi warriors" and held key positions on planning staffs during the Gulf War, arguably contributing significantly to the quality of operational and strategic planning. In recent years, however, the number of officers applying to this program has steadily declined, as officers fear that an extra year at SAMS will disrupt their "timing."[46]

Anti-intellectual tendencies were also reinforced by the Army's Selective Early Retirement Boards, which sent a very powerful message about where the army's priorities lay in the post–Cold War era—a message not lost on the officer corps. Units throughout the army felt the sting, as competent and valued senior officers were asked to take early retirement. The army's leadership was extraordinarily sensitive to the possibility that certain groups of officers, particularly specialists, would be disproportionately affected by these cutbacks, and "floors" were established to protect a number of functional areas which included foreign area officers (FAOs) and permanent professors at West Point.[47] Although these efforts were largely successful, certain army installations and particular types of assignments were clearly disadvantaged by the SERB process. A substantial and disproportionate number of lieutenant colonels and colonels serving as instructors at Fort Leavenworth and the Army War College, for example, were involuntarily discharged. In 1992, alone, twenty-eight lieutenant colonels, a substantial portion of the faculty of the Command and General Staff College and the Combined Arms Service School, were forced to retire.[48] In addition, ROTC commands were dramatically affected by the SERBs when lieutenant colonels serving as Professors of Military Science (PMSs) on campuses around the country were involuntarily and abruptly retired.[49] These events sent a very clear and unmistakable message to the officer corps: the army is not assigning what it perceives to be its most capable officers to these assignments, and the intellectual and professional development of the officer corps may not be the army's highest priority. Not surprisingly, this has deterred officers from wanting to serve in such assignments.[50]

The relationship between officer "quality" and assignment policy is rarely discussed within the halls of the Army Personnel Command, and more rarely still in the presence of an outsider. This reflects a paranoia, attributable in part to a blowup in the early 1970s when it became known that assignment officers were "unofficially" establishing order-of-merit lists and assigning officers to desirable or less-desirable assignments based on their own subjective assessments (Mylander 1974, 77). The centralized selection process eliminated much of this practice, and the Officer Personnel Management Directorate no longer maintains such lists.[51] Despite this, however, assignment officers have tremendous control over the assignment process, and they continue to assign officers to various billets based on a subjective evaluation of the officer's performance file. In recent decades, teaching duty at the Command and General Staff College, the Combined Arms Service School, the Army War College, and at ROTC commands have not been viewed as career-enhancing assignments. This presents a classic chicken/egg problem. Will officers be disadvantaged on future selection boards because of these assignments, or are officers selected for these assignments because they are seen as being not competitive for future selection boards? In general, the officer corps spends little time worrying about such semantics. Officers simply know that they do not want to be assigned to the army's "intellectual centers," and SERBs have unmistakably strengthened this motivation.

In a letter dated February 21, 1990 and addressed to the Chief of Staff of the Army, Lieutenant General David R. Palmer, the Superintendent of the United States Military Academy, voiced his concern that SERBs at the academy were dealing "a crushing blow to USMA's efforts in recruiting and retaining top army performers as tenured faculty members."[52] How these perceptions will also affect recruiting efforts to attract high-quality instructors to the Command and General Staff College, the War College, and ROTC assignments remains to be seen. There is every reason to expect, however, that it will be increasingly difficult because the army has, inadvertently perhaps, conveyed the impression that it places little value on such assignments.[53]

I spent two years with the British army during their downsizing and there's a noticeable difference. In their army, being an instructor at a service school like CGSC is looked upon positively in your career. In our army, Fort Leavenworth was referred to as "SERBia." From talking to students at the Combined Arms Services and Staff School during the years I was at Leavenworth, they felt that the quality of instructors had gone down. Those guys used to be ex-battalion commanders—really sharp guys on the move. Now there has been a noticeable decline in quality, as a lot of those guys are being SERBed.
(Major, Schofield Barracks)

The problem you're going to have at West Point is you're not going to get technical Ph.D.s anymore in the army because they know if they go to West Point they're not going to get promoted. They're going to get kicked out.
(Major, Schofield Barracks)

It's the fewest number of applications for SAMS that we've ever had. The main concern of these majors is their time line. . . . There are a lot of people who tell them they shouldn't do it—from generals to assignments officers.
(Colonel, Fort Leavenworth)

I was with ROTC and we had a lieutenant colonel that got the word, "You're outta here." And I can remember some students saying: "You know, he was a good officer. I learned a lot from him. . . . Man, if they do this to him after sixteen, seventeen, eighteen years . . ." It was hard and we talked through that and we talked about the downsizing and needing to get smaller. But a perception like that is a difficult thing to overcome. (Major, Fort Sill)

The objective here is not to debate the value of civilian graduate education or attendance at the School of Advanced Military Studies, nor to question the quality of instruction at the army service schools, but to illustrate an undeniable shift in the career choices of junior and mid-career officers. On one hand, some officers are battling uncertainty by engaging in a quest for marketability. By seeking skills and education that have clear parallels in the civilian world, officers are attempting to enhance their personal sense of security. Conversely, a second group, presumably the battalion commanders of the future, are adhering more closely to a strictly muddy boots career pattern. They will more likely have completed a master's degree in business by correspondence from Kennesaw State, than a degree in engineering from Georgia Tech or political science from Georgetown. In all likelihood, they will have done everything in their power to avoid assignments in recruiting, with reserve forces, or with ROTC (the infamous "3Rs"), instructor duty at West Point, Leavenworth, and the War College, or an extra year of study in the School of Advanced Military Studies or training with industry. The battalion commanders of the year 2005 will be the brigadier generals of 2010, and the four-star generals of 2015. That this group of officers is likely to have spent less time doing things that might be broadly classified as "intellectual" seems inevitable. The implications of these trends are considered in the next chapter.

Conclusion

The magnitude of the recent downsizing and the prolonged accompanying uncertainty has undermined the professionalism of the U.S. Army. Morale, career expectations, and organizational commitment within the officer corps have fallen, careerism has risen, and initiative has declined in the post–Cold War army. Moreover, these attitudinal changes are affecting officer career patterns in ways that the army's leadership has failed to grasp. At the very least, these trends impair military effectiveness. At worst, they may, in time, have devastating effects on the quality and professionalism of the army's officer corps and thus on the effectiveness of the army itself.

Two implicit arguments are also threaded throughout this chapter. First, the quantitative approach, particularly the survey data used by the army to study the effects of downsizing, misses much of what is important and interesting about the attitudes and behavior of army personnel, and for that matter, the members of any organization. This is partially the result of the inordinate emphasis that the Army Research Institute appears to place on quantitative research. It reinforces the point that a "messy truth" gained through such an approach as the one presented here may be of greater practical value than the "truths" learned from more quantitative methods, no matter how methodologically rigorous or analytically pure they may be.

Second, the army's leadership appears to be neither fully aware of the changing professional climate in the officer corps nor knowledgeable about what should be done about it. The army's downsizing experience reinforces the maxim that the army's leadership must remain constantly in touch with the "point of the spear"—the attitudes and beliefs of the lieutenants, captains, and majors as well as the enlisted members of the muddy boots army. Ultimately, these individuals are crucial to the army's effectiveness—its victory or defeat, success or failure. With this in mind, the next chapter highlights the importance of these trends, discusses their implications, and suggests some potential solutions to the problems they raise.

5

An Agenda for Reform
An Officer Corps for the Twenty-First Century

> An end of war can be a time of rebirth for the Army or a time of psychological let down. We need to seize the moment for reforming and modernizing our officer corps. . . . That is the best way to build for the future. But time is short. When the transition to peace is ended, it will become increasingly difficult to promote fundamental change.
> —William L. Hauser and Zeb Bradford, *Army*, December 1971

In 1993, Yale professor Paul Bracken created something of a buzz in defense policy circles by criticizing the propensity of policymakers to conceptualize military posture in terms of the "next military"—the one existing trends will produce in ten years given the character of current military problems and the fine-tuning of existing operational strategies. Too little emphasis, he argued, was being given to "the military after next"—the dramatically changed military organization that would emerge in twenty years in light of the transformations likely to occur in technology, the nature of warfare, and the international environment (1993, 157). With this insightful admonition in mind, let us ponder for a moment the qualities the army should seek to develop in its officers to ensure they are prepared for the unknown challenges of the future.[1]

Within a decade, the present generation of lieutenant colonels and colonels will be the army's senior leaders. Likewise, today's captains and majors will be the lieutenant colonels and colonels of the next army, and the colonels and generals of the army of 2015—the army after next. Two notable trends promise new challenges for these future army leaders. First, and most obvious, the world has changed. Despite the dangers of the bipolar standoff during the Cold War, there was an element of stability and consistency in international affairs that was oddly comforting. The abrupt end of the Cold War, however, has created a wholly different world—complex, dangerous and unpredictable—in which we are faced with a plethora of small-scale wars, waged as often by "terrorists, guerrillas, bandits and robbers" as by traditional armies (van Creveld 1991, 197).

Despite these uncertainties, the outlines of future military operations within the new world order are beginning to emerge. It is already clear that the military's role in the conduct of U.S. foreign affairs has changed markedly. As a precondition for domestic acceptability of military interventions abroad, the U.S. Army is likely to deploy forces in small numbers, often as part of multilateral coalitions, for specific and achievable purposes, with commanders held accountable for needless collateral damage (Bacevich 1990, 22). Military force is but one instrument among the many that the United States is likely to employ. And the army is certain to be used for a host of missions that fall outside the purview of traditional combat roles. The changing nature of the military mission, coupled with the dramatic decline of defense resources, have in a few short years caused not only the U.S. Army but armies around the world to change shape, shrink in size, and in some cases wither away.

Second, the rate of technological change in the decades ahead, particularly with respect to microchip technology, will be an order of magnitude greater than that of the past decade and will continue to accelerate. Advances in technology are changing not only the way nations trade and communicate but also the way they fight their wars. The post–Cold War era has been accompanied by what some commentators have labeled a revolution in military affairs. Since World War II, technological change has steadily fragmented the military organization into a growing number of specialties and has required increasing reliance on officers with "nonmilitary" expertise (Wood 1988, 30). Recently, this trend has quickened due to advances in computer and communications technology (Krepinevich 1994b; Bracken 1993, 162). These dramatic changes, first fully evident during the Gulf War, promise profound changes in the shape and size of military organizations as well as in their doctrine. Decentralized command and control, precision-guided weaponry, and a blurring of distinctions between the front lines and rear areas are likely to be characteristics of future battlefields and military organizations.

Together, these trends will alter traditional conceptions of professional military expertise, making it more difficult to distinguish between warriors and nonwarriors, commanders and noncommanders, and technicians and nontechnicians. Future military operations will require not only competencies outside the realm of traditional "military expertise" but also a level of political and technical sophistication unknown and unneeded by military leaders in the past. "The army may require a very different kind of officer in the future ... as we move into these fuzzy situations that put a premium on [officers] with cultural sensitivity and an ability to adapt rapidly" (Andrew Krepinevich as cited in Ricks 1995, 1). Moreover, the increasing sophistication of high-tech warfare will enlarge the body of knowledge pertinent to military operations and require a corps of officers who are comfortable with technology, ambiguity, and decentralized command and control (Toffler and Toffler 1993, 74).

Given this growing complexity, the post–Cold War army will require leaders at all levels with specialized knowledge. There will be a demand for officers with political expertise—men and women with in-depth knowledge of certain regions, language skills, the capacity to work on joint (interservice) staffs, an understanding of international and domestic political affairs, and the ability to provide civilian leaders in the administration and Congress with sage military advice. There will be a growing demand for officers with technical expertise—leaders with skills and experience in personnel, administration, logistics, and technology who can be counted upon to master the growing complexities of the modern computer-based military organization. And, of course, there will be a continuing need for officers with expertise in command—leaders who spend the majority of their careers "with troops" preparing for or serving in command. Tomorrow's commanders, however, must be capable not only of leading soldiers in operations from peacekeeping to high-intensity combat but also of developing tactics and doctrine appropriate for the twenty-first century.[2]

In the past, officers have served in all three of these roles, often rotating among them sequentially as they progressed through the ranks. In the future, however, given the growing complexities of each, few officers will be capable of such a feat. Occasionally, an exceptionally gifted leader will have the ability to contribute in more than one area, but for the most part these roles will be mutually exclusive. As former army Chief of Staff Edward C. Meyer concludes: "Some will argue that a good generalist can keep all three balls in the air at the same time. When our world was bipolar that may have been true, but tomorrow's world is changing so rapidly that we are unlikely to have time to permit generalists to become specialists" (1995, 227). Moreover, the costs associated with training and educating officers in a range of needed specialties is increasing rapidly. Thus, there will be growing pressure to gain maximum return from these specialists through repetitive assignments in their areas of expertise (Thie and Brown 1994, 23). In short, the post–Cold War era will strain traditional occupational categories that have defined the officer corps in the past. The future army will be led by a corps of highly trained specialists with diverse technical and nontechnical expertise.

Across all specialties, however, the army's leadership must comprise officers who not only know one field deeply but who possess the broad range of leadership skills, confidence, experience, and intellectual flexibility required to adapt to present and future uncertainties. As Chairman of the Joint Chiefs of Staff General John Shalikashvilli observes: "The unexpected has become so routine; we need people who are comfortable in an uncertain world" (as quoted in Rokke 1995, 21). Moreover, in the long run, the army's effectiveness will depend on its ability to innovate—more specifically on the existence of bright, ambitious officers with the willingness to ask and pursue difficult questions, the curiosity to seek knowledge outside the nuts and bolts of their own area of expertise or of the military profession more generally, and the self-confidence to test and relentlessly pursue promising new ideas. In sum, the army's future success will depend on the capacity of top leaders to create an organizational culture capable of generating intellectual capital, expertise, adaptability, and innovation.

Troubling Trends

This idealized image of the post–Cold War officer corps is distinctly at odds with the officer corps of today or of the immediate future. Today's officer corps is demoralized and less committed, more careerist and increasingly tentative. In addition, as a result of shortened assignments and more turbulent career patterns, officers are less tactically and technically proficient than they were before downsizing began. Moreover, the retrenchment of junior officers to muddy boots career patterns is particularly alarming in light of the challenges posed by this new era. While these problems are largely a function of downsizing, the army's rigid and outdated officer management system has exacerbated these deleterious trends.

Declining Professionalism

The professional fiber of the army officer corps has been strained by the uncertainty and turmoil of downsizing.[3] Although experts have long argued over the definition of military professionalism, Samuel Huntington's concept, first presented in his 1957 classic, *The Soldier and the State*, is still widely accepted by professional soldiers.[4] In this formulation, the distinguishing characteristics of any profession are expertise, social responsibility, and "corporateness."[5] The competence of the military professional lies in the "management of violence," a distinct sphere of proficiency common to all, or almost all, officers.[6] The professional soldier is not motivated by economic incentives but rather feels a special responsibility, a commitment, to the society he serves and to his craft. The corporate character of the military profession is manifest in a certain organic unity (esprit de corps) and consciousness within the profession of the military as a group apart from laymen (1957, 8-11).

The army officer corps is less professional today than it was when the Cold War "officially" ended with the fall of the Berlin Wall in 1989 and planning for downsizing began in earnest. The corporateness and esprit de corps of the officer corps has been undermined by downsizing. Likewise, the corps' commitment to both the army in particular and the military profession in general has been weakened. These effects might have been anticipated, for in some respects the notion of unexpectedly separating competent and committed officers is antithetical to professionalism. A sense of security is one of several attributes that "anchors" an individual to a certain profession and to a certain organization (Strand 1993, 140).

Additionally, the military is unique among professions in that the "expertise" of the professional soldier has only limited applicability outside the military organization. While other professionals—doctors, lawyers, and accountants, for example—may depart the organization for which they work and remain members of their profession as independents or in a range of other public and private enterprises, the military profession can be practiced only within the military institution. It is for this reason, perhaps, that military professionals place added faith in an informal contract—an implicit agreement between them and the military organization of what each can expect from the other (Elton and Malone 1972). In return for enduring the hardships of military life and fulfilling the obligations of a professional soldier, the state provides special privileges, career opportunity, and a reasonable modicum of security. Downsizing is viewed by officers as a violation of this contract.

What is more difficult to anticipate is the magnitude of these changes in attitude and behavior and whether they will be temporary or enduring. This task is further complicated by the fact that they are neither recent phenomena nor solely the consequence of downsizing; they have simply become more conspicuous because of it. During and after the Vietnam War, military professionalism within the army officer corps declined significantly, which, many argued, contributed to America's defeat.[7] In the late 1970s, sociologist Charles Moskos recast this discussion by arguing that the "econometric mindset" in military manpower policy underlying the introduction of the all-volunteer force had accelerated a "creeping occupationalism" in the armed forces. Moskos argued that the military career had traditionally been legitimated in terms of values and norms and a purpose transcending self-interest in favor of a presumed higher good, a notion consistent with conventional conceptions of professionalism. Conversely, occupations are legitimated in terms of the marketplace, that is, a level of monetary compensation established by market dynamics is awarded for equivalent competencies (1977, 43). With this shift, Moskos maintained that military service was increasingly becoming more like a job than a calling, and that this had serious implications for military effectiveness (Moskos and Wood 1988b).

At the core of this debate is the contention that a shift in the philosophy governing manpower policy has fundamentally changed the ethos of U.S. military organizations. On one level, this shift in rationale—which some label (after Max Weber) bureaucratic rationalism—is manifest in the language, analyses, and decisionmaking processes of military policymakers (Faris 1988).[8] On another level, this trend is evident in the corrosion of traditional values and norms among military personnel (Segal 1989, 57). Downsizing is viewed by some as a manifestation of a fundamental shift toward organizational rationalization and depersonalization that runs throughout American society (A. Bennett 1990). If one extends this reasoning to the army, it would not be surprising if downsizing has contributed to occupationalism within the officer corps.[9]

The potential consequences of these trends for military effectiveness are significant. Occupationalism undermines morale, cohesion, expertise, initiative, and the moral climate within the officer corps. Numerous examples of less-than-successful military operations during and after the Vietnam War show the devastating effects of these trends.[10] Quite simply, "a functioning military requires bonds of trust, sacrifice and respect within its rank, and similar bonds of support and respect between an army and the nation it represents" (Fallows 1981, 171). Professionalism within today's officer corps is in decline because the bonds on which it depends have been severely strained by downsizing.

Declining Military Competence

Downsizing has also undermined military competence or expertise, another crucial component of military professionalism. Turbulence within the officer corps has increased dramatically as a consequence of the growing requirements for officers coupled with the limited professional development opportunities available to them. Ironically, in an attempt to "develop" as many officers as possible to serve as future battalion commanders, the army has diluted the quality of preparation available to those select few who will actually be given this opportunity.

The length of officer assignments has always been somewhat controversial within the army. During and after the Vietnam War, for example, critics chastised the army for its shortened assignment policy (most company, battalion, and brigade commanders and staff officers served between six and twelve months in Vietnam) as both a cause and a consequence of pervasive careerism. Moreover, the less time officers spend in key command and staff positions, the less likely they are to develop a close knowledge of their responsibilities, their men, and their unit's abilities (Gabriel 1985, 9). In the mid-1970s, tour lengths for both battalion and brigade commanders were first lengthened to eighteen months and then to thirty months and finally reduced to twenty-four months where they have remained for the last fifteen years (Hauser 1985, 5).

Despite these changes, the rapid rotation of captains though company command positions and majors through battalion staff jobs has persisted, and has been substantially worsened by the stresses and strains of downsizing. The persistence of this phenomenon is due to fundamental shortcomings in officer management practices, the content of which are considered shortly. For now it is enough to note that the time officers spend in key professional development jobs has declined precipitously. This change has alarming implications for the "seasoning" of the army's future combat commanders.

Based on current assignment policy, the battalion commanders of the year 2005 are likely to have had substantially less of the crucial preparatory time in troop units than was enjoyed by their predecessors. The majority of captains will serve fifteen to eighteen months as company commanders, a

TABLE 5.1
Battalion Commander "Seasoning": Past, Present, and Future

	1988 Battalion Commanders	1995 Battalion Commanders	Future Battalion Commanders (2000–2010)	Preparation Time Before Command
Average time captains serve as company commanders	22 Months per command—common to have more than one command	25 months per command—over 50 percent had two commands	15–18 months—exception to have more than one command	23 to 32 percent decline in seasoning
Average time majors serve as battalion staff officers	21 Months—common to serve as both S-3 & XO	22 months—approx. 33 percent served as both S-3 & XO	12 months—rarely serve as both S-3 & XO	43 to 45 percent decline in seasoning

SOURCE: Department of the Army Inspector General, Briefing for Secretary of the Army, Togo West, February 9, 1995.
NOTE: Data only for Infantry, Field Artillery, and Armor Branches.

23–32 percent decline in the amount of time officers have traditionally served in this position. Likewise, most majors will serve a mere twelve months as a battalion operations officer (S-3) or a battalion executive officer (XO), a 43–45 percent decline from the past. In short, the battalion commanders of the future are likely to have had as little as twenty-four months of crucial professional development experience in combat battalions. The impact of these changes on the quality, competence, and confidence of future battalion commanders remains to be seen. It is clear, however, that in an attempt to qualify and develop as many future battalion commanders as possible, the army is on average giving significantly less preparation to those few who will actually have that opportunity.

Muddy Boots Career Patterns

Despite the explicit rules governing officer career management, individual officers (and the senior officers who "sponsor" them) exercise considerable initiative in selecting their assignments. The army's downsizing experience has influenced these choices. There is a growing emphasis being placed in strictly muddy boots career patterns, at the expense of full-time civilian graduate schooling and nontraditional assignments. Intellectual activities within the army appear to be getting short shrift, not necessarily because officers do not want to participate, but because they don't believe they can do so and remain competitive for promotion. It is particularly noteworthy that the number of officers willing to pursue graduate study in the hard sciences (math, science, or engineering) and the utilization tours that follow has declined markedly (*The Science and Engineering Requirements* 1996, 12). These trends are significant because the career decisions and the development experiences of today's junior and mid-career officers will have profound consequences for the next army and the army after next.

For a number of reasons, this scenario might have been predicted. In times of uncertainty, it is common for individuals to make conservative career choices, and professional soldiers are no exception: "The military professional, confronted with an unpredictable and uncontrollable external environment, has traditionally responded with a drive for internal order and internal consistency" (Lang 1964, 78). Additionally, there is a tendency on the part of organizational leaders to reward individuals with the types of backgrounds with which they are most familiar and comfortable, particularly during a periods of uncertainty. For this reason, it is crucial during such periods that army leaders make a conscious effort to avoid becoming fatally inbred, for as the force shrinks, promotion boards predictably tend to reward "standard issue" career patterns (Peters 1993).

Both these undesirable tendencies have been evident during downsizing. As opportunity has declined and competition increased, a growing number of junior and mid-career officers who aspire to military careers are retrenching to traditional career patterns, fearing to stray far, if at all, from the muddy boots army. Concurrently, assignment officers are encouraging officers on the "fast track" who want to stay there to adhere to traditional career patterns in the expectation that nontraditional assignments will be viewed unfavorably by future promotion boards. These trends are directly at odds, however, with developing the kinds of specialized, intellectually adaptable officers who will be required in the post–Cold War era. In short, the army has failed to create the professional climate and the formal and informal institutional structures needed to develop an officer corps for the twenty-first century.

Outdated Assumptions and Misplaced Priorities

To a large extent, the decline in professionalism and the described alterations in career choices are inevitable consequences of the uncertainty created by prolonged and incremental downsizing, a process largely outside the army's control. At the same time, the traditional norms within the officer corps and the rigidity of the Officer Personnel Management System (OPMS) have exacerbated these problems. And army leaders have been unacceptably slow in adjusting officer management practices to meet the challenges of this new age.

Recent history offers some insight into the present situation. Career management systems are important not only because they affect the technical competence of the officer corps but also because they shape the character, content, and values of the institution. With this in mind, perhaps, army Chief of Staff William Westmoreland directed the Deputy Chief of Staff for Personnel in August 1970 to develop a new officer management system that would increase professional competence by instituting more concentrated assignment patterns in various specialties and by ensuring equitable promotion opportunity across these specialties, that is, to create a number of viable paths to the top.[11] The eventual outcome of this directive was the Officer Personnel Management System, which was implemented after several sets of revisions in 1974. For the past twenty-three years, OPMS has, with only marginal changes, remained intact. It established dual career patterns in which officers select a functional area, or secondary specialty, between their fifth and eighth years of service. From that point forward, most officers rotate between assignments in their functional areas and their basic branches through the remainder of their careers.

Military organizations are unique in that they grow their own executive talent. For the army, OPMS provides both the framework and the formula for acquiring, developing, and ultimately separating or retiring each generation of army leaders (Strand 1993, 4). Three main policy areas—strength management (identifying officer requirements and overseeing officer procurement, separation, and distribution), performance evaluation, and professional development (education, training, and assignments)—fall under the purview of OPMS. The system was designed to be evolutionary, adjusting as necessary to meet unforeseen officer development needs (*Commissioned Officer Development and Career Management* 1995, 1). Officer professional development is the key pillar within this triad, reflecting the emphasis army doctrine places on the ability of decentralized leaders at every level to make decisions (*Military Leadership* 1990).

To its credit, the army places a higher premium on the professional development of its officer corps, particularly future commanders, than the other services. Institutional training, rotation through key operational assignments, and self-development make up the army's approach to leadership development.¹² Despite its benefits, however, the emphasis placed on the professional development of the officer corps and, more specifically, on preparing future commanders, has bred inefficiencies. As noted, the professional development process is designed around the goal of preparing officers to command battalions or higher units through a set sequence of schooling and operational assignments. This persists despite the fact that only a small fraction of the officer corps will be afforded the opportunity for such commands. In part, this is a reflection of the army's desire to indoctrinate all junior and mid-career officers with the "heroic leader" mindset through successive field assignments early in their careers.¹³ More than anything else, however, the army's officer development process is the product of the army's history, tradition, and organizational culture.

Officer personnel policy is profoundly influenced by the deeply ingrained institutional value that the army places on command: "Deep in the soul of most professional military men is the desire to lead. The military institution . . . remains primarily committed to the belief that a command career is the best road to success and personal fulfillment" (Sarkesian 1975, 80). Moreover, the system assumes a close correlation between command experience and the army's management needs; a proven commander is capable, this philosophy holds, of performing successfully in most other assignments in the army. As a consequence, battalion command assignments are virtually mandatory for the officer who hopes to advance to the rank of colonel, despite the original intent of OPMS (Strand 1993, 121).¹⁴

Not surprisingly, the officer corps adheres to this relatively narrow conception of military professionalism and officers generally equate command with success. And, senior army leaders perpetuate these notions. For example, in an article on professionalization and the army, Chief of Staff Carl Vuono describes a military professional as "an expert in the profession of arms . . . responsible for soldiers and units" (1990, 3). Given such statements, it is no wonder that the majority of officers participate in relentless rivalry for command or preparatory assignments leading up to command. Predictably, the system is generally unforgiving for those who deviate from this practice.

Additionally, three interrelated organizational priorities, conceived by military and civilian leaders in the aftermath of World War II, continue to influence profoundly officer personnel practices, despite the fact that they are arguably outdated in the post–Cold War era. First, the army places significant institutional emphasis on maintaining its mobilization capability.¹⁵ The army began World War II with an officer corps that was not only too small but too old.[16] To avoid repeating this mistake, it sought to develop a core of well-trained officers at all levels able to serve as operational commanders in case it needed to expand rapidly in the future (Rostker et al. 1993, 3–8).[17] This logic still persists in the army today, despite the growing reliance placed on reserve forces (with their own complement of officers) and the fact that future wars are increasingly likely to be "come as you are," over and done with before there is an opportunity to mobilize conscripts or reserves.[18]

The "generalist" ideal also remains a powerful tradition and significantly influences the design of the officer management system. This also springs from the army's World War II experience when it was observed that "broad-gauged" officers, rather than specialists, coped better when thrust into unforeseen roles (Hauser 1984, 452). The generalist ideal is therefore grounded in the aforementioned notion that gifted operational commanders could fulfill most officer roles throughout the army and that they should be exposed to a variety of command and staff assignments as they advanced through the ranks. While OPMS attempted to alter this tradition by placing greater emphasis on specialization by creating "many roads to the top," generalist career patterns remain distinct criteria for promotion (Strand 1993, 121). The army's reluctance to acknowledge or accept the challenge of a wider, more demanding body of relevant professional knowledge is in distinct contrast to the specialization that has evolved in other professions.

Finally, officer management and development are greatly affected by the army's up-or-out system and the institutional emphasis placed on a young and vigorous officer corps. This priority affected not only the way the army downsized but also the way it develops its officer corps. Legislated guidance on promotion timing (and the mandatory curtailment of officers' careers) cramps the officer development sequence, forcing officers to race through their development requirements at each rank in order to be fully qualified for promotion to the next rank.[19] While DOPMA legislation is outside the army's control, "youth and vigor" is also a priority the army's leadership has supported, and sometimes enthusiastically embraced, over the past decade. As with the other post–World War II insights, however, youth and vigor is arguably no longer an appropriate criterion for manning the modern military. Yet, if one compares the officer career management system put in place in 1948 with that which exists today there are striking similarities.[20] While there is still some justification for considering mobilization capability, generalist career patterns, and youth and vigor, an officer management system founded primarily on these principles is inappropriate in the post–Cold War era.

Furthermore, the army has contributed to the dysfunctional aspects of this management system by taking the notion that "leaders are made and not born" to unhealthy extremes. Over the past several decades, the army has created an officer professional development model guided by the notion that a predetermined set of experiences is optimal for "building" future leaders.[21] This logic has resulted in an increasingly rigid and unforgiving management system in which officers must adhere with great precision to career "templates" and timelines during each phase of their careers to remain competitive for promotion. The army even publishes schematic diagrams showing ideal career patterns, which suggests that to deviate from these traditional patterns is to decrease the quality of an officer's professional experience and therefore to limit his or her career potential. The current system allows little latitude for the officer of exceptional talent to rise to the top without having done all the things that the "prototypical" career pattern requires. And promotion boards reinforce the importance of strict adherence to this progression. It is alarming to think that an Eisenhower or a Marshall, who both had somewhat nontraditional career patterns, would be unlikely to be successful in today's army (Strand 1993, 132).

It is understandable that as the number of opportunities for key development positions has decreased during downsizing, so too has the willingness of career-minded junior and mid-career officers to test uncharted waters in making their career choices. Increased competition for key "branch-qualifying" jobs has contributed to careerism, attenuated cohesion, and stifled initiative. The effects of downsizing are troubling because they have significant implications for the army's current effectiveness. Even more disturbing, however, is the effect that downsizing will have on successive generations of future army leaders. If these patterns persist, the next several generations of leaders are likely to be less diverse collectively, as well as within their individual career patterns, than the leaders of today. Future battalion commanders will have spent significantly less time in key development assignments than their predecessors, as a relatively larger number of officers are rotated through a decreasing number of operational development opportunities. Moreover, it is increasingly less likely that future army leaders will have attended full-time civilian graduate schools (particularly in the hard sciences) or have served in fellowships or trained with industry. They will be less likely to have worked closely with, or studied among, their civilian contemporaries. As Sarkesian writes: "Nothing could be more dangerous to military professionalism than to develop a world view that is unidimensional, omni-competent, and limited in its intellectual scope" (1981, 189). It is not unreasonable to conclude that this observation will likely apply to the next generation of army leaders, or even more likely, to the leaders of the army after next.

Reform for the Twenty-First Century

The problems that exist in today's army are due at least partially to forces outside its control. Regardless of their causes, however, these problems will not be solved by others. Moreover, they will require the army to respond in a manner that is most difficult for a large organization—through self-generated change. How should officer management practices be reformed, not only to address the immediate aftereffects of downsizing but also to prepare better army leaders for the post–Cold War era? What should army leaders do to strengthen professionalism within the officer corps in the short run and modify the officer management system in the long run? And what is the desired role of civilian policymakers—in Congress and the Department of Defense—in addressing these very serious questions?

Reprofessionalization

Recently army leaders have begun to recognize the devastating effects of downsizing on military professionalism and to address these problems with surprising and admirable candor. In a February 1996 article in the journal *Military Review*, Chief of Staff Dennis Reimer conceded publicly that micromanagement, careerism, and a zero-defects mindset are among the unfortunate side effects of the turmoil created by the downsizing of the army (1996, 9). Obviously, recognizing that such problems exist is the first important step toward correcting them. (Indeed, the army's leadership should make an even greater effort in the future to convey its sensitivity to the special problems and uncertainties brought about by downsizing.) Despite this recognition, however, the army has taken little action thus far to arrest the decline in professionalism or to modify existing officer management practices. Further, the changes that are likely to result from current reform efforts are too cautious, too static, and too shortsighted to overcome the army's current problems or to meet the challenges of the post–Cold War era.

One of the paradoxes of change is that trust among juniors and seniors alike is hardest to establish when you need it the most (Duck 1993, 115). This observation accurately describes the army's downsizing dilemma. Since 1989, the "ground rules" concerning opportunity, stability, and security have changed continually, and this has eroded trust within the officer corps. Officers are less trusting of one another, of civilian leaders in Congress and the administration, and of the army's leadership—what it tells them and how it evaluates, assigns, and promotes them. Declining professionalism is the outcome of this loss of trust. Yet, trust is what is needed most during this time of extraordinary organizational change.

As a first step toward addressing this problem, the army's leadership should assess the indirect effects of downsizing on the officer management system, focusing on those aspects of the professional climate cited above.[22] Armed with this assessment, it should take steps to "reinstitutionalize" the officer corps by stressing traditional military values. It should also seek to broaden the definition of professionalism and success by introducing some modest changes into current officer management practices.[23] As in the early 1980s, when the army and the other services undertook like-minded institution-building efforts to counter a perceived increase in occupational tendencies over the previous decade (Moskos 1988, 23), the army should now renew its efforts in this area to counter the ill effects of downsizing. From their "bully pulpits," army leaders (civilian and military) should articulate the distinctive characteristics of the military organization and profession. In this time of uncertainty, they must clarify the meaning and importance of military professionalism and reinforce selfless service and absolute integrity. They should emphasize an officer corps ethos that is nation-centered, not organization-centered; mission-centered, not career-centered; group-centered, not individual-centered; and service-centered, not work-centered (Cotton 1988, 53). Recent articles in military journals by senior army generals addressing these issues are indications that the leadership is moving in this direction (Reimer 1996; Stroup 1996).

But army leaders must not deceive themselves that such efforts are sufficient, for they have been only marginally successful in the past and are likely to be similarly so today. The army leadership must also broaden the notion of professionalism and modify entrenched assumptions about the definition of a successful military career. Because the "management of violence" is perceived throughout the army to be the military professional's distinctive competence, officers are more unwilling than ever to deviate from muddy boots career patterns and the quest for command. Moreover, as the army has attempted to "qualify" as many officers as possible for command, it has inadvertently heightened turbulence by rotating officers at an accelerating pace. This has undermined the professional development of future commanders by significantly reducing the amount of time they spend in key preparatory assignments.

These outcomes are telling indications that the narrow conception of professionalism on which the army has relied in the past is insufficient to describe what is actually required of a modern fighting force in the post–Cold War era. Certainly combat expertise is the single most vital skill for the officer corps, but this should not exclude all the other skills essential to the present and future army. Obviously, members of the officer corps who are not commanders but instead serve as staff officers or who step off the muddy boots track altogether to become foreign area officers, permanent faculty members at West Point or at the other service schools, acquisition officers, and the like make a crucial contribution to the army's short-term and long-term effectiveness, and ultimately to its fighting power. While its leaders acknowledge this is the case, the army's institutional priorities—as demonstrated by who gets promoted, where the most highly touted officers are assigned, and the perceptions held by the majority of officers—belie this assertion.

Along these same lines, the army should make a concerted effort to redefine success for career military officers as something other than simply selection for battalion command. There continues to be a commonly held belief within the officer corps that "to lead is to command." But this longstanding premise is increasingly imprecise in its conception, obscure in its perspective, and inadequate in its application, particularly in the post–Cold War era (Sarkesian 1981, 219). Not only is there a diminishing need for operational commanders, but there is also a growing demand for officers of exceptional quality to serve in assignments distinctly different from "traditional" command. This outmoded conception of what constitutes a "successful" military career accounts for many of the problems the army faces.

The army is likely to see some progress in these two areas by simply ensuring that a greater proportion of qualified officers who do not adhere to strictly traditional career patterns, and who have not served as battalion commanders, are promoted to colonel or higher. The promotion system is a clear-cut demonstration of institutional priorities, and these priorities should be made more transparent. By manipulating the promotion system in this way, the army's leadership will send a message that will not be lost on the officer corps. Over time, officers will modify their behavior and perceptions accordingly. A 1994 RAND study describes this phenomenon well:

> The outcomes of the promotion process . . . are carefully studied in an effort to identify trends and prepare for the future. . . . Career patterns of promoted officers are studied to identify the type of assignments that are prevalent. If certain types of assignments (duty with the reserves, recruiting assignments, ROTC duty, teaching at service schools) are common among selected officers, this type of assignment is considered "career enhancing." The converse is also true. (Thie and Brown 1994, 278)

Finally, the army's leadership should take steps to reduce the rigidity—to loosen the bolts—in the current officer development process. The effects of downsizing have been exacerbated by the fact that officers must satisfy an inflexible set of requirements at each level of professional development in order to be considered "branch-qualified," and, for all practical purposes, to get promoted. Each development requirement is well-conceived and serves an important and useful purpose. Collectively, however, this deluge of requirements is dysfunctional. "Timing," rather than technical skills and expertise, professional maturity, or general knowledge (or cost-effectiveness, for that matter) has become the crucial criterion in officer management. Officers race from one assignment to the next frantically trying to "pass through all the gates" before being considered for the next promotion.

There are three possible approaches to solving these problems. Each poses varying degrees of difficulty and probability of success, and each addresses different aspects of the same problems. First, policymakers in Congress and the administration should modify the existing up-or-out officer management system mandated by the Defense Officer Personnel Management Act to allow for longer and more secure careers. Second, the army should independently make dramatic changes in the Officer Personnel Management System, modifying those aspects of it predicated on outdated assumptions. Third, the army should make minor adjustments in the existing system in order to create added flexibility. The first two will undoubtedly require more time for consideration and implementation than the third. Thus, army leaders should begin with the third course of action immediately and begin on the other two over the next year.

What are these minor adjustments? First, across all branches, the army should expand the types of assignments at each rank that it classifies as mandatory for advancement, or branch-qualifying, particularly at the rank of major.[24] This would reduce competition for these assignments and would lengthen the amount of time that majors who do adhere to "command" career patterns spend in key development jobs. Second, the army should consider adjusting its requirements concerning "utilization" tours following full-time civilian graduate school. As the policy now stands, officers go immediately from graduate school to a tour in which they purportedly utilize their newly acquired skills. This large block of time away from troop assignments not only deters officers from pursuing this option but also creates management dilemmas, as the officers who do attend civilian graduate school attempt to squeeze their other "requirements" into an abbreviated period before being considered for promotion to lieutenant colonel. By allowing officers to defer, or perhaps occasionally waive, the utilization requirement, the army would inject some much-needed flexibility in the current system.

Third, the army should consider waiving occasionally the requirement that officers complete mandatory military schooling before serving in key development assignments.[25] Brigade commanders on every army installation (at the post commander's discretion) should be permitted to select a small number of outstanding junior captains or senior captains and majors (say, 10–20 percent) to serve as company commanders, battalion operations officers, and executive officers.[26] Finally, the army should make promotion boards for lieutenant colonels six to twelve months later, thereby adding some flexibility to the officer development process. Between 1990 and 1995, the army shifted lieutenant colonel promotion boards forward by seven months. This reduced the amount of time officers of this rank had to wait for promotion, but it unnecessarily "cramped" majors in their professional development and contributed to the army's present management dilemmas.

Collectively, these minor adjustments would introduce some diversity and flexibility into career patterns, de-emphasizing the need to follow one, and only one, career path for promotion. These steps would also decentralize marginally the selection process for key development jobs by allowing brigade commanders to identify and reward the army's finest performers and future commanders. These changes would introduce additional efficiency and flexibility into officer management. At best, however, these suggestions are only short-term measures for addressing a number of very serious and deep-seated organizational problems. They do not address the myriad shortcomings in the current Officer Personnel Management System—shortcomings that have become increasingly evident and detrimental during downsizing.

Officer Management Reform

The army's leadership appears to have recognized that current officer management practices are outmoded. In 1996, it initiated an in-depth study of the current officer management system. It is uncertain what the Officer Personnel Management System (OPMS) XXI Task Force charged with this review will recommend. If past history is any guide, however, we might expect to see a relatively conservative set of recommendations that do little to challenge the status quo. Even under the most optimistic of scenarios—one in which a bona fide program for reform is recommended—it is likely to be years before any significant alterations in officer management practices are made. What follows, therefore, is a broad set of recommendations for creating a viable and visionary officer management system for the post–Cold War era.

Officer management consists of strength management, officer evaluation, and professional development. In each of these areas, there is a compelling need for reform. In the case of strength management, the manner in which officer requirements are identified by the army, particularly TDA billets, must be improved. This argument, which was made in chapter 3, is not repeated in detail here. Simply stated, requirements for officers in the army's infrastructure, or TDA, are distorted by the fact that the senior officers who oversee TDA organizations play a significant role not only in identifying their officer requirements but also in authorizing them. Not surprisingly, the system is undisciplined and has placed a heavy burden on the officer management system, particularly during downsizing. Past efforts at reform in this area have failed. But in this period of declining resources, and with the demand for officers in other areas growing rapidly as a result of congressional mandates, the army must rationalize this process and streamline the officer-rich TDA army.

The army wisely refrained from instituting a new officer evaluation report in the midst of downsizing. This decision appears to have been based largely on its post-Vietnam experience, in which the introduction of a new report in the midst of dramatic personnel cuts had a disastrous effect. As downsizing has continued, however, the existing report has become increasingly inflated, contributing to a zero-defects mindset and a less innovative organizational culture. The army has had a new report ready to implement since the late 1980s. The new evaluation system should be implemented in conjunction with the re-professionalization efforts described above.[27]

The army's professional development system is the third component of OPMS. Dramatic changes in the professional development system—the way officers are educated, trained, and assigned—must be made in light of the demands likely to be imposed on the army in the future. The army is likely to require officers who not only are highly trained specialists but are capable of adapting to the uncertainties that inevitably accompany new technologies and unprecedented military missions. The shortcomings in the current system, particularly the institutional emphasis on preparing officers for command, runs counter to this requirement. Moreover, the original intent of OPMS—to establish varied and widely recognized "paths to the top"—has been subverted. This phenomenon was troubling enough during the Cold War, but it will spell disaster for the army in the post–Cold War era. An updated paradigm for officer professional development is needed for the next generation of army leaders, and for the generation after next.

An officer corps of specialists, with expertise across a range of technical and nontechnical areas, is needed for the future. In a recent book, former Chief of Staff Edward C. Meyer and several colleagues make a similar observation, suggesting that the army of the future will require an officer corps of specialists in three areas of expertise—politico-military, manager/technician, and operational command (1995, 225). The role of the professional development system would be to assist officers in gaining specific expertise, while also equipping them with the depth of experience and breadth of perspective necessary for the future. Meyer's proposal is a useful point of embarkation for sketching the skeleton of a future officer corps professional development system. The following pages are not a blueprint for transforming the army but rather a construct for exploring how a significantly modified professional development system might evolve. Clearly, the current system is outmoded, and a new system that develops an officer corps of diverse specialties with multiple paths to the top is absolutely necessary.

The argument for a specialist officer corps, comprising officers not only on a command track but in a host of other specialties as well, has been considered by the army in the past. Indeed, this was one of the primary, though unrealized, objectives of OPMS. Additionally, during the reform movement of the 1970s, a number of authors made recommendations for a "pluralist" officer corps comprised of small core of institutionally oriented command specialists serving mostly in the fighting army and a larger group of occupationally oriented specialists serving mostly in the support army (Hauser 1973, 208; Bradford and Brown 1973, 193).[28] Fortunately, effective professional development for the twenty-first century requires nothing quite so bold as dividing the military profession into two parts. Indeed, in retrospect, these past proposals appear somewhat simplistic.[29] What is needed, however, is an institutional and professional framework that allows officers to concentrate during their careers in one of the three broad areas of expertise outlined above. Moreover, rather than explicitly dividing officers into separate categories of traditional military professionals and those with civilian-oriented specialties, an attempt should be made to broaden institutional conceptions of professionalism in recognition of the critical contributions made by each facet of the officer corps.

Ideally, a professional development system consistent with these principles would seek to identify officers for each area of expertise between their fifth and seventh years of service. This is a controversial point for many traditionalists who argue that making this decision so early in an officer's career does not permit the "late bloomer" to demonstrate a strong propensity for command. The obvious response to this argument, of course, is that a downsized Army does not have the luxury of retaining hundreds of unneeded junior and mid-career officers in command career patterns in the hope of discovering the occasional late bloomer.

As currently, officers would be commissioned into basic branches and spend their first two active duty tours as company grade officers in the field army. As is also presently the case, each officer would be required to command a company during this period in order to be branch-qualified.[30] At this point, however, the traditional officer development models would change dramatically. During this initial five years, the army should ruthlessly cull each cohort, as officers will have had ample opportunity to demonstrate specific aptitudes and potential for continued service. Between their fifth and seventh years of service, on the basis of their preferences, academic background, and performance, officers would choose one of the three career tracks—politico-military, manager/technical, and operational command. The majority of officers would be dedicated to the first two career patterns, while a minority (approximately twice the number of officers who ultimately would be selected for battalion command) would be permitted to pursue the command track. The outcome of this concept would be an army in which every field grade officer might legitimately be called a specialist.

The numbers of officers dedicated to each career track should be determined, of course, on the basis of the army's projected needs. Thus, after rationalizing the officer requirements process, the army should strive to code all, or most, field grade officer billets into one of these three specialties, from the general ranks on down. Obviously, such changes would have significant implications for the branch structure and the current specialty codes of the officer corps. The current branches should be reevaluated and expanded, shrunk, or eliminated, depending on the army's present and projected needs. A certain percentage of officers from each branch, depending on the new officer requirements, could logically serve in the three major specialties. There would, for example, be positions for officers from the transportation branch or the engineer branch in the command track, the managerial/technical track, and perhaps even in the politico-military track. The same would hold true for most other branches. Functional areas would fall within one of these three broad specialties, thus the choice of a functional area would be consistent with the choice of a career track.[31]

It would be imperative, of course, to create viable career patterns and a reasonable development sequence within each specialty. As is now the case, there should be ample opportunity for officers in each of the three specialties to serve with increasing responsibility in various positions between their tenth and twentieth years of service. Within the army, politico-military specialists would generally serve on high-level staffs, division level and above. They would also fill the majority of assignments external to the army—as members of joint staffs, interagency groups, congressional liaison teams, State Department staffs, or as military attachés. Managerial/ technical specialists would also have ample field assignments down to the brigade level in the areas of logistics, maintenance, and personnel. Moreover, they would fill the large majority of assignments in these areas as well as in budgeting, procurement, and research and development, and other technical areas in the Pentagon and in other major army headquarters.

Finally, officers in the operational command track would serve on operations staffs at the battalion, brigade, and division levels, thereby avoiding staff assignments only peripherally related to command.[32] Moreover, officers in the operational command track would be primarily responsible for staffing the army's training centers and for serving as evaluators and advisors for the Army National Guard and the Army Reserve. It would also be necessary and important to identify additional points during an officer's career (following battalion command, and prior to attending the War College, for example) in which he or she might change specialties. One option would be to allow successful battalion commanders who have demonstrated a certain expertise to change into the politico-military or managerial/technical track. However, this possibility should only be open to a small percentage of talented officers who have demonstrated the ability to make significant contributions across specialties.

It is foolish to think, of course, that a one-star or two-star general who served admirably as a brigade commander or division commander is, on the basis of that performance alone, prepared or qualified to serve in a senior position in logistics, procurement, or politico-military affairs, yet the army currently makes such assignments routinely.[33] Under this proposal, general officer positions would for the most part be designated for officers within each of the three career tracks. Division and corps commanders and regional commanders in chief (CINCs) would clearly be designated as part of operational command track, while other senior positions on the Joint Staff or Army Staff would fall in the politico-military area. Some general officer billets such as the Chief of Engineers, the Deputy Chief of Staff for Logistics, and the Commanding General of the Army Material Command would be designated as part of the managerial/technical track. Some general officer positions such as Superintendent of West Point, the Commanding General of the Army War College, and the Chief of Staff of the Army should be open to officers from all three.

Of course, in instituting such changes myriad factors must be considered. How should officers be trained and educated? What are the common principles that should guide professional development across all three categories? And, in what areas should professional development models vary significantly? Three issues in particular—flexibility within career patterns, civilian graduate education, and professional military schooling—will be crucial in the future.

Flexible Career Patterns

Flexible career patterns will be crucially important for the next officer corps, and for the officer corps after next. The army must avoid cookie-cutter career patterns at all costs. As Tracy Goss et al. write: "There is an obscure law of cybernetics—the law of requisite variety—that postulates that any system must encourage and incorporate variety internally if it is to cope with variety externally" (1993, 106). The logic of this law applies not only to the career patterns of individual army officers but to the officer corps at large, and it should be a guiding principle for the army as it develops new career patterns for the post–Cold War era. In practice, it implies that an effort should be made to introduce flexibility by allowing officers periodically to serve in assignments and participate in educational opportunities outside traditional career patterns. At first blush, this might seem to contradict the notion that officers of the future should be specialists. On the contrary, however, variety need not imply "generalist" career patterns in which officers rotate through myriad developmental assignments, becoming jacks of all trades and masters of none. Rather, it simply means that no "ideal" career pattern exists.

The idea of permitting (even encouraging) officers to partake in educational opportunities and to serve in assignments outside their specialties (after they have developed their expertise through consecutive assignments and schooling) has certain advantages. It would contribute to cross-fertilization, benefiting the army by introducing expertise and new perspectives into different components of the organization while adding valuable breadth to an officer's outlook. Although such developmental practices might be viewed as frivolous in corporate America, they would be vital to professional development in an organization that places such a high premium on adaptive leadership.

Variance and flexibility in career patterns within each specialty and across specialties will also improve the quality of organizational decisionmaking. Senior leaders would be more likely to bring with them to high-level positions a diversity of views and experiences, thereby enhancing the quality of the decisionmaking process. Organizations in which there is homogeneity in terms of members' social background, ideology, and professional development are more susceptible to "groupthink"—a myopic mode of thought that exists when people, deeply involved in a cohesive "in-group," allow their desire for unanimity to override any motivation to appraise realistic alternatives (Janis 1982). Varied career patterns will help the army avoid the dangers of groupthink throughout its hierarchy.

Historical experience also suggests that officers with somewhat varied career patterns are more successful and more effective army leaders. In a 1950 sample of the army's elite, for example, Janowitz found that 72.5 percent had "adaptive" career patterns, concluding that "most officers who have entered the top one-half of one percent of the hierarchy had complied with conventional career forms, but [have] ... frequently had specialized and innovating experiences which have increased their usefulness to the military profession."[34] Moreover, army leaders who had been most decisive were characterized by pronounced unconventionality in their career patterns (1960, 151, 169). Others have even gone so far as to conclude that the effectiveness of military leaders varies inversely with their exposure to a conventional routinized military career (Davis, as cited in Janowitz 1960, 151). Similarly, military historian Russell Weigley concludes that the adaptability and thoughtfulness among senior military leaders resulting from such unconventionality "constitutes a prime assurance of [the army's] ability to serve the country adequately in an uncertain future" (1984, 554).

By introducing flexibility into officer career patterns, and specifically into officer assignment and promotion policies, the army may also improve the likelihood of successful peacetime innovation. In his book, *Winning the Next War*, Stephen Rosen finds that "peacetime innovation has been possible when senior military officers with traditional credentials ... have acted to create a new promotion pathway for junior officers practicing a new way of war" (1991, 251). In other words, peacetime innovation was successful when senior officers were able to convince bright, young, talented officers that they would be protected—that is, continue to advance to the highest levels of the army—if they veered from traditional career patterns.[35] Flexible career patterns would thus enhance the likelihood of innovation.

Given these findings, the army's leadership should introduce both variety and flexibility into future career patterns. They should not be so rigid or so unforgiving as to discourage completely nontraditional career choices on the part of ambitious and talented officers as they do now. With formalized specialist career patterns, the officer corps will have significantly more time to develop true expertise in their fields. The army should encourage officers to participate periodically in schooling or nontraditional assignments outside designated career paths by ensuring that certain managerial/technical or politico-military assignments are periodically filled with officers from the operational command track, and vice versa. An officer corps made up of individuals with myriad development experiences, disparate intellectual skills and training, and diversified specialties will be best prepared to adapt successfully to the uncertainties of the post–Cold War era.

Full-Time Civilian Graduate School

The army should also incorporate full-time advanced civilian graduate education into the careers of most officers, including those on the operational command track. As retired colonel A. J. Bacevich writes, "American army officers pride themselves on being doers rather than thinkers" (1990, 23). But thinking, which is not mutually exclusive with doing, is arguably more important in a peacetime army. In the past, the army has generally offered full-time civilian graduate training to officers who agreed to serve in specific follow-on positions for which specialized training was purportedly needed (Sarkesian 1981, 179). In the future, full-time civilian graduate schooling for the majority of officers across all three main specialties—including command specialists—and in a range of disciplines, will help create and sustain a vibrant intellectual climate. The merits and drawbacks of full-time civilian graduate schooling have been debated within the army for decades and the particulars of that debate will not be repeated here. There are three reasons why full-time civilian graduate schooling for most officers is a good idea in the post–Cold War era.[36]

First, and most obviously, this will be necessary in an officer corps of specialists—officers with politico-military, managerial/technical, and operational command expertise. In the first two categories, there is a clear need for specialized education in political science, foreign area specialties, international affairs, law, management, science, mathematics, and engineering. Not surprisingly, the army is incapable of providing top-quality education as inexpensively and efficiently as civilian institutions. Civilian graduate schooling is equally valuable for the breadth it provides, particularly for officers who remain on the operational command track. There will be the tendency among many senior officers to exclude combat leaders from civilian schooling, on the argument that they will have neither the time or the need for such a luxury. This would be a terrible mistake. As retired general Andrew Goodpaster writes:

> The effective command of complex military units and organizations remains as much an art as a science. Development of the capacity for exercising command effectively is advanced by studies ranging from history and the understanding of the human condition to ethics and psychology of leadership, before the processes of decision, the capabilities of weapons, the elements of alliance relationships, the thought patterns, culture and doctrine of possible opponents, and the whole gamut of professional military knowledge are even broached. (As quoted in Sarkesian 1981, 184)

Civilian graduate schooling also helps the army to avoid intellectual isolation.[37] The injection of new ideas, combined with heightened competence and broadened perspective, instills a dynamism within the officer corps that the military cannot hope to achieve through purely professional military education (Sarkesian 1981, 132). Moreover, it provides the opportunity for active duty officers to establish relationships and interact (in a nonpolitical) environment with present and future civilian leaders—members of Congress, the media, appointed officials—foreign nationals, and other national and international personages—with whom they are likely to have greater interaction in the post–Cold War era. And as the number of civilians with military experience steadily declines, it is important that future policymakers gain some knowledge of and experience with members of the armed forces.[38] Finally, there is evidence that the promise of army-sponsored civilian graduate schooling is a powerful retention tool, particularly among company grade officers.[39]

In brief, the army should place an even greater emphasis on civilian graduate education in the post-Cold War era than it has in the past. Specialist career patterns will provide officers with the flexibility to attend civilian schools and gaining expertise in their fields will often require them to do so. Civilian education should not be viewed as a luxury, or limited to a certain number of slots annually. Nor should it be rigidly programmed into an officer's career pattern. Officers in all career specialties should be encouraged to attend civilian graduate schools. In many cases officers should be required to do so and in most cases they should be rewarded for doing so.[40]

Professional Military Schooling

Robust intellectual centers, dedicated not only to the professional development of the officer corps but also to the cultivation of ideas about tactics, doctrine, and strategy, will be instrumental in creating a vibrant and visionary peacetime army. The army's intellectual community—service schools, operational training centers, and laboratories—should receive high priority, not only in terms of financial resources (within budget limitations) but also in terms of the quality of the officers assigned to it. The army's experience in the period leading up to World War II reinforces the importance of military intellectual centers during peacetime. Despite dissatisfaction over slow promotions, perennial unhappiness over poor pay, and chronic low morale, the army retained and maintained a vibrant, versatile, and extraordinarily talented officer corps. Many attribute this success to the institutional emphasis placed on professional education and the core of outstanding officers who served on the faculties of the army's professional schools during the interwar period (1918–1941). Some of the army's most illustrious historical figures—Marshall, Eisenhower, and Patton, for example—were assigned to the Infantry School, the Command and General Staff College, the War College, and Army Industrial College and "formed a self-conscious elite" that proved instrumental to the army's success in World War II (Miller 1973, 47). Similarly, some have attributed the army's smashing success in the Gulf War to the professional schooling received by a generation of senior officers in the 1970s and 1980s (Kitfield 1991).

With these experiences in mind, several reforms in the army's professional schooling programs should be considered. First, the army should take steps to overcome the perception (reinforced by the SERB experience) that the faculties at the Command and General Staff College at Fort Leavenworth and the Army War College are "graveyards" in which disenchanted majors, lieutenant colonels, and colonels serve out the final years of their stalled careers. Duty on these faculties should be seen as career-enhancing—not only as an opportunity to mentor and teach the army's future leadership but as a chance for independent research, doctrinal development, and personal reflection.[41] Senior army leaders and personnel assignment officers must both play a role in changing these perceptions by continually emphasizing the importance of such assignments in word and in deed. The most talented officers at every rank should be routinely assigned instructor duty at West Point, the War College, and Leavenworth and regularly promoted from these assignments to positions of higher responsibility.

The professional schooling system will also require rethinking to ensure its integration with a new officer management system. Given an officer corps of specialists, army leaders should consider whether attendance at the Command and General Staff College and the War College is appropriate for every part of the officer corps. If so, how should the curricula be adjusted to meet the joint development needs of these three groups of specialists? If the army were to place added emphasis on civilian graduate schooling, its professional schools would be able to shift their focus toward the military topics relevant to the post–Cold War era and away from such "civilian" subjects as management and political science, which are better taught and learned elsewhere.[42] As Meyer et al. write:

> The military education program has evolved into a very responsive system for preparing officers for combat. It is less effective in preparing them for other challenges they are likely to face.... The sophistication required in many of the "peace"-related roles that our troops will be called upon to perform indicates that [officer] education needs to be more complete if our armed forces are to be successful in these roles." (1995, 225)

With this in mind, there will undoubtedly be a need to modify the curricula of the Command and Staff College and the War College. While an initial phase of instruction focusing on subjects common to all three career tracks—ethics, leadership, and military history, for example—would still be plausible, there would also be a need for separate sequences of course work, projects, and independent study, with supporting faculty in each. In the event that the army decides that attendance at CGSC or the War College is no longer appropriate for certain groups of officers, it must take steps to ensure that cohesiveness within the officer corps, which is reinforced through the professional schooling system, is maintained.

Summary

These changes would create an officer corps with true and enduring expertise. Field grade officers would be required to serve in consecutive assignments in their designated fields. A substantial reduction in the number of officers on the "command track" would mitigate the unhealthy competitiveness and careerist tendencies that now exist. This approach would permit the army to extend the period that officers spend in key command, staff, and technical assignments, and to reduce turbulence, as officers would no longer be required to change locations or assignments so frequently.

With this approach, the operational commanders in the military after next would be more seasoned, having had the opportunity to develop "warfighting skills" throughout a career of tough, sequential, operational assignments. The same would be true for officers serving in politico-military and managerial/technical career patterns. The army would add significant flexibility to officer management by separating officers into distinct specialist patterns earlier in their careers. As a consequence, an officer's career progression would be pliant enough, for example, to permit twelve to twenty-four months of full-time civilian graduate schooling, as well as occasional assignments outside traditional career patterns without fear of permanent damage to long-term career prospects. In short, this approach will develop army leaders appropriate for the twenty-first century—a corps of officers with expertise in a range of technical and nontechnical skills, but adaptable and sophisticated enough to function effectively amidst the complexities and uncertainties of future military operations.

John Kotter and James Heskett observe that in any organization "who gets promoted says more about real values than any mission statement or credo" (1992, 144). This is true of the army. Formal and widely publicized modifications to army promotion policy will be necessary if such revolutionary changes are to be accepted and lasting. The army must deliver on promises of equal opportunities for advancement to the highest levels if it is to attract the best young officers into all three specialties.[43] Undoubtedly, the logic of this approach will be lost on many senior military leaders who are products of the current system and cling tenaciously to outdated conceptions of military professionalism and officer development. Likewise, despite the army's assurances, junior officers will be reluctant at first to strike out on managerial/technical or politico-military career patterns for fear that promised advancement opportunities will not materialize. Initially, it is likely that the army will be required to assign a certain percentage of each officer cohort (depending on officer requirements) to each of these three career tracks.[44]

With time, however, as these career patterns are established and refined, and as officers in each specialty climb steadily to the highest echelons of the army, anxiety will subside, each career track will be viewed as credible, and a more healthy and vital professional climate will prevail:

> With equal opportunities for advancement in a command, staff or other specialized career, there would be no stigma attached to whatever path an officer took—in concert with the needs of the army, of course, and the army could build pools from which qualified, motivated officers could be pulled for specific requirements requiring specific backgrounds. In that way, the army will have modern versions of the Pattons and Eisenhowers we require.
>
> (Meyer et al. 1995, 225)

Regardless of promotion opportunities, officers in the command track will remain the army's elite. This is inevitable and appropriate. However, the army will only achieve the much-needed balance of "talent" across the officer corps by equitably distributing promotion opportunities among the three career tracks.

Congress and the Department of Defense: Legislative Reform

Civilian leaders too must take steps to build an officer corps for the twenty-first century. Most important, they must become more sensitive to the strains imposed on the army officer corps by incremental and prolonged downsizing. The army's projected size has steadily been chipped away as the political and budgetary landscapes have grown increasingly treacherous. After having already been cut by 30 percent, the army's "final" target troop strength has declined further since 1993, from 535,000 to 520,000 to 495,000, with further cuts on the horizon. This is not to suggest that significant cuts in endstrength were not necessary, or that additional cuts may not be warranted in the future. It is clear, however, that as policymakers in Congress and the Department of Defense have haggled over endstrength, numbers of divisions, modernization dollars, and readiness, they have overlooked the bonds of trust, sacrifice, and respect that atrophy as those in uniform look around and wonder who will be next. These bonds are important in any organization, but they are essential for an effective fighting force. By prolonging the uncertainty of downsizing, policymakers have undermined the faith of the professional officer corps in its leaders, weakened their confidence that successful, productive careers are possible, and engendered attitudes and behaviors antithetical to a professional volunteer army. Civilian leaders must factor the devastating effects of personnel cuts on these "intangibles" into future downsizing decisions.

Additionally, administration policymakers and congressional leaders must replace the existing officer management legislation (DOPMA) with rules and regulations more appropriate to the downsized military services. The possibility of such reform has already been raised. Two recent RAND studies—a 1993 retrospective assessment of DOPMA and a 1994 analysis of future officer career management systems—found substantial shortcomings in the current system and presented various alternatives (Rostker et al. 1993; Thie and Brown 1994).[45] Among other things, the RAND work confirmed that DOPMA was far better suited for periods of growth and stability than for the period of dramatic personnel reductions carried out between 1990 and 1996, though it also noted that even in periods of stability the legislation had shortcomings (Rostker et al. 1993, 69). The numerous waivers and special provisions that Congress authorized to manage officer cuts during this period are testimony to DOPMA's inflexibility. Moreover, DOPMA is based on the assumption that there is a need for uniformity in promotion opportunity timing and grade structure across the services. While uniformity is an understandable objective, it fails to account for differences in service cultures, missions, and officer requirements. Third, DOPMA was designed with the intent of controlling officer growth and "grade creep." Thus, a sliding-scale grade table included in the legislation is used to control officer inventory directly, as the officer requirements generated by the services are generally, and understandably, not believed (This may be one of the few cases in which deeper congressional involvement and oversight is justified.) Still, the DOPMA approach fails to account for the dynamic nature of officer requirements, which may grow or diminish over time, particularly during periods of dramatic organizational change.

In addition, the 1981 DOPMA legislation codified in a single act a combination of beliefs and assumptions based on the military's experiences in World War II. The up-or-out principle and mandatory early retirement, in particular, reflect the desire to ensure a young and vigorous fighting force. This assumption, in particular, has been outdated for decades:

Military manpower policies have been based on the claim that "youth and vigor" are by far the most important qualifications for military service. But how valid is this claim? The military has opted for a youthful force, judging it is better able to endure the hardships of military duty and hence more effective in maintaining defense readiness.... The relationship in which age is a proxy for physical fitness is neither as clear, nor as simple as that implied by past and current military manpower policies.... The requirement for youthfulness and vigor is neither overwhelming nor applicable to all of the jobs in the military services (Binkin 1986, 24, 28).

The benefits of the up-or-out approach and mandatory early retirement are few. These policies ensure a constant flow of "new blood" through the officer corps, arguably providing officers with incentives to perform at high levels throughout their careers. This approach also ensures generous advancement opportunity at every level, through a process of forced attrition. The disadvantages of these policies, however, are equally apparent. The current system is inordinately expensive, as highly trained and effective officers are continually discharged from active duty, despite the fact that they have the ability to provide valuable service for years, sometimes decades, after retirement.[46] Moreover, shortened military careers crowd the officer professional development process and increase turbulence in the officer corps. As one reformer writes: "The chief obstacle to ... meaningful improvement in [the] development of officers is the short and hurried nature of the military career."[47] Finally, as the 1994 RAND study concludes: "The forced-attrition mechanism diminishes long-term commitment" among officers (Thie and Brown 1994, 78). These phenomena were magnified across the entire officer corps by downsizing.

The creation and implementation of a new officer career management system will obviously require much time and research as well as numerous congressional hearings and negotiations before it becomes a reality. However, the army's current management dilemmas and the insightful and comprehensive work done by RAND suggest several fundamental features that should be part of any new system. First, there should be some variation of "up and stay." While it may be desirable to have a high turnover of officers during the first ten years of service to whittle the corps down to an appropriately sized career force, the large majority of those who remain after that point should be retained for an entire career. Second, army careers should be extended for officers with the capacity for continued service to thirty-five to forty years, though under such a system it would be crucial to develop mechanisms for selectively weeding out poor performers. Third, defense planners should consider a more portable retirement system, under which officers and enlisted members could take with them their accrued benefits regardless of the stage of their careers when they depart the army.

These changes would yield many improvements over the current system. First, the proposed system would be more efficient. The services would no longer be forced to separate competent, highly trained officers simply because they had not been promoted. Retention could be solely performance-based. And, indeed, it would be crucially important to develop an effective mechanism for separating retirement-eligible officers who are no longer productive while retaining those who continue to make an important contribution. In addition, these changes would lengthen the period that officers would have to develop and utilize the specialized skills gained throughout successive assignments in their specialties, with a far greater overall return on investment for the army. By extending officers' careers and permitting retention without the necessity for continued promotion, the incentives for careerism and ticket punching will be reduced dramatically. Additionally, the anxiety many officers feel late in their careers as they approach mandatory retirement and the uncertain prospects of civilian employment at middle age will decline.[48]

Third, there is no reason why the grade structure for the services in the future necessarily needs to be a pyramid. For example, the grade structure could be designed like an aircraft carrier—the junior grades are below the decks, the career force begins with the bulge of majors on the carrier deck, and the higher grades of lieutenant colonel, colonel, and general are represented by the narrower superstructure in the center of the ship (Thie and Brown 1994, 194). Admittedly, promotion timing and opportunity would be less certain with alternative grade structures, but this might cause the importance of these variables to diminish. This is a trade-off that should be considered. Finally, legislative reform must take place sooner rather than later. There is no time to waste—officer management reform should be a top priority of both Congress and the current administration.

Leadership for the Military after Next

Some will call these recommendations a "radical" reform agenda. However, the army's current officer management system, and the legislation that governs it, are too antiquated to create the kind of specialized and adaptable officer corps needed for the future. Moreover, the rigidity of the current system has exacerbated the undesirable effects of downsizing. A new system is clearly needed to confront these shortcomings. If "radical" means ridding the army's personnel management system of outmoded assumptions and worn out ideas, then this agenda is radical indeed.

The recommendations I make are relatively straightforward. The army should modify its officer management system, particularly its current professional development model. During their first five to seven years of service, officers should be assigned to one of three career tracks—politicomilitary, managerial/technical, or operational command. Through sequential assignments, military schooling, and civilian graduate education, officers will develop true expertise in these specialties. In the post–Cold War era, the army should also place added emphasis on maintaining flexible career patterns, avoiding at all costs cookie-cutter approaches to professional development. Likewise, full-time civilian graduate schooling should be a top priority for all officers, even those in the operational command track. Additionally, the army should take steps to build an intellectually vital social architecture within its professional schooling system. Finally, Congress should write, debate, refine, and pass new officer management legislation permitting longer careers based on the principle of "up and stay."

None of these propositions is completely new. Variations of each have been debated inside and outside the army for decades. During the reform movement in the early 1970s, a number of friendly and some not-so-friendly critics offered numerous recommendations for the improvement of officer management and professional development to correct the professional malaise the officer corps suffered during and after the Vietnam War. In the post–Cold War era, the army faces a somewhat different problem. While it is true that professionalism within the officer corps has been strained by downsizing, an equally pressing challenge is to modify the army's officer management system to ensure it develops the kinds of specialized, adaptable leaders who will be needed in the future.

The ideas proposed here are ambitious. Even if civilian and military leaders supported them, time would be needed for their implementation. The army, like any large bureaucratic organization, will be slow to transform itself, particularly in areas as sensitive as officer management. It is more likely that there will be significant resistance among many senior military leaders to some, perhaps all, of these proposals. An increased emphasis on specialization, longer careers, an up-and-stay career system, and a broader conception of military professionalism all run counter to deeply entrenched institutional norms. In addition, these recommendations have some very legitimate dangers associated with them.

First, some might argue that it is impossible to draw such definitive conclusions or make such radical recommendations on the basis of one research effort. However, the attitudinal and behavioral problems I observe are consistent with the findings of studies conducted by the Army Strategic Fellows Program and the Department of the Army Inspector General in 1994. Likewise, the *1995 Army Assessment*, an army-wide survey focusing specifically on this issue, reportedly portrays a professional climate even more alarming than that which is described in this book (Reimer 1996). The army's leadership has already begun to acknowledge these problems. It is time now to do something about them.

Along the same lines, some senior officers and civilians contend that the undesired effects of downsizing will subside once stability has returned to the personnel system, making a reform agenda unnecessary. While this contention is not totally incorrect, it grossly underestimates the damage already done. Most of the problems described here will linger even if personnel reductions were to end once and for all (an unlikely prospect until at least 2000 and beyond). Following the Vietnam War, it took the better part of a decade to correct similar problems in the officer corps (Dunnigan and Macedonia 1993). In any case, the army does not have the luxury of waiting for stability to implement organizational change, for the current officer management system is simply inappropriate for developing officers to meet the challenges of the twenty-first century. This assertion holds regardless of the state of professionalism within the officer corps.

It might also be argued that specialized career patterns will pose significant challenges for the army's leadership, perhaps creating problems that outweigh their benefits. There is a legitimate concern, for example, that subdivisions of this sort would destroy the homogeneity and peer group associations among officer cohorts, creating an "us-them" mentality within the officer corps.[49] In addition, critics would be correct in observing that developing and educating an officer corps of specialists would be costly, an expense some will surely say the army cannot afford.[50] Despite these disadvantages, they are far outweighed by the benefits of a specialized officer corps.

Experts in politico-military affairs, management and technology, and operational command are needed if the army is to be successful when faced by the myriad roles it will be expected to play in the future. Intellectual capital of this sort will be as important as the next generation of high-tech weaponry to the army's effectiveness, perhaps more so. In addition, the costs of these recommendations for the army's personnel budget would be less than one might at first believe, for there are efficiencies to be gained as well. With specialist career patterns, it will no longer be necessary to rotate officers as regularly through branch-qualifying assignments (thereby reducing the frequency of moving expenses). Moreover, with a corps of officers dedicated to particular specialties, the overall number of officers required, and their respective costs, are likely to decrease, particularly if the army streamlines its officer requirements process and Congress approves longer careers and a substantially less expensive up-and-stay management system.[51]

Fourth, some will argue that three specialist career tracks and an added emphasis on civilian schooling will undermine the army's warrior ethos, diverting the officer corps' focus from its single most important mission—fighting and winning the nation's wars. This is a legitimate concern—one that requires the utmost consideration—but this problem, too, is avoidable. It is true that with many paths to the top, significantly more officers in what might be considered nonwarrior career patterns will become senior army leaders. This is both sensible and necessary. Just as it would be unreasonable for the executive ranks of Ford Motor Company to be filled exclusively by managers from the manufacturing division, so too is it nonsensical to suggest that it is appropriate to lead a modern army solely with operational commanders. At the same time, there are very real dangers in creating an army managed by senior officers too far removed from the point of the spear to have an intuitive feel for the needs and appropriate priorities of a military organization.

For this reason, operational commanders should, and undoubtedly will, continue to dominate at the highest levels of the organization and many (though not all) of the army's most promising young leaders should be assigned to the operational command career track. But the army must strike a more appropriate balance between the various types of military leaders that dominate at each level of its hierarchy. The army has always had senior officers who could be roughly categorized as politico-military generals, military managers, and operational commanders. This proposal simply formalizes the developmental process for each. The first two are likely to gain some influence at the expense of the third, but they will not and should not displace operational commanders as the "elite" in the organization. Additionally, within the command track, the army's warriors should have the opportunity through longer, sequential, and demanding troop assignments to become truly proficient operational commanders. In short, the army's warriors should be afforded the opportunity to focus predominantly on fighting and winning future wars. These points notwithstanding, the army's senior leaders should make maintaining the warrior ethos, throughout the officer corps, in reality as well as symbolically a top priority during the transition to a new system. Strong leadership in this area will be crucial to the army's future success.

There may also be criticisms that the proposed officer development process devotes too much energy and too many resources to developing in junior and mid-career officers the talents or skills only needed by the very few who will be promoted to the highest levels of the army. According to a retired general of an earlier era, "Problems arise when too much attention is given the qualifications a man must have in order that he may be considered for selection to general officer rank, rather than to the experience needed in the less exalted ranks of service" (Smith 1971, 28). In the post–Cold War era, however, specialized expertise, political sophistication, and adaptability are needed at all levels of the army hierarchy. The infantry captains charged with monitoring compliance with the Dayton Peace Accords in Bosnia, the staff officers who recently planned humanitarian relief operations in northwestern Iraq, and the lieutenant colonels overseeing the development of the next generation of army weapons systems, for example, all must make rapid and independent decisions in an environment far more complicated and politically volatile than their predecessors. Such challenges will be even more numerous and complex in the future.

Finally, some might argue that this reform agenda—particularly the politico-military career track and the emphasis on civilian graduate education—will ultimately "politicize" the officer corps. In this case, politicization refers to partisan politics—activities that subordinate the interests of the country to the parochial interests of the army or particular individuals, thereby undermining military professionalism. This view is consistent with traditional conceptions of professionalism, which hold that civilian control is best maintained by keeping the military separate from society (Huntington 1957). In contrast to the traditional view, however, this proposal presumes a more mature conception of professionalism, recognizing that it has a political dimension. Military professionals should not become politicians, but in the post–Cold War era they must be more astute, more knowledgeable about and sensitive to the political imperatives of domestic and international societies than ever before. As Bacevich writes: "Those who protest the danger of soldiers becoming involved in politics miss the point.

The exclusion of soldiers from politics does not guarantee peace. It only guarantees that those who command armies in wartime will be politically obtuse" (1990, 19).

In conclusion, this chapter is a call for action. Developing exceptional leaders for the next military, and for the military after next, will require sustained and visionary action. By creating three career tracks—politico-military, managerial/technical and operational command—the army will be better able to prepare officers for the uncertainties of this new era. Officers will have the opportunity to develop the expertise needed to maneuver within increasingly tenuous political situations, manage increasingly complex military organizations, and lead soldiers successfully in increasingly complicated and diverse military operations. Moreover, this approach will be far more efficient because officers will no longer be herded through a rigid and outdated professional development process. Finally, by modifying officer management legislation, congressional leaders may once and for all free the military services of outmoded post–World War II planning assumptions.

Instituting these changes will be difficult. It will require dramatic changes in the way military and civilian leaders think about officer management. Many of these changes will be particularly difficult for the army to make because they conflict with deeply entrenched elements of its institutional culture. Moreover, they will require the transfer of resources for specialized training, civilian graduate schooling, and nontraditional military assignments, the benefits of which are unlikely to be understood by greenshade budgeteers. Although change will be difficult and perhaps unpopular, it is nonetheless necessary. The complexity and difficulty of the tasks ahead are no excuse for inaction.

Epilogue
The Army's Future Course

> Unlike steel, an army is a most sensitive instrument and can easily be damaged; its basic ingredient is men, and to handle an army well, it is essential to understand human nature.
> —Field Marshal Bernard L. Montgomery

This book is a tale of two armies. It is a story of the corporate army, which unsuccessfully resisted deep reductions in its budget and endstrength, cuts even deeper than those experienced by the other services. In response to this political mandate, senior army leaders developed and implemented downsizing with an admirable blend of compassion and precision. But this book is also the story of the muddy boots army—a corps of officers, most stationed far from the Pentagon—who have been dramatically and unfavorably affected by downsizing. Prolonged and incremental personnel cuts have undermined the professionalism of the officer corps. Officer morale, career expectations, and organizational commitment have decreased sharply. Competition and careerism within the officer corps are on the rise, and initiative and cooperation are in decline. Downsizing has also affected the career patterns and choices of officers, particularly junior officers, in insufficiently recognized but terribly detrimental ways. It would be an overstatement, perhaps, to say that America's army is today in crisis. But make no mistake: these trends, alarming in and of themselves, are even more so if seen as harbingers of darker days to come.

Who Is to Blame?

If one accepts the seriousness of these trends, an obvious question is whether they might have been mitigated or avoided altogether, and, if so, then who is to blame? Retrospective assessments like this should be taken for what they are. With the luxuries of hindsight and nonparticipation, it is always easier to understand and identify shortcomings or oversights in a decisionmaking process that was at the time a thicket of uncertainty, competing opinions, and incomplete information. Such assessments are useful, however, for understanding how and why things happened and how similar problems might be avoided in the future.

The simplest way to have avoided the undesirable effect of downsizing is not to have downsized at all. But strategic, political, and budgetary forces converged to ensure that large, rapid cuts in personnel were not only necessary but inevitable. Moreover, one might argue that the negative effects of downsizing (no matter how undesirable) are far outweighed by the benefits of defense savings over the last five years. Thus, the more reasonable question is whether military or civilian leaders could have downsized differently to minimize these negative effects.

The army's leadership participated in the downsizing process in several distinct ways. At the political level, it attempted to influence the magnitude and pace of personnel cuts, as well as the content of legislation aimed at easing the burden of downsizing. Army leaders were largely ineffective with respect to the first of these tasks for a variety of reasons, most of which were outside their control. It is reasonable to ask, however, whether the army might have avoided the incremental nature of post–Cold War cutbacks by yielding to inevitably lower endstrengths earlier in the negotiation process. Theoretically, such a move would have yielded significant cost savings up front while at the same time minimizing the uncertainty of downsizing for the officer corps. However, this course of action might have placed the army in even graver jeopardy, for a perverse logic exists within the Department of Defense which suggests that acknowledging the possibility of cuts becomes a self-fulfilling prophecy. If the services fail to resist loudly proposed cutbacks, it is often perceived that they are not being cut enough or that the cutbacks have been unequally distributed. And, as shown in chapter 4, the morale, confidence, and trust of the officer corps depend on its perceptions about how vigorously and effectively army leaders are advocating its interests. Thus, it is understandable that army leaders resisted further cuts in endstrength at every turn, despite the high probability that additional cuts would follow.

At the organizational level, the army downsized with care and took extensive measures to mitigate the undesirable effects of personnel cuts. Generous separation benefits, authorized by Congress but implemented by the army, eased the pain of the cutbacks. While seeking to minimize involuntary separations, army leaders treated those forced to leave with dignity and compassion. The army has been slow to acknowledge or address the effects of downsizing and to reform its existing officer management system, though at best these steps would have reduced but not prevented the problems that plague its officer corps. In some ways, the army surely could have done better, but in many ways it certainly might have done much worse.

Does this then imply that the Department of Defense or Congress is to blame? Given the necessity for substantial personnel reductions, what might each have done to manage downsizing more wisely? The incremental nature of downsizing has been particularly devastating, aggravating unrest and the loss of trust within the army officer corps. Might civilian leaders have decided upon and adhered to a stable downsizing target from the beginning? Such stability would have allowed army leaders to chart a steadier course with personnel reductions. But reductions in the army's budget and endstrength in the years immediately after the Cold War were destined to be drawn out over the better part of a decade for several reasons. Downsizing began in earnest with the 1989 end of the Cold War, but America's stunning victory in the Gulf and the breakup of the Soviet Union showed the U.S. military to be far and away the most potent military in the world, reinforcing the perception that America's military forces could be dramatically reduced without compromising leadership abroad or security at home. At the same time, growing public discord over U.S. involvement in U.N. operations made the continuation of large standing forces increasingly suspect.

Also, as already noted, defense spending has always been disadvantaged, often gutted, in the transition from war to peace. As public support for defense spending wanes, Congress tends to reallocate funding from defense to domestic programs, regardless of strategic requirements. The rising deficit and increased spending on entitlement programs placed added pressures on policymakers to reduce defense spending in the post–Cold War era (Ippolito 1994, 32). This ensured that the plans/resources gap, a perpetual characteristic of any peacetime army, was particularly acute from 1990 to 1996, forcing policymakers to make difficult trade-offs across and within the military services. The fact that a relatively large percentage of the army's budget is dedicated to personnel and force structure ensured that as budget pressures increased, these categories would be repeatedly subjected to cutbacks.

Furthermore, the period explored by this book was divided by a presidential election. There was a high probability of additional cuts in the size of the army in a second Bush administration, but cuts became more certain with the election of Bill Clinton. The plans/resources gap was further exacerbated by Clinton's promises to find substantial savings in defense while making only marginal reductions in force structure and adopting an ambitious national military strategy. These factors converged to ensure incremental cuts by Congress and the administration in the army's budget and endstrength between 1990 and 1996. As each series of cuts became a reality, additional reductions grew more politically acceptable.

It might have been possible for policymakers to determine the needs of the post–Cold War Army in the several years immediately following the demise of the Soviet Union and stick to those levels over the next decade. This would clearly have mitigated some of the undesirable effects of downsizing. However, it would have required extraordinary foresight on the part of military and civilian leaders and an unprecedented level of cooperation between the two political parties. While it is perhaps not unrealistic to aspire to such standards, it is not surprising that civilian leaders failed to achieve them. That civilian leaders have still been unable to agree on the size, role, and required resources for the post–Cold War army more than seven years after the fall of the Berlin Wall is more distressing and less excusable. The prolonged uncertainty has greatly worsened the effects of downsizing and lies at the root of the army's most serious problems. For this, civilian leaders should be taken to task.

In spite of this criticism, it should be noted that civilian leaders in Congress and both administrations were extraordinarily supportive of the army's downsizing efforts, providing not only legislative and managerial flexibility but also the resources needed to downsize effectively. This sensitivity appears to have been driven by political considerations as much as anything else, but this should not take away from the fact that the civilian leaders have been far more attentive to the difficulties of downsizing than in the past. Voluntary separation incentives, DOPMA relief legislation, and genuine empathy for the difficult task the armed forces faced were instrumental in substantially reducing the burden of downsizing.

In sum, there are no clear-cut villains, no obvious heroes, and only one visible victim in this story. Military and civilian policymakers did reasonably well under trying circumstances. Significant cuts in the size of the army were inevitable and justifiable. In an ideal world, military and civilian leaders would have agreed upon a final downsizing target, allowing the army to map a steadier course. Personnel planners could have developed, publicized, and adhered to a credible downsizing plan, and the effects of downsizing documented here would have been far less severe. Such a possibility, however, was confounded by public opinion, the absence of perfect foresight, the exigencies of world events, and the democratic process.

Some will feel discomfort with the fact that these conclusions are not black or white, that military and civilian leaders are judged to have been neither simply right nor clearly wrong. But to draw such stark conclusions from a process as multifaceted and complicated as the downsizing of the army, while psychologically comforting, would inevitably misrepresent and distort the truth. It is possible both to succeed and fail, to be right and wrong, and to have alarming problems in an organization with no one, really, to blame. This is the case with the downsizing of the army. In retrospect, the army's downsizing is somewhat akin to a Shakespearean tragedy in which the actions of each of the characters collectively are leading toward misfortune, but none of them is able to deviate from these fated steps to escape the pending disaster. The post–Cold War downsizing played itself out on the army's stage, and military and civilian leaders interacted unwittingly to create their own tragedy—the declining professionalism of America's army.

What Should Be Done?

The fact that military and civilian leaders may in some ways be excused for the effects of downsizing in no way absolves them from taking immediate and dramatic action to arrest the decline of the army. For civilian leaders, the challenges are two-fold. Members of Congress and senior officials in the administration should take heed of the reform agenda described in the preceding chapter. Much-needed changes in current officer management should be debated and implemented immediately. We no longer have the luxury, if we ever did, of a legislative framework based on outdated assumptions and incapable of adjusting to the dynamic changes taking place within our armed forces. Additionally, civilian policymakers should encourage the army, and the other services, to think far more creatively about real and sustainable reform in their officer management systems, reform that is needed if the U.S. military is to remain the world's premier fighting force in the next century.

Second, and most important, when faced with military policy decisions, civilian leaders must continually remind themselves that the armed services are living, breathing entities comprising talented, committed Americans, young and old, with hopes, fears, and expectations not unlike their contemporaries in the civilian sector. The health and success of the all-volunteer army depends most on its ability to convince its members that membership is worthwhile. The value these individuals place on membership depends largely on stability in personnel funding and endstrength, which directly affect how secure a military career is likely to be, the pace of promotion, and the abundance of professional development opportunities.

Instability and continued reductions in these areas dampen new recruitment, particularly of officers, breed uncertainty, mistrust, and anxiety, and ultimately undermine military effectiveness. Unlike cutbacks in material goods—weapons, research and development, or infrastructure—prolonged and incremental personal reductions in people diminishes military capability by far more than mere numbers suggest. The effects of downsizing on the intangibles of military effectiveness are costly indeed. To paraphrase Field Marshall Montgomery, an army is a most sensitive instrument. Civilian leaders must handle it with care, for its quality and effectiveness are easily jeopardized.

This conclusion might easily be misunderstood as an argument that the army has been cut too much or that further cutbacks should be absolutely avoided. While some might use this book to support such claims, that is not its primary objective. The principal argument here is that prolonged and incremental downsizing has undermined military effectiveness. This finding by itself should not stand in the way of additional cutbacks in the years ahead. Indeed, this book has only addressed a small part of much larger debates, and using personnel considerations alone to determine the size and structure of the army is equivalent to the tail wagging the dog. Some balance of strategic, budgetary, political, and technological considerations will, and should, continue to drive such decisions.

At the same time, downsizing has been extraordinarily damaging to the army in ways not completely understood, and continued cutbacks are likely to have even more devastating effects. To thoroughly overcome the problems identified by this book, it will be necessary for civilian leaders to consider something paradoxical to the idea of downsizing—terminating personnel reductions altogether and providing some modicum of security, promise, and certainty to the soldiers who remain. As Secretary of Defense Dick Cheney observed in 1992: "The biggest thing we can do for [service members] is to make a decision and then live with it.... That's the quickest way we can restore the overall morale and quality of the force" (Remarks of Secretary of Defense Richard Cheney 1992). Sadly, these words went unheeded. The need for stability, even more pressing today, should be given much weight as policymakers consider additional reductions in the years ahead.

The challenges faced by military leaders are even more daunting. Senior army leaders must restore confidence, trust, and loyalty within an officer corps that has every reason to feel disillusioned and betrayed. Declining morale, career expectations, and organizational commitment combined with growing competition and careerism will, if left unabated, eat away at the heart and soul of America's army. A culture of unforgiving perfection, one that discourages initiative and innovation, will surely continue to undermine that which has historically made the U.S. Army great—aggressive leadership, from top to bottom, combined with cutting-edge tactics and technology. Nothing should be a greater priority to army leaders than arresting these deleterious trends. The re-professionalization efforts recommended in chapter 5 are a necessary first step in this direction, and the reform of the officer management system a second.

Perhaps even more distressing than the immediate effects of downsizing, however, is its impact on successive generations of army leaders. If the patterns described earlier persist, the next several generations of leaders will be less diverse collectively and will have less diverse individual career patterns than the army leaders of today. Future battalion and brigade commanders will have spent significantly less time in key development assignments; fewer generals will have attended full-time civilian graduate schooling (particularly in the hard sciences) or have served in fellowships or trained with industry; senior officers across the corps will be less likely to have worked closely with, or studied among, their civilian contemporaries. One would be hard-pressed to imagine career patterns less appropriate for army officers for the next century.

Addressing these problems will require the kinds of leadership that senior army generals have thus far failed to demonstrate. They are going to have to be more honest with the officer corps about the political and budgetary uncertainties they face and far more sensitive to the deleterious effects that downsizing has already wrought. Lastly, army leaders must be creative in instituting real rather than superficial reform of the officer personnel management system. There are preliminary indications that the army's current review of this system will result in a number of well-intentioned but conservative modifications. This outcome will prove to be a terrible mistake. We are, after all, standing on the threshold of a new millennium. America's army must change profoundly, not only to address the effects of post–Cold War downsizing but also to meet the unpredictable and unprecedented challenges of this new age.

Notes

NOTES TO CHAPTER 1

1. Without political effectiveness, Millett et al. conclude, all other types of effectiveness are potentially jeopardized (1988, 4).
2. Endstrength refers to the overall number of personnel on active duty. This number also includes those individuals in the national guard or reserves who are serving on active duty status as well as West Point cadets.
3. Likewise, downsizing has become commonplace at the state level among fiscally minded governors, mayors, and city managers.
4. One obvious explanation for this is the deep involvement of Congress in officer management. The fact that officers are assigned regularly to the Office of the Secretary of Defense, to the army's secretariat, and as liaisons to Congress may also perpetuate this interest.
5. The army was attentive to planning for demobilization as a result of the debacle following World War I. By spring 1943, Marshall had created a Special Planning Division to prepare the army's personnel and logistical demobilization plans (Trask 1983, 21).
6. "Demobilization of the Army," remarks by General of the Army George C. Marshall, Chief of Staff, to members of Congress, September 20, 1945 (Washington, D.C.: Government Printing Office).
7. Soldiers accrued points for each month of service served overseas, for each medal, and for each child under the age of eighteen.
8. Officer retention was not a significant problem. There was a substantial core of regulars and a military career was held in relatively high regard following the war. In 1947, Congress passed legislation expanding the *regular* officer corps from 25,000 to 50,000.
9. The *Stars and Stripes,* an independent service newspaper, exacerbated this problem by publishing demobilization plans prematurely and inaccurately (Sparrow 1952, 191).
10. At the unit level, personnel readiness is defined as the number, grade, and skill qualifications of the individuals assigned to that unit compared with its authorizations. Personnel readiness may also be gauged in the aggregate by comparing the army-wide authorizations across grades with the operating inventory in those grades.

11. Major General Clair Street to Henry H. Arnold, Commanding General, Army Air Force, October 8, 1945, World War II Demobilization files, U.S. Army Center for Military History.

12. The demobilization officially lasted from July 1953 to June 1955. The overall strength of the army was reduced by 28 percent (Trask 1983, 40).

13. General Maxwell Taylor and Lieutenant General James Gavin also resigned in protest of Eisenhower's defense plan (Weigley 1984, 536).

14. Many Reserve officers were commissioned without having college degrees.

15. See *Oral History of LTG (ret.) George Forsythe 1974*.

16. The army ended 1972 with a shortfall of 36,000 soldiers and only one division fully combat-ready (McNeill et al. 1974, 141).

17. Abrams's short-term objective was to stabilize the army's endstrength at 785,000. In the long term, he wanted to ensure that political leaders could not again commit the army to combat without first calling up the Reserves.

18. The army developed a program called Project Transition in the late 1960s to assist soldiers in making the transition to the civilian workforce. The benefits of this program were questioned, however, and it never gained the full support of the army's leadership (Bradford and Brown 1973, 207).

19. The army downsized over ten thousand junior officers, mostly combat-experienced captains, and only six hundred field grade (major and above) officers (Gabriel and Savage 1978, 160).

20. This was less the case after World War II because General Marshall was generally sympathetic to the need for smaller regular forces coupled with a robust mobilization capability (Huntington 1961, 57).

21. In the years 1945–48, 1953–58, and 1970–75, the army's budget was cut far more dramatically than the budgets of the other services. See *National Defense Budget Estimates for FY 1997* (April 1996, 66–68).

22. It should be noted that political pressures to demobilize personnel more rapidly following World War II made controlled and regulated downsizing untenable.

23. Of course, measures of success in downsizing are less clear in the public sector.

24. In support of this assertion, a 1994 American Management Association study found that 96 percent of the companies surveyed suffered a significant decline in morale (Hickok 1995, 5).

25. Cameron (1994b) studied the effects of downsizing on thirty firms in the U.S. automobile industry between 1987 and 1990.

26. Paradoxically, risk-taking and creativity are arguably needed most in the increasingly competitive marketplace that compelled corporate managers to downsize in the first place.

27. As part of this "rethinking" the organization should conduct an organizational audit to determine the specific people, and kinds of people, that will be crucial to future organizational success.

28. As Wilson writes, these variables are all "vested to an important degree in entities external to the organization—legislatures, courts, politicians, and interest groups" (1989, 115).

29. As already noted, even these measures may not account for some of the long-term effects of downsizing resulting from competence anemia, recruiting difficulties, and the like.

30. The specifics of the 1981 Defense Officer Personnel Management Act are described in chapter 3.

31. Officers of all ranks alternate regularly between assignments in the muddy boots army and assignments in the Pentagon.

NOTES TO CHAPTER 2

1. Memorandum from Lieutenant Colonel Thomas Davis, Chief Army Program Development, to Chief of Staff of the Army, Gordon R. Sullivan, July 12, 1994. Unless otherwise noted, the internal army or Department of Defense documents cited in this chapter are from the Office of the Assistant Secretary of the Army for Manpower and Reserve Affairs or the Army Office of the Deputy Chief of Staff for Personnel.

2. In April 1995, Secretary of Defense William Perry directed the army to cut its endstrength by an additional twenty thousand, to 475,000. The army has resisted this directive, and the cut was delayed until the release of the Quadrennial Defense Review.

3. This cost-cutting mindset was reinforced that same year by the passage of the hard-hitting Gramm-Rudman-Hollings deficit reduction law, which threatened automatic spending cuts if congressional appropriations exceeded specified targets. Because of exemptions for entitlements, Gramm-Rudman had a more severe effect on defense, which accounted for over half of the reductions, though it was allocated only 23 percent of the overall budget (Adams and Cain 1989, 33–34).

4. On May 11, Powell gave a speech about the army's future, "National Security Challenges in the 1990s: The Future Ain't What It Used to Be," to a group of generals at the Army War College. Although skeptically received, this speech accurately predicted the demise of the Soviet Union, an expanded NATO, and retrenchment for the U.S. Army. The speech was later printed in *Army* (July 1989), 12–14.

5. The term "Base Force" was chosen to convey the idea that the proposed force structure represented a floor below which the United States could not go and still carry out its responsibilities as a superpower (Jaffe 1994, 21).

6. The new strategy was built around four central concepts: strategic deterrence, forward presence, crisis response, and reconstitution. Only the first of these was a carryover from the Cold War (Snider 1993b, 82).

7. Powell's support for the former position was made clear in a May 7 interview with a *Washington Post* reporter. The story was front-page news, and reported that

"the nation's top military officer" predicted a restructuring that would lead to "a 25 percent lower defense budget" (Powell 1995, 454).

8. See Hearings of the House Armed Services Committee (February 27, 1990). For the report on which this testimony is based, see CBO (1990b).

9. There was also controversy between Congress and DOD over how much budget savings would result from a 25 percent reduction in force structure. While [Cheney] proposed a 10 percent cut in the budget, Representative Les Aspin and others argued that much higher savings (18–27 percent) could be realized. A June 1990 report from the CBO (1990a) reinforced this argument.

10. Bush had requested $306 billion for FY 1991. The agreement set FY 1991 outlays at $306 billion, at $296 billion for FY 1992, and at $293 billion for FY 1993 (Snider 1993a, 30).

11. So long as the Base Force stayed within set spending limits for the 1992 and 1993, there would be little incentive for Congress to attack its strategic rationale. Moreover, deferred modernization and maintenance would eventually require moderate real growth in defense spending (Ippolito 1994).

12. Prior to 1990 the Bush administration instructed the services not to begin post–Cold War planning, so initially the army's efforts did not involve civilian leaders. Secretary of the Army John O. Marsh, a holdover from the Reagan administration, particularly resisted such efforts in the early part of Vuono's tenure. Interview, former Chief of Staff, General (ret.) Carl E. Vuono, August 1995. Correspondence, Colonel (ret.) Raoul Alcalá, Chief, Chief of Staff's Analysis and Integration Group, September 1996.

13. Memorandum from Secretary of the Army Michael Stone to Director, Army Staff, Subject: *Quicksilver II*, March 12, 1990.

14. According to Vuono, the Secretary of the Army and his staff played a relatively inconsequential role in the planning process. For the most part, the army's military leaders developed force options and the secretariat, with little modification, supported them. Interview, Vuono, August 1995.

15. Vuono had the analytic support to go "head to head" with Powell over the emerging Base Force since it was in the same range of options already analyzed by the army (Snider 1993a, 16).

16. Snider attributes the army's emphasis on the pace of downsizing to the unique concerns it had for its manpower training and replacement policies (1993b, 100).

17. The thirty-five thousand a year ceiling was conceived within the army's Office of the Deputy Chief of Staff for Personnel (ODCSPER) in fall 1989. Based on ODCSPER analysis, Vuono argued that cuts greater than thirty-five thousand annually would degrade readiness, disrupt training, and require painful reductions in force (RIFs). Interview, Vuono, August 1995.

18. Interviews, Reno, July 1995, and Thomas Wilson, Deputy Assistant Secretary of the Army, Military Personnel Management and Equal Opportunity Policy, May 1995.

19. Vuono's proposed endstrength of 580,000 was the lowest that could be achieved while adhering to the thirty-five thousand a year ceiling. During this same period, the army was quietly considering alternative ramps to significantly lower endstrengths. Internal memorandum from Robert Emmerichs, Deputy Assistant Secretary, to the Assistant Secretary of the Army for Manpower and Reserve Affairs, Kim Wincup, June 28, 1990.

20. See Hearings of the House Appropriations Committee (February 21, 1990).

21. See Hearings of the House Armed Services Committee (March 5, 1990); and Hearings of the House Appropriations Committee (March 6, 1991).

22. Interviews, Office of the Deputy Chief of Staff for Personnel, July and August 1995.

23. Interview, Colonel (ret.) Michael Harper, Chief, Chief of Staff's Study Group, 1991–95, July 1995.

24. Interview, Colonel (ret.) Raoul H. Alcalá, Chief, Chief of Staff's Analysis and Initiatives Group, 1987–91, August 1995.

25. Despite Secretary Cheney's endorsement of the Base Force, he had not yet instructed the services to adjust their Program Objective Memorandums (POMs) accordingly (Jaffe 1994, 42). The air force accepted the Base Force first, followed by the navy in fall 1990. The army and the Marine Corps were the last to accept, and only then after being forced to do so by Cheney (Lewis et al. 1992, 49).

26. Gray managed to convince Powell to increase the Marine Corps' endstrength from 150,000 to 159,000 (Jaffe 1994, 38).

27. Interviews, Vuono and Alcalá, August 1995.

28. These numbers were subsequently adjusted again in the FY 1992–1993 Amended Biennial Budget to 535,00, 509,000, 429,000, and 170,000 (Eitelberg 1993, 137). See table 2.1.

29. Due to the Gulf War, the army put the Stop-Loss Program into effect, suspending most separations. As a consequence, it was unable to achieve the mandated end strength of 702,000 by the end of FY 1991. See Hearings of the House Armed Services Committee (March 20, 1991).

30. See Hearings of the House Armed Services Committee (July 31, 1991).

31. Ironically, concern that minorities would be disaffected by downsizing followed public hand-wringing over whether minorities would suffer disproportionate casualties in the Gulf. See Shane 1991, 4–5 and GAO 1992.

32. Hearings of the Senate Appropriations Committee (March 14, 1991).

33. For background on the latter see, *Officer Management Legislation: Why Needed?* (February 1990).

34. Memorandum from Kenneth Krieg, Office of the Secretary of Defense to Distribution List, Subject: *Paper for Wednesday's Principal Strategic Issues Session*, January 16, 1990; Memorandum from Donald Atwood, Deputy Secretary of Defense, to Secretaries of the Military Departments, Subject: *Management of Military Manpower Reductions*, January 22, 1990.

35. See *An Assessment of the Service Manpower Plans* (August 1990); Briefing by Secretary of the Army, Michael Stone, to Secretary of Defense Richard Cheney, *Shaping the Force*, May 14, 1991.

36. Ippolito argues that Bush's election-year defense plan was weak due to the administration's failure to articulate the strategic rationale for the Base Force to Congress or the public (1994, 69).

37. The Bush administration argued that the coup attempt provided evidence of continued instability and the need to retain robust military capabilities. This argument was largely overshadowed by the breakup of the USSR several months later.

38. Aspin benefited more than any politician in Washington from the U.S. victory in the Gulf. Not only was he the most prominent Democrat to back Bush's decision to intervene, he also accurately predicted a relatively "short, easy war." Consequently, he was well-positioned to criticize the administration's other defense policies, including the Base Force, a situation he exploited brilliantly (Ippolito 1994, 85).

39. Remarks of Representative Les Aspin (D-WI) to the Air Force Association, Washington D.C., September 17, 1991.

40. Despite his criticisms, Aspin continued to hold together a bipartisan conservative coalition in 1992 to fend off more severe cuts advocated by Representatives Ron Dellums, Barney Frank and other liberals (Towell 1992a, 478).

41. See *An Approach to Sizing American Conventional Forces for the Post-Soviet Era* (February 27, 1992).

42. There were also reports that Powell was amenable to additional cuts in force structure (including a ten-division army) after the election (Schmitt 1992, 16; Garrity and Weiner 1992, 57).

43. Cheney and Powell were, to a certain extent, victims of their own rhetoric. Both had testified a year earlier that cuts below the Base Force would be potentially "disastrous" to long-term national security (Healy 1992, 4).

44. Clinton promised $60 billion in savings by cutting SDI, reducing troop levels by an additional two hundred thousand, having ten carriers rather than twelve, and reducing European troop levels to seventy-five thousand (McCain 1992).

45. The number of interviews I conducted with key decisionmakers in the Bottom-Up Review process is admittedly scant. Although several key figures did agree to interviews, many are still in the army or the administration and were therefore unwilling or unable to discuss these decisions.

46. After cutting Aspin's budget proposal by an additional $2.6 billion, the Bottom-Up Review was adopted by Congress (*1993 Congressional Quarterly Almanac*, 433–41). See also Hearings of the Senate Armed Services Committee (April 1, 1993); and Hearings of the House Armed Services Committee (March 31, 1993).

47. See Hearings of the Senate Armed Services Committee (April 1, 1993).

48. Interview, Colonel William Foster, Army Representative, Force Structure Working Group, Bottom-Up Review, April 1996. Foster was the Chief of the War

Plans Division, Office of the Army Deputy Chief of Staff for Operations and Plans, during this period.

49. The navy argued that peacetime commitments for carrier battle groups abroad, not computer-generated war games, should be the defining criterion. Likewise, the Marine Corps reportedly was able to generate sufficient pressure from Congress to stabilize its force levels (Alcalá 1993).

50. In December 1993, little more than two months after the release of the BUR, Aspin was fired by Clinton, at least partially in response to his inept handling of U.S. operations in Somalia. There are also reports that Aspin lost credibility after losing a battle with the Office of Management and Budget (OMB) over additional defense funding. After several misfires in finding a replacement, Clinton settled on Deputy Secretary of Defense William Perry (Alterman 1994).

51. Since the BUR's release, conservative lawmakers, retired generals, and the GAO have all expressed this view. See Gabriel et. al (1995) and GAO (1995b). For a somewhat more optimistic assessment, see CBO (1994a).

52. The GAO found that underfunding was due to overly optimistic assumptions about savings generated from base closures and management reforms, and the escalating costs of weapons development and environmental restoration (GAO 1994a, 7–9).

53. Prior to assuming the position of Chief of Staff, Sullivan served as Vice Chief of Staff of the Army and the Deputy Chief of Staff for Operations, positions from which he was deeply involved in the army's efforts to resist Base Force reductions.

54. Hearings of the Senate Armed Services Committee (February 26, 1992).

55. Hearing of the House Armed Services Committee (February 26, 1992).

56. These same capabilities were also factored in to earlier planning exercises. BUR planners simply highlighted them and used them as justification for additional cuts in force structure (Alcalá 1993, 3).

57. Foster acknowledges that the army did not make a particularly strong case for its position on Capitol Hill. Interview, April 1996.

58. The Bottom-Up Review had been released, but the manpower levels associated with it had not yet been determined. Endstrength decisions were made in individual negotiations between the services and OSD several months later. As a result of this hearing, the House and Senate Conference Report on the FY 1994 Defense Authorization Bill included a nonbinding provision warning against reductions in the army below 540,000 (1993 *Congressional Quarterly Almanac*, 441).

59. Hearings of the Senate Appropriations Committee (March 9, 1994).

60. The CBO concluded that at its current size, the army's costs are likely to rise $8–12 billion above the administration's projections between 1995 and 2010, with costs peaking sometime around 2005.

61. Although there is a zero-sum trade-off in terms of which accounts receive funding, these areas are also interdependent. Cuts in modernization and procurement, for example, increase maintenance costs as older vehicles become more ex-

pensive to maintain. Similarly, cuts in force structure reduce operations and maintenance costs because there are fewer soldiers to house, clothe, and train.

62. For example, for FY 1994 the army's budget was $61 billion (approximately 24 percent of DOD's overall budget). Forty-four percent of this was allocated to military personnel (West 1994, 24).

63. As concern over the army's dwindling modernization program grew in late 1994 and 1995, Perry took steps to address the problem by proposing additional cuts in army force structure.

64. The three divisions were the First Infantry Division at Fort Riley, Kansas, the Second Armored Division at Fort Hood, Texas, and the Fourth Infantry Division at Fort Carson, Colorado.

65. There is speculation that Perry announced the readiness problem directly to Congress to outmaneuver the Office of Management and Budget, which had shot down Aspin's request for additional funding in 1994 when he made it directly to the administration (*The Economist* 1994, 22).

66. See *Republican Defense Proposals May Worsen Plans Funding Mismatch* (1995) and *Comparison of the House and Senate Armed Services Committee FY 1996 Defense Authorization Bills* (1995).

67. Not surprisingly, the other services later balked at this proposal, and Sullivan reportedly felt as if he had been "gamed." Interview with senior army officer, October 1995.

68. Interview, Lieutenant General Theodore Stroup, May 1995.

69. Reimer has resisted the cut to 475,000, arguing that a force of this size will not be large enough to man ten divisions. See "General Dennis Reimer: Army Chief of Staff" (1995).

70. In February 1992, the *New York Times* published an article based on a Pentagon lead which asserted that the Base Force was explicitly (though not publicly) threat-based, designed around seven "illustrative" scenarios (Correl 1992, 15).

71. This has not always been the case. Up until the mid-1960s, congressional involvement in defense policy was minimal, as the legislative branch deferred to the executive branch on most issues (Blechman 1990). By the mid-1980s, however, the capabilities of Congress had multiplied many times over, inspiring one observer to note, "No legislature in the world devotes as much time, energy, and talent to decisionmaking on the defense budget as does the U.S. Congress" (Danzig 1989, 99).

72. There appear to be at least three explanations for the Marine Corps' success: its traditional expeditionary mission was very much in line with a post–Cold War "force projection" strategy; it was extraordinarily effective at presenting and fighting for its position on Capitol Hill; and it already had a strong base of congressional supporters sympathetic to its cause.

73. Interview, senior army officer, April 1996.

74. Interview, senior army officer, February 1995.

75. Conversely, Vuono and others argue that because the army had already done

extensive analysis, it was well-positioned to argue persuasively against Joint Staff proposals. Interview, Vuono, August 1995.

76. This paragraph is drawn almost entirely from an internal memorandum from Lieutenant Colonel Robert Johnson to Chief of Staff of the Army Gordon R. Sullivan, Subject: *Who's Who and What's What*, October 9, 1992, Gordon R. Sullivan Papers, Box 03A, Military History Institute, Army War College.

77. Congressman Ike Skelton made this very point in a meeting with Major General Daniel Christman in January 1993 and encouraged army leaders to develop a companion document to highlight the army's role in the emerging environment. Christman to General Gordon Sullivan, "Eyes Only", February 8, 1993, Sullivan Papers, Box 04B.

78. Interview, senior army officer, March 1996.

79. Huntington, for example, notes that between 1946 and 1960 military leaders played a "relatively unimportant role ... in proposing changes in policy. In no case did military leaders initiate major new policies and in no case did they effectively prevent changes in old ones" (1961, 114–15).

80. Interservice conflict had in the past freed civilian leaders to pick and choose among program options, thereby enhancing civilian control. Paradoxically, in an effort to centralize and consolidate civilian control, Robert McNamara arguably undercut it by shifting the locus of conflict from interservice to civilian-military (Lucas and Dawson 1974).

81. Interviews, senior army officers, June–August, 1995.

82. It is important to acknowledge that Powell's influence was not necessarily at the expense of Cheney's. As Powell observes in his autobiography, Cheney had a firm grip on every aspect of military policy (Powell 1995).

83. Goldwater-Nichols strengthened the role of the Chairman, at the expense of the services, by identifying him as an independent advisor to the Secretary of Defense and the President and by placing the Joint Staff directly in his control. For more on this, see Snider 1987 and Batcheller 1991.

84. The spending and deficit dynamics shaping federal budget policy show no signs of weakening, and significantly smaller high-tech military forces are proving to be significantly more costly than predicted.

NOTES TO CHAPTER 3

1. TDA units are manned by civilian as well as military personnel, they perform missions that TOE units cannot, and they are nondeployable. The TDA is a relatively small percentage of the overall force structure (roughly 40 percent), but it includes a disproportionate number of authorizations for officers (approximately 60 percent in 1996).

2. Commanders of the Major Commands (MACOMs) submit their TDA requirements for the Army's Program Objective Memorandum (its resource distrib-

ution plan) annually. Although their "mission" is defined by the Department of the Army Headquarters, the MACOMs identify the resources needed to carry it out.

3. Interview, May 1995. In this case, as in others, the individual cited requested anonymity. In such instances, the names are omitted, but the date and the individual's rank or the office in which he or she works is cited in the text.

4. The "joint billet" requirements mandated by the Goldwater-Nichols Act and the requirements to send active duty officers as trainers to the Reserve Component under Title XI of the 1992 National Defense Authorization Act are two examples.

5. A branch is a grouping of officers that make up an "arm" of the army. There are sixteen primary or "line" branches (infantry, chemical, armor, and so forth) and three special branches for chaplains, attorneys, and medical officers. Functional areas are secondary career specialties, such as Operations Research or Foreign Area Officer. Line officers are managed by the Officer Personnel Management Directorate (OPMD), which is responsible for their distribution, assignment, and development.

6. The emphasis Vuono placed on the six imperatives is evident in his speeches, articles, and letters while Chief of Staff. See *Collected Works of the Thirty-first Chief of Staff of the United States Army* (1991).

7. Correspondence, Colonel (ret.) Raoul Alcalá, Chief, Chief of Staff's Analysis and Integration Group, 1987–91, September 1996.

8. The terms "objectives," "goals," and "principles" are used interchangeably. The principles that guided the downsizing process were also the goals or objectives of it.

9. This was in stark contrast to the partiality shown toward regular army officers in the past, particularly after Vietnam.

10. The army does establish minimum requirements, or "floors," to protect officers of certain branches or functional areas. Boards rank officers on the basis of quality, identifying those who are "fully qualified" for promotion and a smaller group of those who are "most qualified." If the mandated floors have not been satisfied, the board replaces officers who are "most qualified" with those of the appropriate skill set who are "fully qualified."

11. Interview, July 1995.

12. This created a bubble (comprising year groups 1967–70) that slowed promotions as it advanced through the system. Interview with Colonel Charles Henning, Chief, Officer Division, Office of the Deputy Chief of Staff for Personnel, May 1995.

13. Curiously, this commitment persists despite the widespread acknowledgment that all the services do an inadequate job of defining readiness and an even worse job of measuring it. See GAO (1994b).

14. This is somewhat ironic considering the public anxiety that African-American soldiers, due to their high representation in the army, would suffer disproportionate casualties in the Gulf War. See Walters (1990).

15. This objective was discussed more openly than concern over race. In briefings distributed in the field, for example, improved promotion opportunity was emphasized as one of the benefits of downsizing. See *The Chain Teaching Program:*

Drawing Down the Army, 1991–94, Updates 1–4. Also, improved promotion rates for early, or below the zone (BZ), promotions during downsizing were an explicit goal of Vuono's as early as 1989. Notes from a meeting between the Director of Military Personnel Management, Brigadier General Stroup, and the Chief of Staff, Subject: *Chief of Staff Guidance*, August 11, 1989. Unless otherwise specified, the internal army documents cited in this chapter are from ASA/M&RA, ODCSPER, and PERSCOM.

16. Interview, May 1995.

17. See, for example, the testimony of Air Force Deputy Chief of Staff for Personnel, Lieutenant General Thomas Hickey (Hearings of the House Appropriations Committee, March 8, 1990). Interview, Lieutenant Colonel Joseph Brown, Chief of Air Force, Officer Retirement and Separation Office, June 1995.

18. Interview, Lieutenant Commander Stephen Green, U.S. Navy, Officer Promotion Plans, June 1995.

19. Vuono expressed his concerns about not "mortgaging the future" as early as 1988. Memorandum from the Chief of Staff for the Deputy Chief of Staff for Personnel, January 7, 1988.

20. All boards have minority "goals"; the Secretary of the Army directs selection boards to be particularly sensitive to the possibility of past institutional discrimination when reviewing files. If a board fails to promote minorities at a rate equal to or greater than the majority, it is required to submit a memorandum to the Secretary of the Army explaining why. Interviews with senior military and civilian officers, May 1995.

21. The number of senior and middle-grade officers is constrained by DOPMA; thus, the separation of officers in these ranks improves promotion opportunity for those in the junior ranks.

22. The relative value placed on these three areas varies. For example, as performance ratings become inflated (as they have during downsizing), it becomes increasingly difficult to distinguish outstanding from mediocre performance. Consequently, the value placed on qualifications, particularly operational assignments, rises. Interview, Jack Miller, Chief, Management Support Division, PERSCOM, May 1995.

23. Churchill made a similar comment about democratic governance.

24. Under the SERB program, in particular, selection boards had a difficult time choosing officers for separation who, by virtue of their rank, had already demonstrated strong performance. "Quality" is increasingly tenuous at the higher ranks, as most officers who make it that far are strong performers. For every hundred lieutenants commissioned, only forty-eight are promoted to lieutenant colonel and twenty-one to colonel. The rest either leave voluntarily or as casualties of up-or-out.

25. Memorandum from the President of the Board for the Deputy Chief of Staff for Personnel, Subject: *After-Action Report, FY 1992 Lieutenant Colonel SERB*, February 6, 1992.

26. This is not to say that SERBs were not, at least in some cases, discriminatory. It is widely acknowledged throughout the army that selection boards "select in their

own image," favoring officers with backgrounds similar to their own. In the past this has resulted in what is commonly referred to as a "muddy boots bias," in which officers with "traditional" career patterns are viewed more favorably by selection boards than officers with less traditional career patterns.

27. This paragraph and the next are based on numerous interviews with assignment officers, branch chiefs, and division chiefs within the Officer Personnel Management Directorate, June 1995.

28. In practice, the evaluations were skewed in favor of A files, thus the targeted population was generally smaller than 50 percent of the cohort. Assignment officers' assessments are a reasonable proxy for "quality." They know the files of the officers they manage intimately and are well positioned to rank them. Moreover, they keep abreast of where the most recent boards appear to be placing an emphasis. Finally, each assessment was verified by the branch manager. Interviews, PERSCOM, June 1995.

29. The United States Military Academy, in particular, has reportedly lost a large number of promising young officers who resigned while serving there as instructors. Likewise, there have been questions raised by the fact that the large majority of West Point graduates who had previously been selected for Rhodes or Marshall Scholarships since 1987 have since resigned their commissions after short stints in the army. Interviews, faculty members, United States Military Academy; staff officers, Officer Division, Office of the Deputy Chief of Staff for Personnel, June–August 1995.

30. This is also not meant to suggest that the officers who left the army were substandard performers. As one retired colonel remarked, "We had a great Army. The bottom third was pretty damn good." Interview, June 1995.

31. The Commander in Chief of U.S. Forces, Europe raised this concern in a memorandum to the Vice Chief of Staff of the Army, Subject: *Retention of Foreign Area Officers*, August 31, 1992.

32. These officers had been deemed fully qualified for retention. Memorandum from President of the 1992 Lieutenant Colonel Selective Early Retirement Board to the Deputy Chief of Staff for Personnel, Subject: *After Action Report, FY 1992 SERB*, February 6, 1992.

33. Interviews, June–August, 1995.

34. Interviews, Office of the Deputy Chief of Staff for Personnel, June–August 1995.

35. A June 1995 GAO report concluded that all four services effectively maintained service-wide aggregate personnel levels during downsizing (1995a).

36. For example, the army was far more successful than the navy and the air force in avoiding RIFs of junior and mid-career officers. See Kitfield 1993b.

37. As an example, on at least one occasion, Chief of Staff Gordon Sullivan called post commanders throughout the army the evening before the release of the SERB results and asked them to ensure personally that the notification process was han-

dled sensitively. Interview, Colonel William Fennel, former staff officer, PERSCOM, July 1995.

38. ACAP has assisted a large number of officers but undoubtedly has been most beneficial for enlisted soldiers, as officers have often relied on civilian placement firms. In 1992, for example, 14,974 officers departed the army, and 12,547 (84 percent) of them were served by army job assistance centers. Interview, Pauline Botehlo, ACAP Director, May 1995.

39. In recent years, federal transition assistance programs like ACAP (particularly within DOD) have come under fire as being poorly managed, inordinately expensive, and ineffective, but ACAP appears to be an exception. For a critical review of DOD's management of transition programs, see GAO 1995b. For a blistering critique of DOD programs, see *A Report for the Joint Chiefs of Staff on Post Transition Experiences of Military Seeking Jobs in the Private Sector* 1995.

40. Indeed, a senior officer in the office of Department of the Army Inspector General (DAIG) observed that Inspector General teams around the Army have reported that downsizing significantly depressed the level of confidence in army "affirmative action" programs. Interview, June 1995.

41. For example, the 1992 RIF of majors resulted in the selection of a disproportionate number of black officers. Blacks comprised 13.7 percent (338 of 2,462) of eligible officers, but were 27 percent (152 of 567) of those initially selected for RIF. *Briefing for Chief of Staff Gordon Sullivan* from the Office of Economic and Manpower Analysis, USMA, January 3, 1992. Prior to releasing these results, the army again made voluntary incentives available and by doing so ultimately reduced the number of officers RIFed to 244 (Gordon R. Sullivan Papers, General Officer Files, Box 04A).

42. The DOPMA "goals" are relatively ambitious; desired promotion opportunity (or percentage of those considered who were selected) for majors, lieutenant colonels and colonels is 80 percent, 70 percent, and 50 percent, respectively. The optimal timing is ten years +/- 1; sixteen years +/- 1; and, twenty-two years +/- 1, respectively.

43. Between 1980 and 1985, the average promotion opportunity to colonel, lieutenant colonel, and major was 57.8, 81.4, and 84.4, respectively—well above DOPMA goals. Likewise, promotion timing was 22 years 11 months; 16 years 4 months; and, 11 years 4 months (Rostker et al. 1993, 29).

44. The increase in BZ promotions to the maximum allowable 10 percent for every promotion board reflected the aforementioned priority that Vuono placed on retaining the best and brightest officers, particularly during downsizing. Interview, Alcalá, August 1995.

45. Garrison commanders generally assume administrative responsibilities in TDA organizations.

46. See *OPMS XXI Precursor Study Issues* (Rough Draft) (1994, 2).

47. Rufus Miles's famous law describes an age-old truism in American politics: "Where you stand depends on where you sit" (Neustadt and May 1986, 157).

48. Many who served in ODCSPER during this period recall that Stroup, rather than Ono, was the key figure in developing the plan. Stroup was particularly close to Chief of Staff Carl Vuono, as signaled by the fact that the Chief of Staff had a "hotline" installed in Stroup's office several months after he arrived in the Pentagon to facilitate their direct communication. Several officers observed that Stroup was the only one-star general in the army with a *direct* line to the Chief of Staff. Interviews, former staff members ODCSPER, May–July 1995.

49. Interview, Lieutenant General (ret.) Allen Ono, former Deputy Chief of Staff for Personnel, July 1995.

50. Interview, Lieutenant General Robert Ord, III, former commander, PERSCOM, July 1995.

51. Correspondence with the author, Colonel (ret.) Raoul Alcalá, Chief, Chief of Staff's Analysis and Integration Group, September 3, 1996.

52. PERSCOM also established a hotline soon after, so soldiers of any rank could call and have their questions concerning downsizing answered. Interview, Colonel William Fennel, July 1995.

53. For example, in a memorandum to the Deputy Chief of Staff, dated June 9, 1984, the Director of the Military Personnel Management Directorate, Major General Robert Porter argued that SERBs would create suspicion that the army's objective was to raise promotion rates.

54. SERBs for special branches, but not line officers, were held in 1985 and 1987. The first line officer SERB was held in 1986, but Army Secretary John O. Marsh did not approve the results (*Officer Management Legislation: Why Needed* February 1990).

55. Interviews, Thomas Wilson, Deputy Assistant Secretary of the Army for Personnel Policy and Equal Opportunity, May 1995; Ono, July 1995.

56. Interview, Lieutenant Colonel (ret.) Steven Shupack, former Chief of the Distribution Programs Branch, Officer Distribution Division, PERSCOM, June 1995.

57. It is impossible, even now, to identify who left the army as a result of SERBs and who retired voluntarily; the SERB lists were never published, and officers selected generally had the option of remaining on active duty for five to six months before retiring.

58. The Secretary of the Army had the option of removing these individuals from the SERB list through a process called "redlining." Interviews, ODCSPER, May–August 1995. The army's desire to protect "diversity" was also apparent in the SERB process. The army secretariat monitored the results of the SERB particularly closely for indications of discrimination, though no special measures, other than the affirmative selection process already in place, were taken. Interview, Wilson, May 1995.

59. As Reno recalls, there was also resistance simply because "it was not invented here." ACAP was viewed skeptically because it was a civilian-sponsored program. Interview, July 1995.

60. Memorandum from John Shannon, Under Secretary of the Army, to Director Army Staff, March 23, 1990; Briefing, April 24, 1990, U.S. Total Army Personnel Command (ACAP History File, U.S. Total Army Personnel Command).

61. Few bureaucracies die willingly, and ACAP is no exception. As downsizing appears to near conclusion, a growing number of ACAP supporters have fervently marketed this "cradle-to-grave" approach as a critical and permanent component of the recruiting process. As of 1997, the debate is unresolved and ACAP's future uncertain.

62. Interview, Lieutenant General (ret.) William H. Reno, former Deputy Chief of Staff for Personnel, July 1995.

63. Stroup, who served as the Director of Military Personnel Management from August 1989 to January 1992, provided continuity between Ono and Reno.

64. Interview, Harper, July 1995. Correspondence with the author, Colonel (ret.) Raoul Alcalá, September 3, 1996.

65. Interview, Lieutenant General (ret.) William H. Reno, conducted by Dwight Oland, January 5, 1993.

66. Interview, Gary Purdum, former Director, Manpower Directorate, June 1995. This may be to some degree the product of what some scholars have described as the army's "consensual" approach to decisionmaking. See Builder 1989.

67. Information Paper, Office of the Deputy Chief of Staff for Personnel, Subject: *Desert Storm End Strength Management*, Colonel Joe Terry, February 15, 1991.

68. Including the members of the Army Reserve and National Guard who were called to active duty, the army's endstrength was over 930,000.

69. Interview, Colonel Michael Shane, former speechwriter, ODCSPER, May 1995; Information Paper, PERSCOM, LTC McLinn, October 16, 1992; See *FY 1992 Department of the Army Historical Summary* (Draft), 29.

70. To what extent the army's leaders believed 535,000 was the final number is unclear. Throughout this period numerous commentators projected endstrength levels well below 500,000. But to plan for lower endstrengths would have been a self-fulfilling prophecy. Interview, Reno, July 1995.

71. This did not apply to the SERBs. Some retirement-eligible lieutenant colonels and colonels were considered by SERBs as many as four times.

72. Thurman created a similar cell—comprising analysts with backgrounds in econometrics, operations research, automation, and programming—in 1982, but it was dissolved after he left (Demma 1994a, 5).

73. This was one of the rules Thurman preached to incoming staff officers. General Thurman, Vice Chief of Staff of the Army, *Staff Officer Orientation*, May 11, 1987, Maxwell R. Thurman Papers, Selected Speeches, 1983–1987, Military History Institute, Army War College.

74. Much of the robust analytic capacity within the personnel community was put in place between 1981 and 1983 when Thurman was the Deputy Chief of Staff for Personnel and Reno was his executive officer.

75. Outside ODCSPER, the Office of Manpower and Economic Analysis at West Point (a small think tank created by Thurman), the RAND Corporation, and an analytic cell within PERSCOM were periodically called upon as well.

76. Interviews, June–August 1995.

77. Interviews, former branch chiefs, ODCSPER, May–July 1995.

78. Interviews, ODCSPER, June–August 1995.

79. Interview, General (ret.) Gordon R. Sullivan, former Chief of Staff of the Army, July 1995.

80. Interview, Fennel, June 1995.

81. Interview, Gary Purdum, June 1995

82. Interview, staff officer, Office of the Deputy Chief of Staff for Personnel, June 1995.

83. Memorandum from Robert Emmerichs, Deputy Assistant Secretary of the Army for Military Personnel Management and Equal Opportunity, to the Assistant Secretary (M&RA), Subject: *Strategy for DOPMA Legislation*, 1990 (no date).

84. Hearings of the Senate Appropriations Committee (March 14, 1991).

85. Memorandum from Secretary of the Army Michael Stone to the Deputy Secretary of Defense, June 18, 1991. The army later backed off on its desire to restrict the "quality" of those who departed. Interview, Wilson, May 1995.

86. Memorandum from the Secretary of the Army to the Deputy Secretary of Defense, June 18, 1991. OSD and the air force resisted this proposal, viewing it as an attack on the existing retirement system. A temporary early retirement program was approved by Congress in the 1993 Defense Authorization Act.

87. A captain with eight years of active duty received total compensation amounting to $44,235. If this officer voluntarily departed the army through the VSI program, he or she would receive $7,446 annually for sixteen years (an annuity worth $119,129 in present dollars). That same officer would have received $44,673 through the SSB program. Both the VSI and SSB were more lucrative than standard separation pay, which for the same individual would have been $29,782. In financial terms, the net present value of the VSI is significantly higher than that of the SSB.

88. Memorandum from Assistant Secretary of Defense for Force Management and Personnel to the Service Secretaries, Subject: *VSI/SSB Policy Guidance*, January 3, 1992. For a useful source on VSI/SSB, see Grismer (1992).

89. Interview, Lieutenant General (ret.) Thomas Carney, former Deputy Chief of Staff for Personnel, May 1996.

90. OPMD assignment officers are career managers charged with simultaneously satisfying the professional development needs and desires of the officer corps with the operational requirements of the army.

91. This appears to have had two antecedents. First, if the assessments of assignment officers were proved incorrect by promotion boards it would undermine their credibility. And, the army is potentially liable if an officer sues for having received "poor advice" about the likelihood of being RIFed.

92. This and the next paragraph are based on interviews with assignment officers, branch chiefs, and division chiefs within OPMD, June 1995.

93. There are three divisions within OPMD—combat arms, combat support arms, and combat service support arms—that manage officer careers through selection for colonel (Thie and Brown 1994, 275). The officer population eligible for VSI/SSB varied from year to year, but generally included officers who had been passed over once for promotion, officers in surplus specialties, and officers from year groups that were being considered for RIF.

94. Carney was also the army's spokesperson on the contentious issues of gays in the military and women in combat roles.

95. Memorandum from Assistant Secretary of the Army (M&RA) to Assistant Secretary of Defense (FM&P) Subject: *Army Implementation of Fiscal Year 1993 Temporary Early Retirement*, April 6, 1993.

96. Correspondence with the author, Colonel (ret.) Raoul Alcalá, September 3, 1996.

97. Interview, Lieutenant General (ret.) Theodore Stroup, former Deputy Chief of Staff for Personnel. May 1995.

98. Interview with Colonel Gary Carlson, Chief Sustainment and Development Branch, ODCSPER, May 1995.

99. Memorandum from the Assistant Secretary for Manpower and Reserve Affairs to the Secretary of the Army, December 23, 1994. Interviews, Major General Thomas Sikora, Director, Military Personnel Management Directorate, May 1995 and Major General John Thompson, Commander, PERSCOM, June 1995.

100. Briefing from Department of the Army Inspector General to Secretary of the Army Togo West, *Impact of the Personnel Drawdown*, February 9, 1995.

101. Interview, May 1995.

102. Briefing from Officer Distribution Division, U.S. Total Army Personnel Command to Commander, PERSCOM, *SERB Impact Analysis*, June 21, 1995.

103. Memorandum from Director Manpower Directorate, Office of the Deputy Chief of Staff for Personnel to Comptroller of the Army, October 19, 1992.

104. In 1993, for example, the four-star generals in command of the Army Training and Doctrine Command (TRADOC) and Forces Command (FORCCOM) sent messages to Chief of Staff Gordon Sullivan expressing their concern that they would be incapable of carrying out their responsibilities with the allocated shortages. Message from TRADOC Commander to the Chief of Staff, August 2, 1993, and message from FORCCOM Commander to the Chief of Staff, October 19, 1993.

105. Interview, Karen Heath, former staff member, House Armed Services Committee, May 1995.

106. Interview, Vuono, August 1995.

107. As assignment officers, Sullivan and Stroup were responsible for selecting officers from among those they managed to be considered for the RIF. Career Résumés, U.S. Army, General Officer Management Office.

108. Like DOPMA, the legislation at the time protected RA officers, but gave the Secretary of the Army the authority to separate reserve officers indiscriminately (Shoemaker 1972, 1).

109. In 1973, the Army submitted a proposal to Congress for authority to RIF Regular Army officers, but its passage was delayed until 1975. With the approval of Congress, the army conducted a Regular Army RIF in 1976 (Tice 1975, 1).

110. See "First-time Selections for Colonel Only 30%" (1973, 10), and "Officer Selection Rates on Decline" (1975, 6).

111. This contributed to the promotion bubble comprising year groups 1967–70 that continue to give personnel planners great difficulties in the 1990s.

112. Interview, Colonel (ret.) William Merrill, former staff officer, ASA/M&RA, June 1994.

113. This was a shocking admission, particularly considering that the army was allocated funding for only thirteen and a half divisions.

114. Clearly, these departures were also due in large part to a perceived decline of professionalism within the officer corps. See "33 West Point Instructors Quit" 1972, 22; Deagle 1972, 13.

115. Although, as noted earlier, the army's leadership may have placed too much stock in the importance of marginal improvements in promotion opportunity and timing.

116. This is a relative assessment, of course. As noted in chapter 2, there is some question whether the army clung too tenaciously to force structure at the expense of modernization and readiness.

117. Individual branches—armor, infantry, special forces, for example—have unique cultures, as do various units from division down to platoon.

118. Such broad generalizations are caricatures, of course, as heroic warrior tendencies and analytic mind-sets exist, to a certain extent, in every army organization. Despite this, the concept of culture is useful for capturing some of the essential features of the decisions made in the post–Cold War period.

119. See *Changing an Army: An Oral History of General William E. DePuy* 1979.

120. In 1979, Chief of Staff General Edward Meyer charged Thurman with tackling one of the army's most serious and alarming problems—recruiting for the all-volunteer force. Thurman responded with the "Be All You Can Be" recruiting campaign, an effort credited by some for the army's rise from the ashes of Vietnam in the 1980s (Kitfield 1995a).

121. This paragraph is based predominantly on the *Oral History of General Maxwell Thurman* (1992), and an interview with Colonel (ret.) Anthony Durso, former Chief of ODCSPER Program and Analysis Division, May 1995.

122. This practice is analogous to what Janowitz calls "tapping", the process by which junior and mid-career officers are recognized as potential members of the "military elite" (Janowitz 1960, 145).

123. As of 1987, the army had authorizations for 4,794 colonels and 49 lieutenant generals, thus there is roughly one chance in a hundred of a colonel being promoted

to the higher rank. Of course, there are certain assignments for colonels that are designated as "kingmaker" jobs. Executive officer to the Vice Chief of Staff (in which three of these four served) was obviously one such job.

124. Remarkably, Thurman was a general for fifteen of his thirty-seven years of service, and a four-star general for seven. Between 1983 and 1987, he held three of the premier four-star assignments in the army.

125. Interview, Stroup, May 1995.

126. Students of military organizations in particular have argued that "the preeminence of bureaucratic rationalism in planning and managing the all-volunteer force has had serious and deleterious effects" (Faris 1988, 68).

NOTES TO CHAPTER 4

1. For a discussion of the role of intangibles in battle, see Keegan 1976 and van Creveld 1985.

2. The Army Research Institute is one of the army's multidisciplinary research arms; it falls under the purview of the Deputy Chief of Staff for Personnel. The two surveys were the Longitudinal Research on Officer Careers Survey (LROC), administered to roughly twenty thousand junior officers between 1988 and 1992, and the ARI Sample Survey of Military Personnel (SSMP), which was distributed semi-annually to approximately 10 percent of the officer corps, or approximately ten thousand officers (with roughly a 50–60 percent response rate).

3. Briefing slides presented to the Secretary of the Army, Togo West, Jr., *Impact of Personnel Drawdown*, February 9, 1995. Also, interview with senior officer, Department of the Army, Office of the Inspector General (DAIG), June 26, 1995. DAIG's overall assessment was based on the consolidation of reports from offices throughout the army.

4. Briefing slides presented to the Chief of Staff, 1994, *Army Leadership Survey*. The Chief of Staff Strategic Fellows are a small "think tank" of six to eight colonels, assigned to the Army War College, who engage in studies at the direction of the Chief of Staff. Their findings were based on group interviews with 1,625 captains at seventy-two locations.

5. See Reimer 1996 and Stroup 1996.

6. Interview, August 1995.

7. In some respects, this research is comparable to the Army War College's 1970 *Study on Military Professionalism*, initiated by General Westmoreland in response to charges that professionalism within the officer corps had eroded during the Vietnam War. To its credit, it is a remarkably candid critique of the gap between ideal and actual professionalism in the army's officer corps. Although the study recommended otherwise, the report was not made public until the late 1970s.

8. Interviews were conducted with twenty-five focus groups of three to nine members and with fifteen individuals. Overall, six (4 percent) of the officers inter-

viewed were O–6s; twenty-six (19 percent) were O–5s; forty-one (30 percent) were O–4s, and fifty-nine (43 percent) were O–3s. In addition, interviews were conducted with six battalion, brigade, and division command sergeants major.

9. Officers report to these schools from assignments throughout the army, thus their views are likely to be more representative of the army at large. At Fort Sill, interviews were conducted with students in the Field Artillery Advance Course as well as field grade officers assigned to the Field Artillery Center. At Fort Leavenworth, interviews were conducted with students in the Combined Arms Services and Staff School (CAS[3]) and the Command and General Staff College, as well as with field grade officers permanently assigned there. At Carlisle Barracks, interviews were conducted with Army War College students. Approximately 90 percent of the interviews were recorded and 80 percent of the recordings were transcribed.

10. The Twenty-fifth Light Infantry Division is located at Schofield Barracks, and the First Cavalry Division and the Second Armored Division are located at Fort Hood.

11. The officers interviewed were promised complete anonymity (only their branch, rank, gender, and race were recorded). Minorities were represented in roughly the same proportion as serve in the army. Female officers were underrepresented, as the combat units visited had significantly fewer women.

12. There is an inherent bias in the fact that many of these officers are serving in coveted assignments and so have likely suffered least from organizational downsizing. The officers selected for the Command and General Staff College and the Army War College, in particular, have already been identified as the army's top performers. Likewise, officers at Fort Hood and Schofield Barracks were members of three premier combat divisions.

13. Interview, Schofield Barracks, HI.

14. Interviews, Office of the Deputy Chief of Staff for Personnel, June 1995. There are three combat training centers—the National Training Center (NTC) at Fort Irwin, California, the Joint Readiness Training Center (JRTC) at Fort Polk, Louisiana, and the Combat Maneuver Training Center (CMTC) in Hohenfels, Germany.

15. This is most often the case with captains and majors who generally change "duty stations" every twelve to twenty-four months. Interviews, Officer Distribution Division, Officer Personnel Management Directorate, August 1995.

16. The amount of turbulence in the personnel system is referred to as personnel tempo or PERSTEMPO. The operational tempo or number of operational deployments is commonly referred to as OPTEMPO. As OPTEMPO increases so too does PERSTEMPO.

17. Numerous officers assigned to Fort Hood and Schofield Barracks, places from which units are deployed regularly, made this point.

18. In 1996, 81 percent and 64 percent of the officer and enlisted force, respectively, were married. This is a notable increase from 1945, when 65 percent of all of-

ficers and 23 percent of all enlisted soldiers were married. Statistics from the Office of the Deputy Chief of Staff for Personnel.

19. The Officer Personnel Act of 1947 required that Regular Army officers twice nonselected for promotion be discharged without being eligible for retirement benefits. A modification to this policy was conceived in 1980 which allowed for the "selective continuation" of those officers in shortage branches.

20. Interview, Colonel Tony Buckles, Chief, Combat Arms Division, PERSCOM, November 1995.

21. This finding is consistent with the conclusions of a survey conducted by Wong and McNally (1994) of 791 majors at the Command and General Staff College in spring 1992.

22. The 1993 National Defense Authorization Act (NDAA) authorized the services to retire middle-rank officers prior to twenty years of service with full retirement benefits. The authority was extended in 1994 to last through 1999, though the army has not officially stated if and to whom this benefit will be available in the future. There is great uncertainty among majors about this issue.

23. It is particularly interesting that willingness to recommend the military as a career appears to have been on the rebound until fall 1993, at which time the results of the Bottom-Up Review were released. Soon after, "willingness" suffered a substantial decline.

24. Roughly 50 percent of each year group is selected for a year of attendance at the Command and General Staff College. Selection to CGSC is in part a self-fulfilling prophecy, as officers develop personal alliances there that are important for their future career advancement. Branch-qualifying assignments vary across branches, though there is a very clear hierarchy of jobs. Assignments as a battalion operations officer or executive officer are coveted by majors who aspire to battalion command.

25. The centralized selection process was created in 1974 when the army officially adapted the Officer Personnel Management System. Centralized boards are used to select officers for promotion, command, and crucial schooling assignments. A typical promotion board is presided over by a general officer and consists of eighteen to twenty-one officers at least one grade higher than those being considered. Boards are designed with a mix of officers of different branches, race, and gender (Yost 1991, 5).

26. To allow comparison of these ratings with those given to other subordinates, the boards also review a profile of the senior rater's previous rating record. There are three aspects of a senior rater's evaluation that count in the selection process: How the senior rater evaluates the officer on a ten-block scale (the mean rating given by most senior officers is the second block from the top); the rater's profile, or how he has rated officers of that rank in the past; and, a narrative portion in which the senior rater describes the officer's performance and potential.

27. Below-the-zone promotions were begun in the 1950s by Army Chief of Staff Maxwell Taylor, who allowed promotion boards to "dip down 10 percent below the

formal zone ... to let you look down and see if there was someone just standing out like a sore thumb who ought to be looked at and considered" (Meyer et al. 1995, 89).

28. For arguments in favor of below-the-zone promotions, see Roades 1973.

29. There clearly is some basis for this perception: in 1996, 41 percent (a 6 percent increase from 1995) of the lieutenant colonels selected for command had been promoted at least once "below the zone." Memorandum, U.S. Army Personnel Command, Subject: *OPMS Precursor Issues*, (no date) 1995.

30. The "labor exchange" is consistent with what Selznick calls the informal structures within an organization (as cited in Dawkins 1979, 142).

31. Interview, Officer Personnel Management Directorate, U.S. Total Army Personnel Command, July 1995.

32. While the 1970 Army War College study noted the difficulty in sorting out the causal relationships at the time, the report identified the heavy reliance on and misuse of statistical indicators as detrimental to a professional climate.

33. OER inflation is a chronic problem in the army and other services. For examples see Brown 1975 and Byron 1992.

34. Interviews, Combat Arms, Combat Support, and Combat Service Support Divisions, U.S. Total Army Personnel Command, July 1995.

35. Senior officers—lieutenant colonels and colonels—are more ambivalent on this point, perhaps because a zero-defects climate is to some degree a reflection of their own failure to promote a healthy professional environment.

36. While the majority of officers "dual track," a small minority are permitted to serve repetitive tours in chosen specialties.

37. There are fourteen functional areas. The more common are Personnel Programs Management and Operations Plans and Training, particularly for combat arms officers who want to remain competitive for command. In addition, Foreign Area Officer (FAO), Operations Research, Comptroller, Systems Automation, and Research, Development and Acquisition are also commonly chosen (*Commissioned Officer Development and Career Management* 1995, 163; and Interview, Combat Arms Division, Officer Personnel Management Directorate, July 1995).

38. Although the overall number of officers admitted into these specialties has decreased, the demand (measured in terms of number of applications) has increased. Likewise, functional area assignment officers report that the overall quality of officers opting for these functional areas has risen. Interviews, PERSCOM, 1995.

39. Observer controllers evaluate the performance of units rotating through the training center.

40. In the past, senior officers without master's degrees have had the opportunity to pursue them at night as students at the Army and Naval War Colleges.

41. The "3Rs"—Recruiting, Reserve Component, and ROTC—have traditionally been viewed as three of the least desirable jobs in the army. It is almost univer-

sally perceived that the individuals who serve in these assignments, on average, do less well than their contemporaries.

42. Interviews with assignment officers, Officer Personnel Management Directorate, PERSCOM, July 1995.

43. The word "choice" is somewhat misleading. Cadets and officer candidates fill out "dream sheets" in which they request both basic branch and assignment. When possible, preferences are satisfied, but officers are often assigned to a branch they did not request, or was low on their list.

44. Janowitz offers a more sanguine view of military intellectuals within the army, noting that since World War II, they have emerged as a distinct and visible type. He also argues that the navy displays the least respect for intellectuals, military or civilian (1960, 431–33).

45. The majors who complete the SAMs programs are awarded a master's degree and automatically assigned to corps-level planning staffs for the following year.

46. Interviews, Fort Leavenworth, August 1995.

47. Despite the fact that numerous permanent professors and FAOs were selected for early retirement, the percentages were equal to, and in most cases lower than, the army average. Selective Early Retirement Boards, Colonel, Lieutenant Colonel, and Major, After-Action Reports, FY 1991, 1992, 1993, 1994.

48. Interviews, Fort Leavenworth, August 1995.

49. In 1992, for example, lieutenant colonels or majors on seventy-four campuses were involuntary separated from the army. Headquarters, U.S. Army Recruiting Command, Memorandum to the Office of the Assistant Secretary of the Army for Manpower and Reserve Affairs, December 21, 1994.

50. Numerous mid-career officers interviewed expressed this view. Interviews, July–August 1995.

51. Interviews, Officer Personnel Management Directorate, U.S. Total Personnel Command, July 1995.

52. Palmer's comments were about the effect of SERBs in general and not meant to imply that West Point was disproportionately affected by selected early retirement. Floors were established to protect USMA's permanent professors, though a small percentage were still forced to retire.

53. A related question is how SERBs on ROTC campuses affected the willingness of ROTC cadets to request active duty.

NOTES TO CHAPTER 5

1. This chapter focuses primarily on the management of line officers, who make up the majority of the officer corps, by the Officer Personnel Management Directorate (OPMD).

2. These three categories are taken primarily from the final chapter of Meyer et al. 1995, 225–27.

3. In this discussion, professionalism is considered primarily at the individual level in terms of the attitudes and behavior of officers. For a discussion the various levels of analysis for considering professionalism, see Sarkesian 1981, 11.

4. See, for example, Vuono 1990, 3.

5. Numerous scholars argue for modified definitions of professionalism. See, for example, Janowitz 1977; Bradford and Brown 1973; and Hauser 1973.

6. This is the component of Huntington's definition that causes the most contention. Huntington portrayed officers with technical, "civilian" skills as distinct from line officers and as an impediment to professionalism. He likened the relationship between combat and support skills to that between the expertise of doctors and medical support staff, such as nurses (Huntington 1957, 12; Gough 1992, 432). For a powerful critique of this narrow definition, see Bacevich 1990.

7. Concern over this issue was the catalyst for the army's 1970 *Study of Military Professionalism*, countless books by military "reformers" in the early to mid-1970s, and the introduction of the Army's Officer Personnel Management System (OPMS) in 1974.

8. This trend is, of course, consistent with the evolution of analytic culture discussed in chapter 3.

9. Although these effects might have been anticipated, it is ironic that the same rationale that allowed the army to cut the officer corps with precision and relative success at the organizational level has undermined military professionalism at the individual level.

10. These tendencies have also been used by some analysts to account for military "failures" not only in Vietnam but in the Iranian hostage rescue mission, the 1983 bombing of a Marine barracks in Beirut, the U.S. invasion of Grenada, and elsewhere. See Luttwak 1985; and Gabriel 1985.

11. The guidelines for the original OPMS system circulated in 1971 state: "The guiding philosophy of OPMS is to: (1) improve the professional climate of the officer corps; (2) identify early, and develop carefully, officers most qualified for command; (3) allow for specialization in some technical areas without undue restriction on promotion and schooling opportunities; (4) provide a satisfying career for that large segment of the officer corps who are neither commanders nor specialists (*The Officer Personnel Management System*, June 25, 1971).

12. The army's leadership development process is a continuous cycle of education, training, and operational experience. During their careers, officers progress through four phases, in each of which they must complete certain branch-qualifying assignments and satisfy specific educational requirements before being eligible for promotion to the next phase (*Commissioned Officer Development and Career Management* 1995).

13. This second point was made by a senior civilian official in the U.S. Total Army Personnel Command, Interview, June 1995.

14. The large majority of officers who are selected for the Army War College are former battalion commanders. Selection for the War College is generally a pre-

requisite for promotion to colonel, and attendance at the War College, or one of the other senior service colleges, is generally a prerequisite for promotion to general. Interview, Colonels Division, U.S. Total Army Personnel Command, May 1996.

15. DOPMA formalized this objective. The DOPMA graded tables are based on a sliding scale in which the relative number of field grade officers permitted increases as the overall endstrength of the officer corps decreases. This reflects Congress' intent to retain a "base" of field grade officers for remobilization (Roskter et al. 1993, 9).

16. For a discussion of various types of mobilization, ranging from selective to total, see Goldich 1992.

17. Of course, this contributes to turbulence, as the maximum number of officers possible are rotated through existing command assignments to gain as much experience across the officer corps as possible.

18. For an example of the mobilization mentality, see General Gordon Sullivan's comments concerning reconstitution in his prepared statement before Congress. Hearings of the House Armed Forces Committee (March 31, 1993).

19. Under DOPMA, mandatory retirement for generals, colonels, lieutenant colonels and majors is 35 years, 30 years, 28 years, and 20 years, respectively (Strand 1993, 122).

20. Although promotions are marginally faster and retirement slightly earlier, the overall pattern of assignments and schooling is remarkably the same.

21. This problem was exacerbated in 1986 by the passage of the Department of Defense Reorganization Act (also known as Goldwater-Nichols) which mandated that officers would be denied promotion to general unless they had previously served in a joint assignment. This legislation further cluttered prototypical army officer career patterns (Strand 1993, 46).

22. The army's most recent attempt in this area is the *Army Assessment 1995*, a survey distributed across the service by the Army Research Institute and focusing on the professional climate (Reimer 1996).

23. The term "reprofessionalization" is used interchangeably with institution building (Cotton 1988).

24. The army began to move in this direction by expanding the jobs for majors across branches that are considered to be branch-qualifying (*Commissioned Officer Development and Career Management* 1995). There is great anxiety in the field, however, over how these new assignments will be viewed by promotion boards. Interviews, June–August, 1995.

25. At two points during an officer's first twelve years of service, he or she is required to complete mandatory military schooling before serving in critical branch-qualifying jobs. Between their fourth and fifth years, most captains spend approximately twenty weeks in their branch's advancement course. This requirement must be satisfied before they serve as company commanders. Likewise, the majority of of-

ficers are selected for the Command and General Staff College between their eleventh and fourteenth years of service (those not selected must complete the course by correspondence). Officers must be CGSC-qualified before serving in critical branch-qualifying jobs as majors.

26. This was the policy in the early 1980s, but it was terminated after the curricula at the army's advance courses and the Command and General Staff College were revamped to prepare officers for these follow-on jobs. Interview, Colonel Charles Henning, former Chief Officer Division, Office of the Deputy Chief of Staff for Personnel, June 1996.

27. This is clearly the army's intent. It will purportedly introduce a new report in fall 1997. Interview, senior officer, OPMS Task Force, February 1997.

28. These proposals called for splitting the army organizationally into the "fighting army," comprising predominantly combat arms officers, and the "support army," made up predominantly of the other branches. "Command specialists" were to be treated differently in terms of promotion, professional education, and tenure from the rest of the officer corps.

29. A pluralist officer corps would arguably exacerbate the lamentably narrow interpretation of military professionalism that already exists.

30. The initial five to seven years in the "field army" serve a valuable purpose by socializing the officer into the army and reinforcing the military ethos. They also provide a foundation of basic skills and experience through which the officer can develop his or her expertise.

31. In other words, an infantry officer who chooses operations research as his functional area would automatically be assigned to the managerial/technical career track. Additionally, an analysis of officer requirements for the post–Cold War era is likely to yield requirements for new officer specialties.

32. Officers in the operational command track would also serve as executive officers and deputies at the battalion and brigade levels. For some additional insights into how the operational command track might evolve, see Nowowiejski 1995.

33. Interview, senior army officer, July 1995.

34. Janowitz defines "elites" as officers who were major generals or above and who were identified, on the basis of numerous interviews within the defense establishment, as key decisionmakers.

35. Rosen documents six peacetime case studies in which new and important doctrinal innovations resulted from this phenomenon with varying degrees of success. The process is a lengthy one, however, as it takes a long time for changes in promotion practices to occur and for young officers (who pursued these options) to rise to the top (1991, 105).

36. The same argument also applies more broadly to fellowships in think tanks or academic institutions, advanced education programs, and training with industry.

37. This runs counter to Huntington (1957), who maintains that insularity and isolation contribute to professionalism (Gough 1992, 421).

38. As the World War II generation has been replaced by the Vietnam generation, the number of senior public officials with military experience has declined precipitously (Gibson and Snider 1996).

39. See *Report to the Officer Corps, Results of the Professional Development of Officers Study Surveys* (April 1985, 13).

40. This recommendation is consistent with the findings of the Ad Hoc Study conducted by the Army Science Board in early 1995. The report warned that technical literacy is no longer valued by military line officers, or by the institution at large, and recommended that higher priority be placed on civilian graduate schooling in mathematics, science, and engineering, and that more flexible career patterns be adopted for technically proficient officers (*Military Officers for the High Tech Army of Today and Tomorrow*, January 5, 1995).

41. Moreover, in contrast to current trends, special education programs such as the School for Advanced Military Studies should take on added importance and prestige in a peacetime army. Before downsizing began, the *Leader Development Study* recommended increased participation in the School of Advanced Military Studies (1988, 20).

42. A detailed discussion of the curricula of the army's professional military schools lies outside the scope of this book. For more on this issue see Murray 1986/87; Forsythe 1992, 45–48; and Rokke 1995.

43. John Peck finds that, historically, promotion opportunity to "elite status" is equal across branches. While this is true in a relative sense, the vast majority of general officers are drawn from the combat arms branch, which comprises the large majority of line officers (1994, 232).

44. Dawkins demonstrated the difficulty of convincing officers to accept assignments voluntarily that they view to be outside the mainstream in his study of the military advisor system during the Vietnam War (1979).

45. Both studies were conducted for the Assistant Secretary of Defense (Force Management and Personnel).

46. Interview, former Army Chief of Staff General (ret.) Edward C. Meyer, May 1996.

47. Memorandum from William L. Hauser to the House Armed Services Committee Staff, June 26, 1994 (copy held by author).

48. This approach is consistent with those of democratic armies in other NATO countries (Thie and Brown 1994; Strand 1993).

49. Indeed, this points lends support to the idea that the army's current professional schooling system should remain largely intact. When possible, officer cohorts should undergo education and training experiences together to build the corporateness and esprit de corps that is an essential element of professionalism.

50. The British army, faced with the same issue, is fearful that as it becomes

smaller it will be necessary to have relatively more specialists in its officer corps, an option it hopes to avoid due to the added expense. Discussion, British field marshall, June 1996.

51. A significantly smaller number of officers required is also likely to be an outcome of the rationalization of the TDA requirements process.

Acronyms

AC	Active Component
ACAP	Army Career and Alumni Program
ACS	Advanced Civilian Schooling
ADCSOPS	Assistant Deputy Chief of Staff for Operations
ADSO	Active Duty Service Obligation
ARI	Army Research Institute for the Behavioral and Social Sciences
ARSTAF	Army Staff
ASA/M&RA	Assistant Secretary of the Army for Manpower and Reserve Affairs
ASD/FM&P	Assistant Secretary of Defense (Force Management and Personnel
BF	Base Force
BUR	Bottom-Up Review
BZ	Below-the-Zone
CA	Combat Arms
CAS³	Combined Arms and Services Staff School
CBO	Congressional Budget Office
CG/FG	Company Guide to Field Grade Ratio
CGSC	Command and General Staff College
CINC	Commander in Chief
CMTC	Combat Maneuver Training Center
CSA	Chief of Staff of the Army
CS	Combat Support
CSS	Combat Service Support
DA	Department of the Army
DAIG	Department of the Army Inspector General
DCSOPS	Deputy Chief of Staff for Operations
DCSPER	Deputy Chief of Staff for Personnel
DCSRM	Deputy Chief of Staff for Resources Management
DMPM	Directorate of Military Personnel Management
DOD	Department of Defense
DOPMA	Defense Officer Personnel Management Act
E/O	Enlisted to Officer Ratio

FA	Functional Area
FAA	Functional Area Analysis
FAO	Foreign Area Officer
FM	Field Manual
FORCCOM	Forces Command
FY	Fiscal Year
GAO	General Accounting Office
JCS	Joint Chiefs of Staff
JRTC	Joint Readiness Training Center
LRDC	Longitudinal Research on Officer Careers
LTC	Lieutenant Colonel
LTG	Lieutenant General
LTRB	Lieutenant Retention Board
MACOM	Major Command
MP	Manpower Directorate
MRC	Major Regional Contingency
NCO	Noncommissioned Officer
NDAA	National Defense Authorization Act
NG	National Guard
NMS	National Military Strategy
NTC	National Training Center
O-1	Second Lieutenant
O-2	First Lieutenant
O-3	Captain
O-4	Major
O-5	Lieutenant Colonel
O-6	Colonel
OASA/M&RA	Office of the Assistant Secretary of the Army (Manpower and Reserve Affairs)
OCSA	Office of the Chief of Staff of the Army
ODCSPER	Office of the Deputy Chief of Staff for Personnel
ODP	Officer Distribution Plan
OER	Officer Evaluation Report
OMB	Office of Management and Budget
OML	Order of Merit List
OPMD	Officer Personnel Management Directorate
OPMS	Officer Personnel Management System
OPTEMPO	Operations Tempo
OSD	Office of the Secretary of Defense
OTRA	Other Than Regular Army
PA&E	Program Analysis and Evaluation
PERSCOM	U.S. Total Army Personnel Command

PERSTEMPO	Personnel Tempo
PMS	Professor of Military Science
POM	Program Objective Memorandum
PPBS	Planning, Programming, and Budgeting System
QDR	Quadrennial Defense Review
R&D	Research and Development
RA	Regular Army
RIF	Reduction in Force
ROTC	Reserve Officer Training Corps
SAMS	School of Advanced Military Studies
S-3	Operations Officer
SERB	Selective Early Retirement Board
SSB	Special Separation Bonus
SSMP	Sample Survey of Military Personnel
TDA	Table of Distribution and Allowances
TERA	Temporary Early Retirement Authority
TOE	Table of Organization and Equipment
TRADOC	Training and Doctrine Command
USA	United States Army
USAF	United States Air Force
USMC	United States Marine Corps
USN	United States Navy
USAR	Army Reserve
USMA	United States Military Academy
VERRP	Voluntary Early Release/Retirement Program
VCSA	Vice Chief of Staff of the Army
VSI	Voluntary Separation Incentive
XO	Executive Officer

Bibliography

Adams, Gordon, and Stephen Alexis Cain. 1989. "The Defense Budget in the 1990s." In *American Defense Annual, 1989–1990*, ed. Joseph Kruzel, 33–54. New York: Lexington Books.

Alcalá, Raoul H. 1993. U.S. Army Participation in the Bottom-Up Review, Report prepared for Center for National Security Studies, with addendum, Los Alamos National Laboratory (copy held by author).

———. 1994. Comments on the Historical Monograph, "The Development of the Base Force, 1989–1992" by Dr. Lorna Jaffe, June 11 (copy held by author).

Alterman, Eric. 1994. "Military Ties: Why Is the President Letting Conservative Hawks Hold His Domestic Agenda Hostage to Pentagon Fantasies?" *Mother Jones*, March, 66.

Anderson, Jon. 1995. "A Major Decision: What's Next?" *Army Times*, April 10, 10–14.

Approach to Sizing American Conventional Forces for the Post-Soviet Era, An. 1992. Les Aspin, House Armed Services Committee, February 27.

"Are U.S. Forces Ready to Fight?" 1994. *New York Times*, December 27, editorial page.

Armstrong-Stassen, Margerie. 1994. "Coping with Survivor Transition: A Study of Layoff Survivors." *Journal of Organizational Behavior* 15: 597–621.

Army Command, Leadership, and Management: Theory and Practice, 1994–1995. U.S. Army War College, Carlisle Barracks, Pa.

Asmus, Ronald. 1993. *The New U.S. Strategic Debate*. Santa Monica, Cal: RAND Corporation.

Assessment of Service Manpower Reduction Plans, An. 1990. Office of the Assistant Secretary of Defense for Force Management and Personnel, August.

Auster, Bruce. 1993. "The Commander and Chiefs." *U.S. News and World Report*, February 8, 37–39.

Axel, Helen. 1993. *Human Resources Executive Review*. Conference Board Report. New York.

Bacevich, A. J. 1990. "New Rules: Modern War and Military Professionals." *Parameters* 20: 12–23.

Bandow, Doug. 1996. "Dole's Military Card," *New York Times*, July 16, 19.

Barnes, James. 1996. "The Spirit of '96." *National Journal*, February, 12.

Bassford, Christopher. 1988. *The Spit-Shine Syndrome: Organizational Irrationality in the American Field Army*. New York: Greenwood Press.

———. 1990. "Cohesion, Personnel Stability, and the German Model." *Military Review* 80: no. 10: 73–81.

Batcheller, Gordon. 1991. "The Eclipse of the Joint Chiefs." *Marine Corps Gazette*, July, 32.

Bechloss, Michael, and Strobe Talbott. 1993. *At the Highest Levels: The Inside Story of the End of the Cold War*. Boston: Little, Brown.

Bennett, Amanda. 1990. *The Death of Organization Man*. New York: Simon and Schuster.

Bennett, James. 1990. "So Many Officers, So Little to Do." *The Washington Monthly* 22, no. 1: 22–27.

Best Practices in Corporate Restructuring: Wyatt's 1993 Survey of Corporate Restructuring. 1993. New York: Wyatt Company.

Betts, Richard. 1995. *Military Readiness: Concepts, Choices, and Consequences*. Washington, D.C.: Brookings Institution.

Binkin, Martin. 1984. *America's Volunteer Army: Progress and Prospects*. Washington, D.C.: Brookings Institution.

———. 1986. *Military Technology and Defense Manpower*. Washington, D.C.: Brookings Institution.

Binkin, Martin, and Irene Kyriakopoulos. 1981. *Paying the Modern Military*. Washington, D.C.: Brookings Institution.

Birtle, A. 1988. *Lineage and Functions of the Office of the Assistant Secretary of the Army (Manpower and Reserve Affairs), 1941–1988* (information paper). Washington, D.C.: U.S. Army Center for Military History.

Black, Chris. 1994. "Budget Issues Drive Flap over Army Readiness." *Boston Globe*, November 27, 2.

Blechman, Barry. 1990. *The Politics of National Security: Congress and the U.S. Defense Policy*. New York: Oxford University Press.

Borosage, Robert L. 1994. "Getting Over the Cold War: How to Curb the Pentagon's Fantasies—and Free Up Billions." *Washington Post*, February 20, C2.

Bowen, Wyn Q., and David H. Dunn. 1996. *American Security Policy in the 1990s*. Brookfield, Vt.: Dartmouth Publishing.

Bracken, Paul. 1993. "The Military after Next." *Washington Quarterly* 16 (autumn): 157–74.

Bradford, Zeb B., and Frederic J. Brown. 1973. *The United States Army in Transition*. Beverly Hills, Calif.: Sage Publications.

Bresler, Robert. 1993. *The New Freshmen, the 103rd Congress, and National Defense: Separating Rhetoric from Reality*. Carlisle, Pa.: Strategic Studies Institute, U.S. Army War College.

Brewer, Thomas. 1975. "The Impact of Advanced Education on American Military Officers." *Armed Forces and Society* 2, no. 1: 63–80.

Bridges, William. 1987. *Surviving the Survivor Syndrome* (pamphlet). New York: William Bridges and Associates.

Brockner, Joel. 1990. "Scope of Justice in the Workplace: How Survivors React to Co-Worker Layoffs." *Journal of Social Issues* 41, no. 1: 95–106.

———. 1992. "Managing the Effects of Layoffs on Survivors." *California Management Review* (winter): 9–28.

Brown, Walter T. 1975. "OER Inflation, Quotas, and Rating the Rater." *Air Review* 26: 38–47.

Builder, Carl. 1986. "On the Army Style of Analysis." Banquet talk given at the Twenty-Fifth Annual U.S. Army Operations Research Symposium, Fort Lee, Va., October 8 (copy held by author).

———. 1989. *The Masks of War*. Baltimore: Johns Hopkins University Press.

Byron, John L. 1992. "What Men or Gods Are These." *Proceedings*, December, 28–32.

Callahan, David. 1994. "Saving Defense Dollars." *Foreign Policy*, no. 96: 94.

Cameron, Kim. 1994a. "Guest Editor's Note: Investigating Organizational Downsizing—Fundamental Issues." *Human Resource Management* 33, no. 2: 183–88.

———. 1994b. "Strategies for Successful Organizational Downsizing." *Human Resource Management* 33, no. 2: 189–211.

Cameron, Kim, and Sarah Freeman. 1994. *The Downsizing of an Army Organization: An Investigation of Downsizing Strategies, Processes, and Outcomes*. Technical Report 1003. Alexandria, Va.: U.S. Army Research Institute for the Behavioral and Social Sciences.

Chainteaching Program: Drawing Down the Army, The. 1991–94. U.S. Total Army Personnel Command, Updates 1–4.

Coakley, Robert, Earnest Fisher, Karl Cocke, and Daniel Griffin. 1968a. *Resume of Army Roll-Up Following World War II*. Washington, D.C.: U.S. Army Center for Military History.

———. 1968b. *Demobilization Following the Korean War*. Washington, D.C.: U.S. Army Center for Military History.

Cocke, Kevin. 1991. "Demobilization After the Vietnam War." (information paper). Washington, D.C.: U.S. Army Center for Military History.

Cocke, Karl. 1994. "Evolution of U.S. Total Army Personnel Command" (information paper). Washington, D.C.: U.S. Army Center for Military History.

Collected Works of the Thirty-first Chief of Staff of the United States Army. 1991. Carl E. Vuono, General, United States Army Chief of Staff, June 1987–June 1991.

Collins, James. 1971. *Historical Analysis of Problems Facing the Army after Major Recent Conflicts*. Washington, D.C.: U.S. Army Center for Military History.

Commissioned Officer Development and Career Management. 1995. Department of the Army Pamphlet 600-3. Washington, D.C.: Headquarters, Department of the Army.

Comparison of the House and Senate Armed Services Committee FY 1996 Defense Authorization Bills. 1995. Defense Budget Project, Washington, D.C., July 26.

Congressional Budget Office (CBO). 1990a. *Savings from a 25 Percent Reduction in the Defense Department's Forces*. CBO Staff Memorandum (June). Washington, D.C.

———. 1990b. *Meeting New National Security Needs: Options for Military Forces in the 1990s*. CBO Papers (February). Washington, D.C.
———. 1990c. *Managing the Reduction in Military Personnel*. CBO Papers (July). Washington, D.C.
———. 1991. *Fiscal Implications of the Administration's Proposed Base Force*. CBO Staff Memorandum (December). Washington, D.C.
———. 1994a. *Planning for Defense: Affordability and Capability of the Administration's Program*. Memorandum (March). Washington, D.C.
———. 1994b. *The Costs of the Administration's Plan for the Army through the Year 2010*. Memorandum (November). Washington, D.C.
———. 1994c. *Trends in Selected Indicators of Military Readiness, 1980 through 1993*. CBO Papers (March). Washington, D.C.
———. 1995. *An Analysis of the Administration's Future Years Defense Program for 1995 through 1999*. CBO Papers (January). Washington, D.C.
Congressional Quarterly Almanac. 1993. 103rd Congress. Vol. 49: 433–45.
Cordesman, Anthony. 1994. *U.S. Defence Policy: Resources and Capabilities*. London: Royal United States Institute for Defence Studies.
Correl, John. 1992. "The Base Force Meets Option C." *Air Force Magazine*, June, 15.
———. 1994. "The High-Risk Military Strategy." *Air Force Magazine*, September, 34.
Cotton, Charles. 1988. "The Institutional Organization Model and the Military." In *The Military: More Than Just a Job?* ed. Charles Moskos and Frank R. Wood, 39–56. McLean, Va.: Pergamon-Brassey's International Defense Publishers.
Crowell, Lorenzo. 1993. "The Lessons and Ghosts of Vietnam." In *Looking Back on the Vietnam War: A 1990s Perspective on the Decisions, Combat, and Legacies*, ed. William Head and Lawrence Grinter, 230–40. Westport, Conn.: Praeger.
Dandeker, Christopher, 1994. "A Farewell to Arms? The Military and the Nation-State in a Changing World." In *The Military in New Times*, ed. James Burk, 117–39. New York: Westview Press.
Danzig, Richard. 1989. *Reforming the Pentagon: The Knowledge Gap*. Report to the Analytic Sciences Corporation (under contract to the Ford Foundation), Alexandria, Va.
Davis, J. E. 1994. "Where Leaders Come From." *Fortune*, September 19, 241–42.
Davis, Paul, David Gompert, and Richard Kugler. 1996. "Adaptiveness in National Defense: The Basis of a New Framework." RAND Issue Paper, National Defense Research Institute (August).
Davis, Paul, Richard Kugler, and Richard Hillestad. 1997. "Strategic Issues and Options for the Quadrennial Defense Review," RAND, National Defense Research Institute (February).
Dawkins, Peter. 1979. *The United States and the "Other" War in Vietnam*. Ph.D. diss., Woodrow Wilson School of Public and International Affairs, Princeton University.
Deagle, Edwin. 1972. "Anatomy of a Resignation: About Moral Numbness, Confidence, and Price." *Army Times*, August 23, 13.

Dean, Arthur. 1993. "Personnel Readiness—A Shared Responsibility." *Journal of the Adjutant General's Corps* 5, no. 4: 15–18.

Dean, Scott. 1988. "U.S. Generals Still Outnumbered in International Lineup." *Armed Forces Journal*, March, 20, 25.

Decisive Victory: America's Power Projection Army 1994. A White Paper (October).

Defense Officer Personnel Management Act. 1980. Report of the House Committee on the Armed Services. November 13.

De Meuse, Kenneth, and Walter Tornow. 1993. "Leadership and the Changing Psychological Contract Between Employer and Employee." *Issues and Observations* (Center for Creative Leadership) 13, no. 2: 3–6.

Demma, Vincent. 1994a. *Trace of the Organization and Strength of the Office, Deputy Chief of Staff for Personnel and Its Predecessor Organizations, 1921–1994* (information paper). Washington, D.C.: U.S. Army Center for Military History.

———. 1994b. *Army Personnel Policies: An Overview, 1984–1993* (information paper). Washington, D.C.: U.S. Army Center for Military History.

Demobilization Series Study No. 9, 1949, Procurement of Officers, 1 September 1945–10 March 1948, Historical Section, Army Field Forces. Washington, D.C.: U.S. Army Center for Military History.

Downs, George, and Patrick Larkey. 1986. *The Search for Government Efficiency.* Philadelphia: Temple University Press.

Drea, Edward. 1991. *Historical Perspective on CSA Roles during Times of Budget or Personnel Austerity* (information paper). Washington, D.C.: Center for Military History.

Duck, Jeanie D. 1993. "Managing Change: The Art of Balancing." *Harvard Business Review*, November–December, 109–18.

Dunnigan, James F., and Raymond M. Macedonia. 1993. *Getting It Right: American Military Reforms after Vietnam to the Persian Gulf and Beyond.* New York: William Morrow.

Dyer, Lee. 1983. "Bringing Human Resources into the Strategy Formulation Process." *Human Resource Management* 22, no. 3: 257–71.

Economist, The. 1994. "Divvying Up the Doughboys in Lean Times: Are Our Troops Stretched Too Thin to Keep U.S. the World's Top Cop?" October 18, 22.

Eitelberg, Mark. 1993. "Military Manpower and the Future Force." In *American Defense Annual, 1993*, ed. Joseph Kruzel, 135–54. New York: Lexington Books.

Ellis, James. 1992. "Where Troop Cuts Will Be Cruelest." *Business Week*, June 8, 72.

Elton, Robert, and Dandridge Malone. 1972. "The Informal Contract." *Army*, September, 10–14.

Etzioni, Amitai. 1964. *Modern Organizations.* Englewood Cliffs, NJ: Prentice-Hall.

Executive Review, Downsizing. 1993. Conference Board, vol. 1, no. 1: 1–14.

Fallows, James. 1981. "The Civilianization of the Army." *Atlantic Monthly*, April, 98–108.

Famiglietti, Gene. 1972. "New OER Okayed." *Army Times*, August 2, 1.
———. 1973a. "Abrams Scores OER Puff Jobs." *Army Times*, March 14, 1.
———. 1973b. "Froelke Backs Officer Equality." *Army Times*, May 9, 1.
———. 1973c. "Raters Inflate OER Despite Warning." *Army Times*, August 8, 1.
———. 1974. "New OER in '75." *Army Times*, December 4, 1.
Faris, John. 1984. "Economic and Noneconomic Factors of Personnel Recruitment and Retention in the AVF." *Armed Forces and Society* 10, no. 2: 251–75.
———. 1988. "The Social Psychology of Military Service and the Influence of Bureaucratic Rationalism." In *The Military: More Than Just a Job?* ed. Charles Moskos and Frank R. Wood, 57–78. McLean, Va.: Pergamon-Brassey's International Defense Publishers.
Fessler, Pamela. 1992. "Hill Struggles to Assist Victims of the Post–Cold War Budget Cuts." *Congressional Quarterly*, March 7, 542–45.
Finnegan, Philip, and Jason Glashow. 1995. "Perry Eyes Boost to Army Budget." *Defense News*, May 1–7, 1.
"First-time Selections for Colonel Only 30%." 1973. *Army Times*, May 23, 10.
Fitton, Robert A., ed. 1990. *Leadership: Quotations from the Military Tradition*. Boulder, Colo.: Westview Press.
Force XXI Operations: A Concept for the Evolution of Full-Dimensional Operations for the Strategic Army of the Early Twenty-First Century. 1994. TRADOC Pamphlet 525–5 (August 1).
Forsythe, George B. 1992. "The Preparation of Strategic Leaders." *Parameters* (spring): 38–47.
FY 1992 Department of the Army Historical Summary (draft), chapter 7, Personnel. Washington, D.C.: U.S. Army Center for Military History.
Gabriel, Charles, Alfred Gray, Carlisle Trost, and Robert RisCassi. 1995. *A Report on Military Capabilities and Readiness*. Prepared at the request of Senator John McCain, February 7.
Gabriel, Richard. 1985. *Military Incompetence: Why the American Military Doesn't Win*. New York: Hill and Wang.
Gabriel, Richard, and Paul Savage. 1978. *Crisis in Command*. New York: Hill and Wang.
Galvin, John. 1995. "What's the Matter with Being a Strategist?" *Parameters* (summer): 161–68.
Gannett News Service. 1994. "Republicans' Contract Loads Up Legislative Agenda." November 18.
Garrity, Patrick, and Sharon K. Weiner. 1992. "U.S. Defense Strategy after the Cold War." *Washington Quarterly* 15, no. 2: 57.
Geelhoed, E. Bruce. 1979. *Charles E. Wilson and Controversy at the Pentagon, 1953 to 1957*. Detroit: Wayne State University Press.
General Accounting Office (GAO). 1986. *Measuring Military Capability: Progress, Problems, Future Directions*. Washington, D.C.

———. 1992. *Defense Force Management: Composition of Groups Affected by Fiscal Year 1991 Force Reductions*. Washington, D.C.

———. 1993. *Military Downsizing: Balancing Accessions and Losses Is Key to Shaping the Future Force*. Washington, D.C.

———. 1994a. *Future Years Defense Program: Optimistic Assumptions Lead to Billions in Overprogramming*. Washington, D.C.

———. 1994b. *Military Readiness: DOD Needs to Develop a More Comprehensive Measurement System*. Washington, D.C.

———. 1995a. *Military Personnel: High Aggregate Personnel Levels Maintained throughout Drawdown*. Washington, D.C.

———. 1995b. *Military Downsizing, Persons Returning to Civilian Life Need More Help from DOD*. Washington, D.C.

———. 1995c. *Workforce Reductions: Downsizing Strategies Used in Selected Organizations*. Washington, D.C.

———. 1995d. *Bottom-Up Review, Analysis of Key DOD Assumptions*. Washington, D.C.

"General Dennis Reimer: Army Chief of Staff." Interview. 1995. *Army Times*, November 11.

Gibson, Christopher, and Don Snider. 1996. *Explaining Post–Cold War Civil-Military Relations: A New Institutionalist Approach*. A paper presented at the School for Advanced International Studies as part of the John M. Olin Institute for Strategic Studies Project on Post–Cold War Civil Military Relations.

Goldich, Robert. 1992. *Defense Reconstitution: Strategic Context and Implementation*. CRS Report for Congress. November 20.

Goss, Tracy, Richard Pascale, and Anthony Athos. 1993. "The Reinvention Roller Coaster: Risking the Present for a Powerful Future." *Harvard Business Review*, November–December, 97–108.

Gough, Terrence. 1992. "Isolation and Professionalization of the Army Officer Corps: A Post-Revisionist View of The Soldier and The State." *Social Science Quarterly* 73, no. 2: 421–35.

Graham, Bradley. 1994. "Republicans Plot Military Maneuvers." *Washington Post*, December 12, A21.

———. 1995. "Military Short of Victory in War on Bias." *Washington Post*, April 29, A1.

Gray, Colin. 1994. "Off the Map: Defense Planning after the Soviet Threat." *Strategic Review* 22, no. 2: 26–35.

Greenfield, David. 1995. "Downsizing, Military-Style." *Operations Research/Management Science Today*, April, 3–4.

Greengard, Samuel. 1993. "Don't Rush Downsizing: Plan, Plan, Plan." *Personnel Journal*, November, 64–76.

Greenhalgh, Leonard, Anne Lawrence, and Robert Sutton. 1988. "Determinants of Work Force Reduction Strategies in Declining Organizations." *Academy of Management Review* 13, no. 2: 241–54.

Grismer, David. 1992. *Evaluating Policies for Voluntary Senior Separations during Drawdown* (working paper). Santa Monica, Calif.: RAND Corporation.

Hadley, Arthur. 1986a. "The Split Military Psyche." *New York Times Magazine*, July 13, 26.

———. 1986b. *The Straw Giant*. New York: Random House.

Hall, Gaineford J., and S. Craig Moore. 1982. *Uncertainty in Personnel Force Modeling*. Santa Monica, Calif.: RAND Corporation.

Halloran, Richard. 1984. *Serving America: Prospects for the Volunteer Force*. New York: Priority Publications.

Hammond, Paul. 1961. *Organizing for Defense: The American Military Establishment in the 20th Century*. Princeton: Princeton University Press.

———. 1994. "Central Organization in the Transition from Bush to Clinton." In *American Defense Annual, 1994*, ed. Charles Hermann, 163–82. New York: Lexington Books.

Harback, Herbert. 1992. "The Threat to Strategic Leadership." *Military Review*, November, 72–79.

———. 1993. "Leadership Lessons from Downsized Corporate America." *Military Review*, August, 24–31.

Hardy, Cynthia. 1990. *Strategies for Retrenchment and Turnaround: The Politics of Survival*. Berlin, N.Y.: W. DeGruyter.

Harris, Beverly. 1994. *Perceptions of Army Officers in a Changing Army*. Alexandria, Va.: U.S. Army Research Institute.

Hauser, William L. 1973. *America's Army in Crisis*. Baltimore: Johns Hopkins University Press.

———. 1984. "Careerism vs. Professionalism." *Armed Forces and Society* 10, no. 3: 449–63.

———. 1985. *Restoring Military Professionalism*. Heritage Foundation Backgrounder, number 449. Washington, D.C.: Heritage Foundation.

———. 1992. "Career Management: Time for a Bold Adjustment." *Parameters* (spring): 50–59.

———. 1994. Memorandum to the House Armed Services Committee Staff, June 26 (copy held by author).

———. 1996. "Professional Management for a Revolution in Military Affairs." *Inter-University Seminar on Armed Forces and Society Newsletter* (winter): 13, 15.

Hauser, William L., and Zeb Bradford. 1971. "Officer Corps Reform Is Our Job." *Army*, December, 34–39.

Hayes, James. 1978. *The Evolution of Military Officer Management Policies: A Preliminary Study with Parallels from Industry*. Santa Monica, Calif.: RAND Corporation.

Healy, Melissa. 1992. "Pentagon Manpower Plan May Force Dismissals." *Los Angeles Times*, January 12, 4.

Hearing of the House Armed Services Committee. February 26, 1992. *National Defense Authorization Act for Fiscal Year 1993*.

Hearings of the House Appropriations Committee. February 21, 1990. *FY 1991 Army Posture.*
———. March 8, 1990. *Military Manpower: Department of the Army.*
———. March 6, 1991. *Fiscal Year 1992 Army Posture.*
Hearings of the House Armed Services Committee. February 27, 1990. *Congressional Budget Office Force Structure Overview.*
———. March 5, 1990. *The FY 1991 Authorization Act.*
———. March 20, 1991. *Manpower Budget Overview.*
———. July 31, 1991. *Implementing the Force Drawdown.*
———. March 31, 1993. *FY 1994 National Defense Authorization, Army.*
Hearings of the Senate Appropriations Committee. March 14, 1991. *Department of Defense Appropriations for FY 1992.*
———. March 9, 1994. *Department of Defense Appropriations for FY 1995.*
Hearings of the Senate Armed Services Committee. February 26, 1992. *National Defense Authorization Act for Fiscal Year 1993.*
———. April 1, 1993. *Department of Defense Authorization for Appropriations for Fiscal Year 1994 and Future Years Defense Program.*
Hearings of the Senate Armed Services Committee, April 1, 1993. *1994 Defense Authorization Act.*
Hewes, James. 1975. *From Root to McNamara: Army Downsizing and Administration, 1900–1963.* Washington, D.C.: U.S. Army Center of Military History.
Hickok, Thomas A. 1995. *The Impact of Work Force Reductions on Those Who Remain: A Study of Civilian Workers at Two Department of Defense Bases.* Ph.D. diss., School of Public Administration, University of Southern California.
———. 1996. *Annotated Bibliography on Work Force Reductions* (draft). Greensboro, N.C.: Center for Creative Leadership.
Hix, William M., and Richard Sortor. 1991. *Strategic Planning for the United States Army Personnel Function.* Santa Monica, Calif.: RAND Corporation.
Hodermarsky, Commander George T. 1990. *Postwar Naval Force Reductions 1945–1950: Impact on the Next War.* Master's thesis, Naval War College.
Horner, Donald. 1995. "Leader Development and Why It Remains Important." *Military Review* 75, no. 4: 76–87.
Hough, Paul G. 1989. *Birth of a Profession: Four Decades of Military Cost Analysis.* Santa Monica, Calif.: RAND Corporation.
Hudson, Neff. 1995. "Equal Opportunity in the Military." *Army Times*, May 1, 8.
Hunt, S. D., and R. Morgan. 1994. "Organizational Commitment: One of Many Commitments or Key Mediating Construct?" *Academy of Management Journal* 37: 1568–1687.
Huntington, Samuel. 1957. *The Soldier and The State.* Cambridge: Harvard University Press.
———. 1961. *The Common Defense: Strategic Programs in National Politics.* New York: Columbia University Press.

Huxley, Aldous. 1959. *Collected Essays*. New York: Harper and Brothers.
Ingraham, Larry. 1985. "The OER Cudgel: Radical Surgery Needed." *Army*, November, 54–57.
Ippolito, Dennis. 1994. *Blunting the Sword: Budget Policy and the Future of Defense*. Washington, D.C.: Institute for National Strategic Studies, National Defense University.
Jaffe, Lorna. 1994. *The Development of the Based Force (1989–1992)*. Joint History Office, Office of the Chairman of the Joint Chiefs of Staff.
Janis, Irving. 1982. *Groupthink: Psychological Studies of Policy Decisions and Fiascoes*. New York: Houghton Mifflin.
Janowitz, Morris. 1960. *The Professional Soldier: A Social and Political Portrait*. Glencoe, Ill.: Free Press.
———. 1972. "Volunteer Armed Forces and Military Purpose." *Foreign Affairs* 50, no. 3: 427–43.
———. 1977. "From Institutional to Occupational: The Need for Conceptual Clarity." *Armed Forces and Society* 4, no. 1: 51–54.
———, ed. 1964. *The New Military: Changing Patterns of Organization*. New York: Russell Sage Foundation.
Jaquette, D. L., G. R. Nelson, and R. J. Smith. 1977. *An Analytic Review of Personnel Models in the Department of Defense*. Santa Monica, Calif.: RAND Corporation.
Jervis, Robert. 1976. *Perception and Misperception in International Politics*. Princeton, N.J.: Princeton University Press.
Johns, John. 1984. *Cohesion in the U.S. Military*. Ft. Lesley McNair, Washington, D.C.: National Defense University Press.
Just, Ward. 1970. *Military Men*. New York: Alfred A. Knopf.
Kamensky, John. 1996. "Role of the Reinventing Government Movement in Federal Management Reform." *Public Administration Review* 56, no. 2: 247–55.
Kanter, Arnold. 1975. *Defense Politics*. Chicago: University of Chicago Press.
Kaufmann, William W. 1992. *Assessing the Base Force: How Much Is Too Much?* Washington, D.C.: Brookings Institution.
Kaufmann, William W., and John D. Steinbruner. 1991. *Decisions for Defense: Prospects for a New Order*. Washington, D.C.: Brookings Institution.
Keegan, John. 1976. *The Face of Battle*. London: Penguin Books.
Kinnard, Douglas. 1977a. *The War Managers*. Hanover: University of New Hampshire.
———. 1977b. *President Eisenhower and Strategy Management: A Study in Defense Politics*. Lexington: University Press of Kentucky.
Kitfield, James. 1991. "Schooled in Warfare." *National Journal*, October.
———. 1992a. "Victory the Next Time." *National Journal*, January.
———. 1992b. "Army: Suffering More Than Its Sister Services." *National Journal*, August.

———. 1993a. "General Dennis Reimer: Focusing on the Drawdown." *National Journal*, March.
———. 1993b. "The Drawdown Deepens." *National Journal*, May.
———. 1993c. "Keeping the Production Fires Burning ... Weakly." *National Journal*, August.
———. 1995a. *Prodigal Soldiers*. New York: Simon and Schuster.
———. 1995b. "Crisis of Conscience." *National Journal*, October.
Korb, Lawrence, ed. 1976. *The System for Educating Military Officers in the U.S.* Occasional paper no. 9. Pittsburgh: International Studies Association, University of Pittsburgh.
Koretz, Gene. 1997. "Big Payoffs from Layoffs: How the Largest Downsizers Fared." *Business Week*, February 21, 30.
Kotter, John, and James Heskett. 1992. *Corporate Culture and Performance*. New York: Free Press.
Kozlowski, Steve, Georgia Chao, Elanor Smith, and Jennifer Hedlund. 1991. *Organizational Downsizing: Individual and Organizational Implications and Recommendations for Action*. Technical Report 929. Alexandria, Va.: U.S. Army Research Institute for the Behavioral and Social Sciences.
Krepinevich, Andrew, Jr. 1994a. *The Bottom Up Review: An Assessment*. Washington, D.C.: Defense Budget Project.
———. 1994. "Keeping Pace with the Military-Technological Revolution." *Issues in Science and Technology* 24 (summer): 23–29.
Krueger, Richard A. 1994. *Focus Groups: A Practical Guide for Applied Research*, 2d ed. Thousand Oaks, Calif.: Sage Publications.
Lancaster, John. 1992. "Top Pentagon Officials Defend Need to Retain Large Military; Cheney, Powell Seek to Counter Charges That They Failed to Adjust." *Washington Post*, February 1, A4.
Landers, Robert. 1990. "Downsizing America's Armed Forces." *Editorial Research Reports* 2 (June 8).
Lang, Kurt. 1964. "Technology and Career Management in the Military Establishment." In *The New Military: Changing Patterns of Organization*, ed. Morris Janowitz, 39–82. New York: Russell Sage Foundation.
Laurence, Janice. 1991. *Implications of the Defense Drawdown on Minorities*. Human Resources Research Organization. Paper presented at the Biennial Conference of the Inter-University Seminar on Armed Forces and Society, Baltimore.
Leader Development Study (Final Report). 1988. Prepared by a Study Group for the Chief of Staff of the Army, April, Ft. Leavenworth, Kans.
Lester, Marianne. 1974. "Getting RIFED: Being Average isn't Good Enough Anymore." *Army Times* (Family Supplement) (January 16): 8–10.
Lewis, John. 1989. *Historical U.S. Force Structure Trends: A Primer*. Santa Monica, Calif.: RAND Corporation.

Lewis, Leslie, Robert Roll, and John Mayer. 1992. *Assessing the Structure and Mix of Future Active and Reserve Forces: Assessment of Political and Practices for Implementing the Total Force Policy.* Santa Monica, Calif.: RAND Corporation.

Lorsch, Jay W. 1986. "Managing Culture: The Invisible Barrier to Strategic Change." *California Management Review* 28, no. 2: 95–109.

Lucas, William, and Raymond Dawson. 1974. *The Organizational Politics of Defense.* Occasional paper no. 2. Pittsburgh: International Studies Association, University of Pittsburgh.

Luttwak, Edward. 1985. *The Pentagon and the Art of War: The Question of Military Reform.* New York: Simon and Schuster.

Lynn, William J. 1985. "The Wars Within: The Joint Military Structure and Its Critics." In *Reorganizing America's Defense: Leadership in War and Peace*, ed. Robert J. Art, Vincent Davis, and Samuel Huntington, 168–206. Washington, D.C.: Pergamon-Brassey's International Defense Publishers.

Marshall, Catherine, and Gretchen B. Rossman. 1995. *Designing Qualitative Research.* 2d ed. Thousand Oaks, Calif.: Sage Publications.

Mathews, William. 1993. "Task Force Will Study Threat of 'Hollow Force.'" *Army Times*, May 31.

Maze, Rick. 1994. "Transition Counseling May Become a Thing of the Past." *Army Times*, August 7, 6.

———. 1995. "Retired Pay Cuts Loom in Budget Plan." *Army Times*, August 14, 3.

McAllister, Bill. 1994. "Can Marvin Runyon Deliver?" *Washington Post Magazine*, July 10, 17–19, 28–35.

McCain, John. 1992. "A New Direction for Defense." *Roll Call*, September 28.

———. 1994. *Going Hollow: The Warnings of the Chiefs of Staff, An Update.* Office of Senator John McCain, September.

McCracken, Grant. 1988. *The Long Interview.* Thousand Oaks, Calif.: Sage Publications.

McIntire, Katherine. 1992. "General William DePuy: Architect of Revolution." *Army Times*, September 21.

McNeill, Charles (Study Group Leader). 1974. *The 50,000 Man-Year Reduction: An Army Example of Crisis Management and Decisionmaking.* U.S. Army War College Research Program Paper. Carlisle Barracks, Penn.: Military History Institute, U.S. Army War College.

Meyer, Edward C., Manning Ancell, and June Mahaffey. 1995. *Who Will Lead: Senior Leadership in the United States Army.* Westport, Conn.: Praeger.

Military Leadership. 1990. Field Manual, 22–100. Washington, D.C.: Headquarters, Department of the Army.

Military Officers for the High Tech Army of Today and Tomorrow. January 5, 1995. (Briefing slides, Ad Hoc Study), Army Science Board.

Military Personnel: End Strength, Separations, Transition Programs, and Downsizing Strategy. 1993. Annex J to Adjusting to the Drawdown, Report. Washington, D.C.: Defense Conversion Commission.

Miller, Robert A. 1973. "The United States Army during the 1930s." Ph.D. diss., Department of Politics, Princeton University.

Millett, Allan, and Peter Maslowski. 1984. *For the Common Defense: A Military History of the United States of America.* New York: Free Press.

Millett, Allan, Williamson Murray, and Kenneth Watman. 1988. "The Effectiveness of Military Organizations." In *Military Effectiveness, Vol. 1: The First World War,* ed. Allan Millett and Williamson Murray, 1–31. Boston: Allen and Unwin.

Mills, Quinn D., and G. Bruce Friesen. 1996. *Broken Promises: An Unconventional View of What Went Wrong at IBM.* Cambridge: Harvard Business School Press.

Mone, Mark. 1994. "Relationships between Self-Concepts, Aspirations, Emotional Responses, and Intent to Leave a Downsizing Organization." *Human Resource Management* 33, no. 2: 281–98.

Morrison, David C. 1993. "How Many Carriers Are Enough?" *National Journal* 25, no. 36: 2162.

———. 1994. "Bottoming Out?" *National Journal* 26, no. 38: 2126.

Moskos, Charles. 1977. "From Institution to Occupation: Trends in Military Organization." *Armed Forces and Society* 4, no. 1: 41–50.

———. 1988. "Institutional and Occupational Trends in Armed Forces." In *The Military: More Than Just a Job?* ed. Charles Moskos and Frank R. Wood, 15–26. McLean, Va.: Pergamon-Brassey's International Defense Publishers.

Moskos, Charles, and Frank R. Wood, eds. 1988a. *The Military: More Than Just a Job?* McClean, Va.: Pergamon-Brassey's International Defense Publishers.

———. 1988b. "Introduction." In *The Military: More Than Just a Job?* ed. Charles Moskos and Frank R. Wood, 3–14. McLean, Va.: Pergamon-Brassey's International Defense Publishers.

Murray, Williamson. 1986/87. "Grading the War Colleges." *The National Interest,* no. 6 (winter): 12–19.

———, ed. 1995. *Brassey's Mershom American Defense Annual, 1995–1996.* Washington, D.C.: Brassey's International Defense Publishers.

Mylander, Maureen. 1974. *The Generals.* New York: Dial Press.

National Defense Budget Estimates for FY 1997. 1996. Office of the Under Secretary of Defense (Comptroller), April.

Naylor, Sean. 1993. "Readiness: Suddenly the Word is on Everyone's Lips." *Army Times,* July 12.

Neustadt, Richard, and Ernest May. 1986. *Thinking in Time.* New York: Free Press.

Noer, David. 1993. *Healing the Wounds: Overcoming the Trauma of Layoffs and Revitalizing Downsized Organizations.* San Francisco: Jossey-Bass.

Nowowiejski, D. 1995. "Leader Development and Why It Remains Important." *Military Review* 75, no. 4: 70–75.

Officer Management Legislation: Why Needed? 1990. Report to the Committees on Armed Services of the U.S. Senate and House of Representatives, Office of the Assistant Secretary of Defense (Force Management and Personnel), February.

Officer Personnel Management System, The. 1971. Department of the Army, Office of the Adjutant General, June 25.

"Officer Selection Rates on Decline." 1975. *Army Times*, September 3, 36.

O'Hanlon, Michael. 1995. *Defense Planning for the Late 1990s: Beyond the Desert Storm Framework.* Washington, D.C.: Brookings Institution.

O'Keefe, Sean. 1994. "Planning without a Plan: A Review of the Clinton Defense Budget." In *American Defense Annual, 1994*, ed. Charles Hermann, 44–64. New York: Lexington Books.

OPMS XXI Precursor Study Issues (rough draft). 1994. U.S. Army Total Personnel Command, U.S. Army OPMS Precursor Study Group.

Osborne, David, and Ted Gaebler. 1992. *Reinventing Government: How the Entrepreneurial Spirit Is Transforming the Public Sector.* New York: Addison-Wesley.

Owens, Mackubin T. 1995. "Strategy and Resources: Trends in the U.S. Defense Budget." In *Brassey's Mershon American Defense Annual, 1995–1996*, ed. Williamson Murray, 155–81. Washington, D.C.: Pergamon-Brassey's International Defense Publishers.

Parkinson, Russell. 1992. *Project Transition* (information paper). Washington, D.C.: U.S. Army Center for Military History.

Partington, Angela, ed. 1992. *The Oxford Dictionary of Quotations.* 4th ed. Oxford: Oxford University Press.

Peck, John. 1994. "Assessing the Career Mobility of U.S. Army Officers: 1950–1974." *Armed Forces and Society* 20, no. 2: 217–37.

Pendley, William T. 1994. "Mortgaging the Future to the Present in Defense Policy: A Commentary on the Bottom-Up Review." *Strategic Review* 22, no. 2: 36–39.

Peppers, Jerome G. 1988. *History of United States Military Logistics 1935–1985.* Huntsville, Ala.: Logistics Education Foundation Publishing.

Peters, Ralph. 1993. "Drawdown Hardships Summon Soldiers' Best." *Army Times*, March 8.

Philpott, Tom. 1993. "Quality Gamble: Leaner, Meaner, or Weaker?" *Army Times*, June 14.

Pine, Art. 1994. "Pentagon's Bottom-Up Review Appears to Be Down and Out." *Los Angeles Times*, August 23, 5.

Post, G. 1973. "Five Officer Branch Shortages Easing." *Army Times*, April 11, 8.

Powell, Colin (with Joe Persico). 1995. *My American Journey.* New York: Random House.

Putnam, Robert. 1988. "Diplomacy and Domestic Politics: The Logic of Two-Level Games." *International Organization* 43, no. 2: 427–60.

Redina, Mark. 1990. "An Officer Corps for the 1990s." *Military Review*, October, 64–72.

Reich, Robert. 1996. "Don't Blame the Corporations." *Des Moines Register*, January 5, 11.

Reimer, Dennis. 1996. "Leadership for the 21st Century: Empowerment, Environment, and the Golden Rule." *Military Review* 76, no. 1: 5–9.

Remarks of Representative Les Aspin (D-WI) to the Air Force Association, Washington, D.C., Office of Representative Les Aspin, September 17, 1991.

Remarks of Secretary of Defense Richard Cheney to the Philadelphia World Affairs Council, Philadelphia, October 16, 1992.

Report for the Joint Chiefs of Staff on Post Transition Experiences of Military Seeking Jobs in the Private Sector, A. 1995. New York: Wesley, Brown, and Bartle Company. (Copy held by author).

Report to the Officer Corps, Results of the Professional Development of Officers Study Surveys. 1985, Washington, D.C.: Office of the Chief of Public Affairs, Headquarters, Department of the Army, April.

Republican Defense Proposals May Worsen Plans/Funding Mismatch. 1995. Defense Budget Project, Washington, D.C., June 30.

Ricks, Thomas. 1995. "In the Wake of the Cold War, An Intellectual Leads Army in New Missions." *Wall Street Journal*, October 2, 1.

Roades, Charles W. 1973. "Fast Burner: Does He Hear a Different Drummer?" *Air University Review*, November–December, 88–93.

Rokke, Mervin. 1995. "Military Education for the New Age." *Joint Forces Quarterly*, no. 9 (autumn): 18–23.

Rosen, Stephen P. 1991. *Winning the Next War: Innovation and the Modern Military.* Ithaca: Cornell University Press.

Rostker, Bernie, Harry Thie, James Lacy, Jennifer Katawa, and Susanna Purnell. 1993. *The Defense Officer Personnel Management Act of 1980: A Retrospective Assessment.* Santa Monica, Calif.: RAND Corporation.

Sadacca, Robert, Janice Laurence, and Ani DiFazio. 1995. *Outcome and Evaluation of the Army Career and Alumni Program's Job Assistance Centers.* Alexandria, Va.: Human Resources Research Organization, June 16.

Sarkesian, Sam C. 1975. *The Professional Army Officer in a Changing Society.* Chicago: Nelson-Hall.

———. 1981. *Beyond the Battlefield: The New Military Professionalism.* New York: Pergamon-Brassey's International Defense Publishers.

Sarkesian, Sam C., and William Taylor. 1975. "The Case for Civilian Graduate Education for Professional Officers." *Armed Forces and Society* 1, no. 2: 251–61.

Schein, Edward. 1985. *Organizational Culture and Leadership.* San Francisco: Jossey-Bass.

Schmitt, Eric. 1992. "A New Battle Ahead for Powell: The Budget." *New York Times*, January 17, 16.

———. 1994. "Pentagon Buoying Troops, Will Cut Arms Development." *New York Times*, August 23, 18.

Science and Engineering Requirements for Military Officers and Civilian Personnel in the High Tech Army of Today and Tomorrow, The. 1996. Ad Hoc Study, Final Report. Army Science Board, February.

Scroggs, Stephen K. 1996. "Army Relations with Congress: The Impact of Culture

and Organization." Ph.D. diss., Department of Political Science, Duke University.
Segal, David. 1986. "Measuring the Institutional/Occupational Change Thesis." *Armed Forces and Society* 12, no. 3: 351–76.
——. 1989. *Recruiting for Uncle Sam: Citizenship and Military Manpower Policy.* Lawrence: University Press of Kansas.
——. 1993. *Organizational Designs for the Future Army.* Special Report 20. Alexandria, Va.: U.S. Army Research Institute for the Behavioral and Social Sciences.
Shane, Michael. 1991. "The Downside of Downsizing the Military." *FOCUS*, April, 4–5.
Shoemaker, R. 1972. "Officer Force-Out Set but Army Denies RIF." *Army Times*, January 6, 1.
Shy, John. 1986. "First Battles in Retrospect." In *America's First Battles, 1776–1965*, ed. Charles Heller and William Stofft, 327–54. Lawrence: University Press of Kansas.
Smith, Lynn. 1971. "What's Wrong with Being an Expert." *Army*, November, 26–29.
Snider, Donald M. 1987. "DOD Reorganization, Part I, New Imperatives." *Parameters* 18, no. 3: 88–100.
——. 1993a. *Strategy, Forces, and Budgets: Dominant Influences in Executive Decisionmaking, Post–Cold War, 1989–1991.* Carlisle, Pa.: Strategic Studies Institute, U.S. Army War College, February.
——. 1993b. "A Comparative Study of Executive National Security Decision-Making during Periods of Fundamental Changes: The Beginning and End of the Cold War." Ph.D. diss., School of Public Affairs, University of Maryland.
——. 1996a. U.S. Civil-Military Relations and the Search for New Strategies and Force Structure. Paper presented at the Conference on Strategy, Force Structure, and Defense Planning for the Twenty-First Century, Fletcher School of Law and Diplomacy (November).
——. 1996b. "The Coming Defense Train Wreck." *Washington Quarterly* 19, no. 1: 89.
Snyder, William P. 1994. "Military Retirees: A Portrait of the Community." *Armed Forces and Society* 20, no. 4: 581–98.
Sorley, Lewis. 1992a. "National Guard and Reserve Forces." In *American Defense Annual, 1991–1992*, ed. Joseph Kruzel, 182–201. New York: Lexington Books.
——. 1992b. *Thunderbolt: General Creighton Abrams and the Army of His Times.* New York: Simon and Schuster.
Sparrow, J. C. 1952. *History of Personnel Demobilization in the United States Army.* Washington, D.C.: Center of Military History, Department of the Army.
Spring, Baker. 1995. *Budget Cuts Could Spell End of American Global Power.* Heritage Foundation Reports, Background Update, vol. 258. Washington, D.C.: Heritage Foundation.
Stavem, Christine. 1995. "In Latest Twist, Army Considers Troop Reductions for 1998." *Defense Week* 16, no. 19.

Steinbeck, John. 1945. *Cannery Row*. New York: Viking Press.
Steward, William G. 1993. *From War to Peace: A History of Past Conversions*. Washington, D.C.: Logistics Management Institute.
Strand, Richard N. 1993. *Military Career Paths in Transition: A Comparative Study of Management Systems*. Ph.D. diss., School of Public Administration, University of Southern California.
Stroup, Theodore. 1996. "Leadership and Organizational Culture: Actions Speak Louder Than Words." *Military Review* 76, no. 1: 44–49.
Study on Military Professionalism. 1970. Carlisle Barracks, Pa.: U.S. Army War College.
Sullivan, Gordon. 1993. *America's Army into the Twenty-First Century*. National Security Paper No. 14. Institute for Foreign Policy Analysis in association with the Fletcher School of Law and Diplomacy, Tufts University.
Sullivan, Gordon, and Anthony Coroalles. 1995. *Seeing the Elephant: Leading America's Army into the Twenty-First Century*. National Security Paper No. 18. Institute for Foreign Policy Analysis in association with the Fletcher School of Law and Diplomacy, Tufts University.
Sullivan, Gordon, and James Dubik. 1995. *Envisioning Future Warfare*. Fort Leavenworth, Kans.: U.S. Army Command and General Staff College Press.
Sullivan, Leonard, Jr. 1993. "The Defense Budget in Transition." In *American Defense Annual, 1993*, ed. Joseph Kruzel, 25–52. New York: Lexington Books.
Taylor, William J., and Donald Bletz. 1974. "A Case for Officer Graduate Education." *Journal of Political and Military Sociology* 2 (fall): 251–267.
Thie, Harry J., and Roger A. Brown. 1994. *Future Career Management Systems for U.S. Military Officers*. Santa Monica, Calif.: RAND Corporation.
"33 West Point Instructors Quit." 1972. *Army Times*, July 12, 22.
Tice, James. 1975. "Next RIF Hits 2200 Officers." *Army Times*, March 5, 1.
———. 1994a. "Minorities Gain Despite Drawdown." *Army Times*, March 29, 18–19.
———. 1994b. "Minorities, Women Gain in Downsizing Active Force." *Army Times*, November 21, 8.
Tocqueville, Alexis de. 1992. *Democracy in America* (reprint of 1840 edition, vol. 2). New York: McGraw Hill.
Toffler, Alvin, and Heidi Toffler. 1993. *War and Anti-War*. New York: Warner Books.
Towell, Pat. 1990. "Cheney's Latest Plan Shows Only Part of Ax Blade." *Congressional Quarterly*, June 23, 1974–77.
———. 1992a. "Move to Cut Pentagon Spending Falls Short of Critic's Goal." *Congressional Quarterly*, February 29, 478–80.
———. 1992b. "Nunn Breaks from Democrats in Backing Bush's Request." *Congressional Quarterly*, March 28, 815.
Trask, David F., ed. 1983. *Historical Survey of U.S. Mobilization: Eight Topical Studies of the Twentieth Century* (draft report). Washington, D.C.: U.S. Army Center for Military History.
Uchitelle, Louis. 1996. "The New Buzz: Growth Is Good." *New York Times*, June 15, D1.

Uchitelle, Louis, and N. R. Kleinfield. 1996. "On Battlefield of Business, Millions of Casualties." *New York Times*, March 3, 1.
van Creveld, Martin. 1985. *Command in War*. Cambridge: Harvard University Press.
———. 1991. *The Transformation of War*. New York: Free Press.
Vuono, Carl E. 1990. "Professionalism and the Army in the 1990s." *Military Review* 70, no. 4: 2–9.
Walters, Ron. 1990. "Why Should Blacks Fight in the Gulf?" *Washington Post*, December 27, 17.
Waterman, Robert H., and Judith A. Waterman. 1994. "Toward a Career Resilient Workforce." *Harvard Business Review*, July–August, 87–95.
Weidenbaum, Murray. 1992. "The Economics of Defense in the 1990s." In *American Defense Annual, 1991–1992*, ed. Joseph Kruzel, 43–56. New York: Lexington Books.
Weigley, Russell. 1984. *History of the United States Army*. 2d ed. Bloomington: Indiana University Press.
West, Richard L. 1994. "Short Rations for the Army." *Army*, April, 19–25.
Whetten, D. A. 1980. "Organizational Decline: A Neglected Topic in Organizational Science." *Academy of Management Review* 5: 577–88.
Whyte, William H. 1956. *The Organization Man*. New York: Simon and Schuster.
Wildavsky, Aaron. 1988. *The New Politics of the Budgetary Process*. Glenview, Ill.: Scott, Foresman.
Wilson, C. George. 1995a. "Although Painful, Latest Drawdown Proving a Success," *Army Times*, March 6, 39.
———. 1995b. "Save Commands for Fighters," *Army Times*, October 30, 54.
Wilson, James Q. 1989. *Bureaucracy: What Government Agencies Do and Why They Do It*. Basic Books.
Wong, Leonard, and Jeff McNally. 1994. "Downsizing the Army: Some Policy Implications Affecting the Survivors." *Armed Forces and Society* 20, no. 2: 199–216.
Wood, David. 1995. "Unlikely Radical Inspires Army to Do More with Less." *Harrisburg Patriot-News*, April 2, A12.
Wood, Frank. 1988. "At the Cutting Edge of Institutional and Occupational Trends: The U.S. Air Force Officer Corps." In *The Military: More Than Just a Job?* Ed. Charles Moskos and Frank R. Wood, 27–38. McLean, Va.: Pergamon-Brassey's International Defense Publishers.
Yin, Robert. 1994. *Case Study Research: Design and Methods*. 2d ed. Thousand Oaks, Calif.: Sage Publications.
Yost, Barbara. 1991. *Senior Rater and Other Impacts on the Army's Officer Selection Process—Where Are We?* The Industrial College of the Armed Forces (Executive Research Project).

List of Interviews

INDIVIDUAL INTERVIEWS CONDUCTED BY THE AUTHOR*

Abell, Charles	August 1995
(Staff Member, Senate Armed Services Committee)	
Adams, Colonel James, USA (ret.)	April 1995
(Chief, Force Integration and Analysis Division, ODCSPER)	
Alcalá, Colonel Raoul, USA (ret.)	August 1995
(Chief, Chief of Staff's Analysis and Integration Group)	
Anderson, Colonel Tully, USA (ret.)	May 1995
(Chief, Program, Budget, Compensation Division, ODCSPER)	
Beard, Lieutenant Colonel, USA	May 1995
(Executive Officer, Directorate of Military Personnel Management, ODCSPER)	
Bergstrom, Colonel Albion, USA	April 1995
(Chief, Officer Division, ODCSPER)	
Botelho, Pauline	May 1995
(Director, Army Career and Alumni Program; Chief, Distribution Division, Army Personnel Command)	
Brost, Captain David, USA	June 1995
(Assignment Officer, PERSCOM)	
Brown, Lieutenant Colonel Joseph, USAF	June 1995
(Chief, Retirements/Separations Programs)	
Bryant, Captain Vincent, USA	June 1995
(Assignment Officer, PERSCOM)	

*Dr. James Yarrison from the U.S. Army Center for Military History also participated in a number of these interviews. The transcripts from the majority of the interviews are maintained at the Center for Military History. Contact the author for more information concerning the availability of these transcripts.

Several additional senior army officers who were interviewed for this study requested anonymity. Their comments are cited in the text, but due to the sensitivity of their positions, their names have been excluded from this list.

Buckles, Colonel Anthony, USA   July 1995
  (Chief, Combat Arms Division, PERSCOM)
Carlson, Colonel Gary, USA   May 1995
  (Chief, Sustainment and Development Branch,
  ODCSPER)
Carney, Lieutenant General Thomas, USA (ret.)   May 1996
  (Deputy Chief of Staff for Personnel)
Carter, Colonel Roland, USA   July 1995
  (Executive Officer, ODCSPER)
Cartland, Colonel John, USA (ret.)   May 1995
  (Deputy Director, Directorate of Manpower,
  ODCSPER)
Christman, Lieutenant General, Daniel, USA   April 1996
  (Assistant to the Chairman, Joint Chief of Staff)
Clark, William   May 1995
  (Deputy Assistant Secretary of the Army, Manpower
  and Reserve Affairs)
Darwin, Lieutenant Colonel Charles, USA (ret.)   June 1995
  (Budget Analyst, ODCSPER)
Davis, Lieutenant Colonel, USA   February 1996
  (Army Program Analysis and Evaluation)
Durso, Colonel Anthony, USA (ret.)   May 1995
  (Director, Plans, Analysis, and Evaluation, ODCSPER)
Emmerichs, Robert   May 1995
  (Deputy Assistant Secretary of the Army, Manpower
  and Reserve Affairs)
Faber, Colonel Morris, USA (ret.)   May 1995
  (Chief, Officer Division, ODCSPER)
Fennel, Colonel William, USA   June and July 1995
  (Branch Chief, PERSCOM)
Foster, Colonel William, USA   April 1996
  (Director, War Plans, Office of the Deputy Chief of
  Staff for Operations)
Fulcher, Lieutenant Colonel, USA   June, July 1995
  (Chief, Distribution Division, PERSCOM)
Goldich, Robert   April 1995
  (National Security Analyst, Congressional
  Research Service)
Greene, Lieutenant Commander, USN   July 1995
  (Head, Officer Promotion Plans)
Harper, Colonel Michael, USA, (ret.)   July 1995
  (Chief, Chief of Staff's Staff Group)

Harris, Beverly — June 1995
  (Researcher, Army Research Institute)
Harvey, Susan — July 1995
  (Program Officer, Army Career and Alumni Program)
Heath, Karen — May 1995
  (Staff Member, House Armed Services Committee)
Henning, Colonel Charles, USA — June 1995
  (Chief, Officer Division, ODCSPER)
Henry, P. T., USMC (ret.) — August 1995
  (Staff Member, Senate Armed Services Committee)
Higgins, Michael — April 1995
  (Staff Member, House Armed Services Committee)
Ingalsbe, Colonel Duane, USA (ret.) — May 1995
  (Chief, Program, Budget, Compensation Division, ODCSPER)
Jehn, Christopher — June 1995
  (Assistant Secretary of Defense, Force Management and Personnel)
Jones, Lieutenant General Donald, USA (ret.) — June 1995
  (Deputy Assistant Secretary of Defense, Force Management and Personnel)
Kelly, Colonel Larry, USA (ret.) — May 1995
  (Chief, Personnel Structure and Integration Division, ODCSPER)
King, Ernest, USA (ret.) — September 1995
  (Army Career and Alumni Program, Fort Hood, Texas)
Landrum, Colonel Michael, USA — May 1995
  (Speechwriter/Legislative Liaison, ODCSPER; Military Assistant to the Assistant Secretary of Defense Plans and Policy)
Larson, Colonel, USA — July 1995
  (Director, Officer Personnel Management System, OPMS XXI, Precursor Study)
Leahy, Colonel Michael, USA — July 1995
  (Chief, Functional Area Management Division, PERSCOM)
Lewis, Colonel Mark, USA — May 1995
  (Executive Officer, ODCSPER)
Loo, Lieutenant Colonel Brad, USA — May 1995
  (Chief, Analysis Branch, ODCSPER)
Maloney, Colonel James — July 1995
  (Chief, Officer Distribution Division, PERSCOM)

Mangano, Major William, USA May 1995
  (Analyst, Officer Division, ODCSPER)
Merrill, Colonel William, USA (ret.) June 1995
  (Chief, Military Personnel Policy and Equal Opportunity,
  Office of the Assistant Secretary of the Army/Manpower
  and Reserve Affairs)
Miles, Colonel, Paul, USA (ret.) October 1995
  (Aide de Camp, General William Westmoreland)
Miller, Jack August 1995
  (Chief, Management Support Division, PERSCOM)
Moore, Colonel, David, USA July 1995
  (Staff Officer, Office of the Assistant Secretary of
  Defense, Force Management and Personnel).
Nelson, Brigadier General Harold, USA (ret.) September 1995
  (Chief, U.S. Army Center for Military History)
Noblit, Major Mark, USMC July 1995
  (Analyst, Officer Plans Division)
Ono, Lieutenant General Allen, USA (ret.) July 1995
  (Deputy Chief of Staff for Personnel)
Ord, Lieutenant General Robert III, USA July 1995
  (Commander, U.S. Army Pacific Command;
  Commander, PERSCOM)
Pang, Fred May 1995
  (Assistant Secretary of Defense, Force Management;
  staff member, Senate Armed Services Committee)
Purdum, Gary June 1995
  (Chief, Directorate of Manpower, ODCSPER)
Putman, Major General Gerald, USA July 1995
  (Commander, PERSCOM)
Rangel, Colonel Hector, USA (ret.) June 1995
  (Chief, Sustainment and Development Branch, ODCSPER)
Reno, Lieutenant General William H., USA (ret.) July 1995
  (Deputy Chief of Staff for Personnel)
Reyenga, Lieutenant Colonel, USA July 1995
  (Assignment Officer, PERSCOM)
Schaefer, Major Gary, USA June 1995
  (Assignment Officer, PERSCOM)
Scribner, Lieutenant Colonel, Barry, USA (ret.) September 1995
  (Chief, Office of Economic and Manpower Analysis,
  West Point)
Shane, Colonel Michael, USA May 1995
  (Chief, Enlisted Distribution Division, PERSCOM)

Shupack, Lieutenant Colonel, USA (ret.) June 1995
  (Chief, Distribution Programs Branch, PERSCOM)
Sikora, Major General Thomas, USA June 1995
  (Director, Military Personnel Management Directorate,
  ODCSPER)
Smith, Lieutenant Colonel Gaylin, USA June 1995
  (Analyst, ODCSPER)
Smith, Captain Tracy, USA June 1995
  (Assignment Officer PERSCOM)
Spencer, Lieutenant Colonel Carmen, USA July 1995
  (Branch Chief, PERSCOM)
Stroup, Lieutenant General Theodore, USA (ret.) May, June 1995
  (Deputy Chief of Staff for Personnel)
Sullivan, General Gordon, USA (ret.) August 1995
  (Chief of Staff of the Army)
Terry, Colonel Joseph, USA (ret.) July 1995
  (Deputy, Directorate of Manpower, ODCSPER)
Thie, Harry July 1995
  (Analyst, RAND Corporation)
Thomas, Lieutenant Colonel Carter, USA (ret.) June 1995
  (Analyst, Directorate of Manpower, ODCSPER)
Thompson, Major General John, USA July 1995
  (Commander, PERSCOM)
Thornton, Lieutenant Colonel, Gene, USA August 1995
  (Chief, Sustainment and Development, ODCSPER)
Tice, James June 1995
  (Reporter, *Army Times*)
Valcourt, Lieutenant Colonel David, USA July 1995
  (Branch Chief, PERSCOM)
Vuono, General Carl E., USA (ret.) August 1995
  (Chief of Staff of the Army)
Wagonhurst, Colonel Jeffrey, USA July 1995
  (Deputy Director, Officer Personnel
  Management Directorate)
Waters, Lieutenant Colonel David, USA May 1995
  (Chief, Operations and Analysis Branch, ODCSPER)
Wilson, Thomas May 1995
  (Acting Deputy Assistant Secretary of the Army,
  Manpower and Reserve Affairs)
Wincup, Kim May 1995
  (Assistant Secretary of the Army, Manpower and
  Reserve Affairs)

Wong, Brigadier General Frederick, USA (ret.)   July 1995
(Director, Office Personnel Management Directorate)

INTERVIEWS CONDUCTED BY OTHER PERSONS

Changing an Army: An Oral History of General William E. DePuy. 1979. U.S. Army Military History Institute, Army War College, Carlisle Barracks, Carlisle, Penn.
Interview with Lieutenant General William H. Reno conducted by Dwight Oland, June 5, 1991. U.S. Army Center for Military History.
Interview with Lieutenant General William H. Reno, conducted by Dwight Oland, January 5, 1993. U.S. Army Center for Military History.
Interview with Lieutenant General (ret.) Reno conducted by Dwight Oland, February 17, 1993, U.S. Army Center for Military History.
Oral History of LTG (ret.) George Forsythe. 1974. U.S. Army Military History Institute, Army War College, Carlisle Barracks, Penn.
Oral History of General Maxwell Thurman. 1992. U.S. Army Military History Institute, Army War College, Carlisle Barracks, Penn.
Oral History of LTG (ret.) Allen Ono, Deputy Chief of Staff for Personnel, June 1987–July 1990. Interviews conducted by Dwight Oland, U.S. Army Center for Military History.

FIELD INTERVIEWS BY THE AUTHOR

Locations (July–September 1995)

Fort Sill, Oklahoma   Fort Leavenworth, Kansas
Schofield Barracks, Hawaii Carlisle Barracks, Pennsylvania
Fort Hood, Texas

Field Interview/Focus Groups

25 Focus Groups
15 Individual Interviews

Breakdown by Rank

Lieutenants and Captains	59	(43 percent)
Majors	41	(30 percent)
Lieutenant Colonels	26	(19 percent)
Colonels	6	(4 percent)
Total	132	

Additionally, six interviews were conducted with battalion, brigade, and division command sergeants major at these installations.

Index

Italicized letters *d, n,* and *t* following page numbers refer to diagrams, footnotes, and tables, respectively.

Abrams, Creighton, 11, 104–105, 117, 204*n*
ACAP. *See* Army Career and Alumni Program
Active duty service obligation (ADSO), 112
African Americans, 74, 84–86, 85*t*, 212*n*, 215*n*. *See also* Minorities
Air Force: Base Force and, 207*n*; Bottom-Up Review and, 42–43; post–Cold War vision of, 58; priorities of, 48, 57, 75
All-volunteer force, 7, 10, 220*n*
American Management Association, 204*n*
American Management Survey, 15
American Telephone and Telegraph, 13–14
Anteus Study, 34
Anti-intellectualism, 147, 152–156, 164–165, 225*n*
ARI. *See* Army Research Institute for the Behavioral and Social Sciences
Army: analytic culture of, 94–97, 106–111, 217*n*–218*n*, 220*n*; attitude changes in, 22–23, 117–136, 122*d*, 124*d*, 156, 191, 201; Base Force and, 33–37, 206*n*–207*n*; behavior changes in, 22–23, 136–156, 137*d*, 191, 201; Bottom-Up Review and, 43–48; communication in, 89–90, 99, 214*n*–216*n*; compassion in, 73–74, 76, 84, 110–111, 197, 214*n*–215*n*; confidence in leadership, 127–129, 128*d*; constituencies of, 68–69; diversity in, 74, 76–77, 84–86, 85*t*, 207*n*, 215*n*–216*n*; new world order and, 157–160, 193; organizational culture of, 58–59; political effectiveness of, 2–3, 11–13, 46, 55–59, 62, 196, 206*n*; post–Cold War vision of, 58; priorities of, 47–48, 57, 71–87, 167–168, 172, 212*n*; quality of, 72; susceptibility to cuts, 56–61; "tail" of, 67, 80–81, 87; "teeth" of, 67, 80–81, 87
Army Assessment 1995, 191, 227*n*
Army Career and Alumni Program (ACAP), 84, 90–91, 215*n*, 217*n*
Army Research Institute for the Behavioral and Social Sciences (ARI), 119, 133, 156, 221*n*
Army Science Board, 229*n*
Army Training and Doctrine Command (TRADOC), 219*n*
Army War College, 153–155, 183–184, 221*n*–222*n*, 227*n*
ASA/M&RA. *See* Office of the Assistant Secretary of the Army for Manpower and Reserve Affairs
Aspin, Les: in Congress, 35–36, 38–39, 53, 206*n*, 208*n*; as defense secretary, 39–43, 52, 54, 99, 208*n*–210*n*; Option C and, 38–39
Assignment officers, 78, 98–99, 214*n*, 218*n*–219*n*
Assignment policy, 146–148, 227*n*; flexibility in, 173–174, 179–181; marketability and, 148–149; military schools and, 152–156, 183–185; muddy boots army and, 150–152, 165, 205*n*; professional development and, 163–164; specialization and, 166, 186, 229*n*

Bacevich, A. J., 181–183, 193–194
Base Force, 28–39, 207*n*; budget and, 31–33, 38–39, 51–54, 206*n*; endstrength and, 29, 29*t*, 36–37, 40*t*, 206*n*–207*n*; force structure and, 29, 29*t*, 32–33, 36, 40*t*, 46; strategy and, 32–35, 38–39, 51–54, 205*n*, 208*n*, 210*n*
Bassford, Christopher, 145

259

260 | Index

Below the zone (BZ), 87, 139–140, 213*n*, 215*n*, 224*n*
Bottom-Up Review, 28, 39–54; budget and, 44, 48–49, 51–54, 208*n*; endstrength and, 40, 40*t*, 46, 49–50, 96, 209*n*; force structure and, 40*t*, 43, 45–46, 209*n*; strategy and, 43–44, 51–54
Bracken, Paul, 157
Branch qualifying, 138, 142, 173, 223*n*, 226*n*–228*n*
Bridges, William, 15
B-2 bomber, 32
Buchanan, Patrick, 14
Budget Enforcement Act (1990), 33
Budgets, defense: 1989–1997, 27*d*; Base Force and, 31–33, 38–39, 51–54, 206*n*; Bottom-Up Review and, 44, 48–49, 51–54, 208*n*; cuts in, 26, 30–33, 38–39, 41, 204*n*–205*n*, 208*n*; in peacetime, 197–198; strategy and, 28, 51–54; trade-offs in, 47–50, 209*n*–210*n*, 220*n*; underfunding in, 43–44, 47, 49, 209*n*, 211*n*
Builder, Carl, 57, 109–110
Bureaucratic rationalism, 162, 221*n*
Burn-out, 126
Bush administration, 28–39, 53, 206*n*, 208*n*
Bush, George, 30, 32–33, 208*n*
BZ. *See* Below the zone

Careerism, 136, 137*d*, 138–143
Carlisle Barracks, 121, 222*n*
Carney, Thomas, 88, 95–100, 107–108, 108*t*, 219*n*
CBO. *See* Congressional Budget Office
CGSC. *See* Command and General Staff College
Chain teaching, 89
Cheney, Richard: Base Force and, 30–33, 36, 53, 206*n*–208*n*; on decision-making, 200–201; influence of, 211*n*; Colin Powell and, 61; on strategy, 51
Christman, Daniel, 211*n*
Clinton, Bill: Bottom-Up Review and, 28, 40–44, 48–49, 54; election of, 38–40, 198, 208*n*; federal government and, 14
Clinton administration, 28, 39–51, 53, 99
Combat Maneuver Training Center (CMTC), 222*n*
Combined Armed Services School, 153–155

Command: opportunity for, 87, 116*d*, 129–132, 146–152; preparation for, 163–164, 164*t*, 167–170, 184, 192–193, 201; as specialty, 159, 176–179, 182, 184–185, 191–194, 228*n*; as success, 129–132, 167, 171–172
Command and General Staff College (CGSC): faculty for, 153–155, 183–184; selection for, 138–140, 142–143, 222*n*–223*n*, 228*n*
Commanders of the Major Commands (MACOMs), 211*n*–212*n*
Commissioned Officer Development and Career Management, 131
Competence, 163–164
Congress: army relationship with, 35–36, 59; Base Force and, 31–33, 38–39, 45, 206*n*; Bottom-Up Review and, 46–47, 208*n*; defense policy and, 210*n*; downsizing role of, 53, 101–103, 197–199; officer management and, 66–68, 203*n*; reform role of, 186–190, 194, 199–200; transition aid and, 37
Congressional Budget Office (CBO), 32, 209*n*
Contract with America, 49
Corporate army, 21–22, 195

DAIG. *See* Department of the Army Inspector General
Dawkins, Peter, 229*n*
Decisive Victory: America's Power Projection Army, 58
Defense Officer Personnel Management Act (DOPMA): changes in, 97, 112–113, 173; goals of, 215*n*; grades and, 227*n*; guidelines of, 5, 66–67; promotion and, 70, 77, 86–87, 173, 213*n*; reform and, 187; retirement and, 114, 227*n*
Deficit, 30, 33, 197, 205*n*
Dellums, Ron, 208*n*
Demobilization, 6–10, 203*n*–204*n*
Department of Defense, 30–31, 36–38, 41, 186, 197, 206*n*
Department of Defense Reorganization Act (1986). *See* Goldwater-Nichols Act
Department of the Army Inspector General (DAIG), 120, 215*n*
Deployments, 123, 126, 158, 222*n*
DePuy, William E., 107
Diversity, 74, 76–77, 84–86, 85*t*, 207*n*, 215*n*–216*n*

DOPMA. *See* Defense Officer Personnel Management Act
Downsizing: attitude changes and, 16–17, 22–23, 117–136, 122*d*, 124*d*, 156, 204*n*; behavior changes and, 22–23, 136–156, 137*d*; best practices in, 17–18; definition of, 2; effects of, 117–156; of officer corps, 2, 5, 12–13, 66–116, 69*d*, 71*t*; politics of, 25–62; in private sector, 4, 13–18, 111, 204*n*; in public sector, 4, 14–15, 19–20, 111–112, 203*n*; reducing the ranks, 2, 63–116; in U.S. military history, 6–13
Dual designations, 68, 147–148, 166, 224*n*
Du Picq, Ardant, 125

Econometric mindset, 162
Education: civilian graduate, 150–153, 164–165, 169, 174, 181–183, 229*n*; marketability and, 148–149; military, 153–156, 174, 183–185, 224*n*, 227*n*–229*n*
Eisenhower, Dwight D., 10
Endstrength: 1989-1996, 27*d*; of active army 1940-1995, 8*d*; attitudes and, 122–123; Base Force and, 29, 29*t*, 36–37, 40*t*, 206*n*–207*n*; Bottom-Up Review and, 40, 40*t*, 46, 49–50, 209*n*; cuts in, 3, 25–26, 34, 186, 217*n*; definition of, 203*n*; Gulf War and, 92–93, 93*d*, 217*n*; of officer corps 1940-1995, 8*d*; Option C and, 40*t*; politics and, 196; proposed cuts in, 205*n*, 210*n*; 1999 target, 49; trade-offs and, 49–50; Vietnam War and, 11, 204*n*
Enlisted to officer ratio (E/O), 81–82, 115*d*. *See also* Officer to enlisted ratio
Ethics, 143–144
Evaluations, officer, 77, 138; downsizing and, 144–146; inflation in, 104–105, 144–145, 213*n*, 224*n*; reform in, 175
Exon, James, 45

FAA. *See* Functional Area Analysis
Field Grade Tables, 67
Fighting army, 176, 228*n*
Flexible Response, 10
FORCCOM. *See* Forces Command
Force enhancers, 45–47
Force projection, 35, 37, 56, 210*n*
Forces Command (FORCCOM), 219*n*
Force structure, 26; army review of, 34; Base Force and, 29, 29*t*, 32–33, 36, 40*t*, 46; Bottom-Up Review and, 40*t*, 43, 45–46, 209*n*; cuts in, 69, 91–92, 206*n*, 208*n*–209*n*; expansion of, 105, 220*n*; officers and, 67; Option C and, 38–39, 40*t*; priorities in, 47–48; shaping of, 72–73, 79–82; trade-offs and, 50, 210*n*, 220*n*
Fort Carson, 50, 210*n*
Fort Hood, 121, 222*n*
Fort Leavenworth, 121, 153, 155, 184, 222*n*
Fort Riley, 210*n*
Fort Sill, 121, 222*n*
Foster, William, 208*n*–209*n*
Frank, Barney, 49, 208*n*
Functional Area Analysis (FAA), 107
Functional areas, 147–149, 152–153, 166, 178, 212*n*, 224*n*
Future Years Defense Plan, 33

GAO. *See* General Accounting Office
Gates Commission, 122
Gavin, James, 204*n*
General Accounting Office (GAO), 44, 209*n*, 214*n*
Generalist ideal, 168
Global Reach-Global Power, 58
Goldwater-Nichols Act, 61, 211*n*–212*n*, 227*n*
Goodpaster, Andrew, 182
Gorbachev, Mikhail, 38, 52
Grade structure, 189
Gramm-Rudman-Hollings law, 205*n*
Gray, Al, 34, 36, 207*n*
"Groupthink," 180
Gulf War: Les Aspin and, 208*n*; downsizing and, 37, 92–93, 93*d*, 97, 102, 207*n*; endstrength in, 92–93, 93*d*, 217*n*

Hard skills, 148–149
Hauser, William L., 157
Heroic leader, 129, 150, 152, 167
Heskett, James, 185
Hollow army, 35, 48, 73, 105
Homosexuals, 42, 219*n*
Huntington, Samuel, 26, 120–121, 161, 211*n*, 226*n*, 229*n*
Huxley, Aldous, 103

Inouye, Daniel K., 37
International Business Machines, 14
Interservice rivalry, 59, 211*n*
Ippolito, Dennis, 208*n*

Janowitz, Morris, 180, 221*n*, 225*n*, 228*n*
Joint Chiefs of Staff, 30–32, 34, 42, 54–61, 211*n*
Joint Readiness Training Center (JRTC), 150, 222*n*
Just, Ward, 152

Kanter, Arnold, 55
Kasserine Pass, 6
Kennedy, John F., 10
Korean War, 10–11
Kotter, John, 185

Labor exchange, 140–141, 224*n*
Leader Development Study, 229*n*
Lieutenant Retention Boards (LTRBs), 71, 71*t*, 114
Longitudinal Research on Officer Career Survey (LROC), 221*n*
Luttwak, Edward, 118

McNamara, Robert, 41, 107, 211*n*
MACOMs. *See* Commanders of the Major Commands
Major regional contingencies (MRCs), 43–44, 46, 50
Manager/technician track, 176–179, 182, 184–185, 191–194, 228*n*
Manpower Directorate, 65–66, 94
Marine Corps: Base Force and, 207*n*; Bottom-Up Review and, 43, 209*n*; congressional support for, 56; political effectiveness of, 210*n*; post–Cold War vision of, 58; priorities of, 48, 57
Marketability, 146, 147*d*, 148–149, 151, 155
Marsh, John O., 114, 206*n*, 216*n*
Marshall, George C., 203*n*–204*n*
Meyer, Edward C., 48, 159, 176, 184, 220*n*
Miles, Rufus, 88, 216*n*
Military effectiveness, 2
Minorities: downsizing and, 74, 76, 207*n*, 215*n*–216*n*; in officer corps, 84–86, 85*t*; promotion and, 213*n*
Mobilization capability, 167–168, 227*n*
Modernization, 47–50, 209*n*–210*n*, 220*n*
Montgomery, Bernard L., 195
Morale: after Korean War, 10–11; definition of, 124–125; downsizing and, 204*n*; in officer corps, 3, 13, 22–23, 104, 124*d*, 124–129; World War II demobilization and, 9

Moskos, Charles, 162
MRCs. *See* Major regional contingencies
Muddy boots army, 21–22, 195; assignment policy and, 205*n*; bias toward, 214*n*; as career choice, 146–152, 147*d*, 164–165

National Defense Authorization Act: 1972, 11; 1991, 37, 112–114; 1992, 113, 212*n*; 1993, 223*n*; 1994, 209*n*
National Guard, 57
National Performance Review, 4
National Training Center (NTC), 150–151, 222*n*
Navy: Base Force and, 207*n*; Bottom-Up Review and, 42–43, 209*n*; post–Cold War vision of, 58; priorities of, 48, 57, 75
New Look, 10
Nixon, Richard, 11
North Atlantic Treaty Organization (NATO), 205*n*
NTC. *See* National Training Center
Nuclear deterrence, 10
Nunn, Sam, 32, 53

Occupationalism, 162
ODCSPER. *See* Office of the Deputy Chief of Staff for Personnel
ODP. *See* Officer Distribution Plan
OERs. *See* Officer Evaluation Reports
Office of Management and Budget (OMB), 209*n*–210*n*
Office of Manpower and Economic Analysis, 218*n*
Office of the Assistant Secretary of the Army for Manpower and Reserve Affairs (ASA/M&RA), 65–66
Office of the Assistant Vice Chief of Staff, 107
Office of the Deputy Chief of Staff for Personnel (ODCSPER), 65–66, 87–102, 206*n*, 216*n*
Office of the Secretary of Defense (OSD): Bottom-Up Review and, 42; downsizing and, 31–32, 34, 74–75, 77; influence of, 40
Officer corps: after Korean War, 10; after World War II, 7–9; army role of, 6; attitude changes in, 22–23, 117–136, 122*d*, 124*d*, 156, 160, 191, 201; behavior changes in, 22–23, 136–156, 137*d*, 160, 191, 201; career choices in, 146–156, 147*d*, 164–165, 176–179,

225*n*; career expectations in, 124*d*, 124–125, 129–132; career intent in, 133–135, 134*d*; commitment in, 124*d*, 124–125, 132–136; confidence in leadership, 127–129, 128*d*; distribution changes in, 81*t*, 81–82, 115*d*; diversity in, 85*t*, 85–86; downsizing of, 2, 5, 12–13, 66–116, 69*d*, 71*t*; endstrength of 1940-1995, 8*d*; families and, 126, 223*n*; line positions filled in, 83*d*; morale in, 3, 13, 22–23, 104, 124*d*, 124–129; number required in, 67–68, 212*n*, 230*n*; quality of, 75, 77–79, 79*t*, 123, 130–131, 212*n*–213*n*, 218*n*; readiness of, 82–84; reform in, 157–194, 199–202; shaping of, 72–73, 75, 79–82; shortages in, 68, 83, 101, 123–124, 219*n*; turbulence in, 123–124, 126, 227*n*; values in, 171; Vietnam War and, 11–12, 103–106; willingness to recommend career, 135–136, 136*d*, 223*n*. *See also* Professional development; Professionalism
Officer Distribution Plan (ODP), 68
Officer Evaluation Reports (OERs), 104–105, 144–146, 224*n*
Officer management system, 5, 66–68, 137–138, 165–186; flexibility in, 173–174, 179–181; reform in, 3, 23, 173–194, 199, 201–202
Officer Personnel Act (1947), 223*n*
Officer Personnel Management Directorate (OPMD), 98, 154, 212*n*, 219*n*
Officer Personnel Management System (OPMS), 68, 137, 147, 166; boards and, 223*n*; guidelines of, 226*n*; professional development and, 175–176; reform in, 173–174; specialization and, 168; XXI Task Force, 175
Officer to enlisted ratio, 9–10, 12–13
OMB. *See* Office of Management and Budget
OML. *See* Order of Merit List
Omnibus Budget Reconciliation Act (1990), 33
Ono, Allen, 72, 88–91, 107–108, 108*t*
Operational command track, 176–179, 182, 184–185, 191–194, 228*n*
Operational tempo (OPTEMPO), 222*n*
OPMD. *See* Officer Personnel Management Directorate
OPMS. *See* Officer Personnel Management System

Option C, 38–39, 40*t*
Ord, Robert, III, 89
Order of Merit List (OML), 99, 154
OSD. *See* Office of the Secretary of Defense

Palmer, David R., 154, 225*n*
Peck, John, 229*n*
Pentagon, 65–66
Perry, William, 3, 48–50, 205*n*, 209*n*–210*n*
Personnel: army management of, 64–68, 66*d*, 87–88; as army priority, 47–48, 57; readiness of, 73, 76, 82–84, 203*n*; tempo (PERSTEMPO), 222*n*. *See also* Endstrength
Personnel Management Directorate, 65–66, 94
Planning, Programming, and Budgeting System (PPBS), 31, 61
Plans/resources mismatch, 44, 47, 49, 61, 197–198
PMSs. *See* Professors of Military Science
Point system, 9, 203*n*
Policymaking, 25–62, 186–189, 196–202, 211*n*
Politico-military track, 176–179, 182, 184–185, 191–194
POMs. *See* Program Objective Memorandums
Porter, Robert, 216*n*
Powell, Colin: on army's future, 30, 205*n*; Base Force and, 30–36, 52, 205*n*–206*n*, 208*n*; Bottom-Up Review and, 42, 53; influence of, 28, 54–55, 60–61, 211*n*
Power from the Sea, 58
PPBS. *See* Planning, Programming, and Budgeting System
Preparedness, 1, 6
Professional development, 166–186, 227*n*–228*n*; army priorities and, 166–167; flexibility in, 173–174, 179–181; models of, 169, 177, 227*n*; process of, 226*n*; reform in, 175–186, 190; specialization and, 175–186, 191–194; timing and, 168–169, 173, 188
Professionalism, 226*n*; broader concept of, 171–172, 190–191; decline in, 3, 23, 161–164, 190, 226*n*; definition of, 161, 226*n*; importance of, 6; political dimension of, 193–194; restoration of, 170–174; Vietnam War and, 143, 162, 220*n*–222*n*, 224*n*
Professors of Military Science (PMSs), 153–154

Program Analysis and Evaluation, 94
Program Objective Memorandums (POMs), 207n, 211n–212n
Project Transition, 204n
Promotion: below the zone (BZ), 87, 139–140, 213n, 215n, 224n; boards, 73, 138, 212n–213n, 223n–224n; bubble, 212n, 220n; career choices and, 172–173; flexibility and, 181, 228n; flow of, 70; generalist ideal and, 168; opportunity for, 13, 74–77, 86–87, 104, 115d, 212n–213n, 215n, 221n; professional development model and, 169, 227n; selection for, 138; Selective Early Retirement Boards and, 90, 216n; specialization and, 184–186, 229n; timing of, 74, 86–87, 104, 116d, 174, 215n; up-and-stay system, 188–189; up-or-out system, 67, 70, 139, 168, 173, 187–188
Putman, Gerald, 98

Quadrennial Defense Review, 3, 28, 50, 120, 205n
Quicksilver I and II, 34

RAH-66 Comanche, 48
RAND Corporation, 107, 172–173, 187, 218n
Readiness, 212n; as army priority, 71–73; Base Force and, 35–36; Bottom-Up Review and, 48–49, 210n; definition of, 73; personnel, 73, 76, 82–84, 203n; trade-offs and, 47–48, 50, 220n
Reagan, Ronald, 30
Recruiting, 149, 155, 220n, 225n
Redina, Mark, 150
"Redlining," 216n
Reductions in Force (RIFs), 113–114, 214n; after Vietnam War, 12; minorities and, 215n; results of, 70, 71t; threat of, 98
Reform, 157–194, 199–202
Reich, Robert, 13
Reimer, Dennis, 50, 170, 210n
Reischauer, Richard, 32
Reno, William H.: analytic culture and, 109–110; on Army Career and Alumni Program, 217n; as Deputy Chief of Staff for Personnel, 88, 91–95, 97; on downsizing, 35; Thurman, Maxwell and, 107–108, 108t
Reserve officers, 105, 204n; after Korean War, 10; after Vietnam War, 12; after World War II, 9; cuts in, 13; Vietnam War and, 104, 220n
Reserves, 45–46, 57, 105, 155, 225n
Retirement: benefits, 121–122, 223n; eligibility for, 20, 129, 134, 223n; involuntary, 70–71, 71t, 89–90, 100–101, 114, 153–155; mandatory early, 188–189; voluntary, 70–71, 71t, 98–99, 112–113, 218n
Ridgway, Matthew, 10
RIFs. See Reductions in Force
Rosen, Stephen, 181, 228n
ROTC, 149, 153–155, 225n
Runyon, Marvin, 15

Sample Survey of Military Personnel (SSMP), 221n
SAMS. See School of Advanced Military Studies
Sarkesian, Sam, 25, 169–170
Schofield Barracks, 121, 222n
School of Advanced Military Studies (SAMS), 153, 155, 225n, 229n
SDI. See Strategic Defense Initiative
Selective Early Annuity, 98
Selective Early Retirement Boards (SERBs), 70–71, 89–90, 114; cancellation of, 100–101; faculty and, 153–155, 225n; notification of, 90, 214n–215n; officer evaluations and, 144–145; promotion and, 90, 216n; results of, 71t; selection for, 90, 213n–214n, 216n–217n; specialization and, 80
Senior raters, 138, 144–145, 223n–224n
Separation, personnel: involuntary, 17–18, 70–71, 71t, 78, 84, 89–90, 97–101, 113–114; voluntary, 17–18, 37, 70, 71t, 84, 97–99, 112–113; World War II and, 9
SERBs. See Selective Early Retirement Boards
Shalikashvili, John, 160
Skelton, Ike, 45–46, 53, 56, 211n
Soviet Union: Colin Powell on, 52, 205n; U.S. policy and, 30–34, 38, 51–52, 208n
Specialization, 158–160, 175–186, 228n; assignment policy and, 166, 186, 229n; command, 159, 176–179, 182, 184–185, 191–194; costs of, 191–192, 229n–230n; downsizing and, 7, 80; education and, 181–183; Officer Personnel Management System and, 168; political, 159, 176–179, 182, 184–185, 191–194; problems of, 191; promotion and,

184–186, 229n; technical, 158–160, 176–179, 182, 184–185, 191–194, 228n
Special Separation Bonus (SSB), 37, 70, 97, 113; Carney, Thomas and, 96; compensation in, 98, 218n; eligibility for, 219n; performance and, 78–79, 79t, 99, 214n; results of, 71t; specialization and, 80
Spence, Floyd, 49
SSB. *See* Special Separation Bonus
SSMP. *See* Sample Survey of Military Personnel
Stars and Stripes, 203n
Steinbeck, John, 21
Stop-Loss Program, 207n
Strategic Defense Initiative (SDI), 32, 49, 208n
Strategic Fellows, 120, 144, 191, 221n
Strategy, 26; Base Force and, 32–35, 38–39, 51–54, 205n, 208n, 210n; Bottom-Up Review and, 43–44, 51–54; budgets and, 28, 32, 51–54; officer views of, 126–127; portfolio management approach, 50; win-hold-win, 42; win-win, 42
Street, Clair, 9–10
Strength management, 166, 175
Stroup, Theodore: as Deputy Chief of Staff for Personnel, 88, 100–101; Allen Ono and, 89, 217n; William H. Reno and, 93, 95, 216n; Maxwell Thurman and, 107–108, 108t; Vietnam War and, 220n; Carl E. Vuono and, 72, 216n
Study on Military Professionalism, 143, 221n–222n, 224n, 226n
Sullivan, Gordon: Base Force and, 44–45, 209n; Bottom-Up Review and, 47, 53; budget trade-offs and, 50; communication and, 214n–215n; officer evaluations and, 105; politics and, 58–59, 210n; strategy and, 56; Vietnam War and, 220n
Support army, 176, 228n
Survivor syndrome, 16–18

Tables of Distribution and Allowances (TDAs): command in, 130, 215n; cuts in, 83–84, 87, 91–92, 111; minorities in, 85; officers in, 67–68, 80–82, 211n–212n, 230n; reform in, 175
Tables of Organization and Equipment (TOEs): command in, 130; cuts in, 87, 91–92, 111; officers in, 67–68, 80–81

Tapping, 221n
Task Force Smith, 6
Taylor, Frederick, 106
Taylor, Maxwell, 10, 204n, 224n
TDAs. *See* Tables of Distribution and Allowances
Technology, 158–160
Temporary Early Retirement Authority (TERA), 70, 99, 113, 218n
"3Rs," 155, 225n
Thurman, Maxwell: analytic culture and, 88–89, 91, 106–109, 217n; career of, 221n; legacy of, 91, 96, 100, 108t; recruiting and, 220n
Thurmond, Strom, 47
Ticket punching, 136, 138–140
Tocqueville, Alexis de, 1
TOEs. *See* Tables of Organization and Equipment
Total Obligational Budget Authority, 26
TRADOC. *See* Army Training and Doctrine Command
Transition aid: downsizing and, 18, 37, 197; history of, 9, 13, 204n; *See also* Army Career and Alumni Program

U.S. Congress. *See* Congress
U.S. Military Academy, 153–155, 184, 214n, 225n
U.S. Postal Service, 15
U.S. Total Army Personnel Command (PERSCOM): analytic culture and, 218n; assignments and, 154; hotline, 216n; role of, 66; separation and, 78, 98–99
Up-and-stay system, 188–190
Up-or-out system, 67, 70, 139, 168, 173, 187–188
Utilization tours, 148, 165, 174

Vanguard Study, 92
VERRP. *See* Voluntary Early Release/Retirement Program
Vietnam War: downsizing and, 11–12, 73–74, 103–106, 204n, 220n; professionalism in, 143, 162, 220n–222n, 224n; zero-defects mindset in, 143
Violence, management of, 161, 171
Voluntary Early Release/Retirement Program (VERRP), 70, 71t, 112–113

Voluntary Separation Incentive (VSI), 37, 70, 97, 113; Thomas Carney and, 96; compensation in, 98, 218n; eligibility for, 219n; performance and, 78–79, 79t, 99, 214n; results of, 71t; specialization and, 80

Vuono, Carl E.: Base Force and, 34–36, 207n; communication and, 89; politics and, 53, 57, 60, 206n, 210n; priorities of, 71–72, 105, 212n–213n; on professionalism, 167; strategy and, 56; Theodore Stroup and, 216n

Warner, Edward, 42
Warrior ethos, 192–193
Weigley, Russell, 180
Westmoreland, William, 166, 221n–222n
West Point. *See* U.S. Military Academy

Wildavsky, Aaron, 51
Wilson, George C., 63
Wilson, James Q., 106
Wincup, Kim, 90–91
Win-hold-win strategy, 42
Win-win strategy, 42
Wolfowitz, Paul, 31–32
Women, 74, 76, 84–86, 85t, 215n, 219n
World War II, 7–10, 203n–204n
Wyatt Company, 14, 16

"Youth and vigor," 168, 187–188

Zero-defects mindset, 136–138, 137d, 143–146, 175, 224n

About the Author

David McCormick is an associate in the Pittsburgh office of the international management consulting firm McKinsey & Company, Inc. A former army officer, he graduated from West Point in 1987, was commissioned into the army corps of engineers and was assigned to the Eighty-Second Airborne Division. As a junior officer, he served in the Gulf War and was awarded the bronze star for meritorious service. He is a senior parachutist and graduate of the U.S. army ranger school.

McCormick holds a Ph.D. from the Woodrow Wilson School of Public and International Affairs at Princeton University and has published articles on U.S. defense policy and foreign affairs.